Shopsmith
3931 Image Drive
Dayton, Ohio 45414-2591

Dear Woodworking Friend,

We hope you enjoy your book, and we'd like to thank you for your interest in Shopsmith. You may already know that Shopsmith is synonymous with Woodworking and the remarkable MARK V woodworking system. But, the truth is, you don't have to own a MARK V to take advantage of all that Shopsmith offers.

We do more than sell woodworking equipment – we provide a complete **system** that includes everything you need to get the most out of woodworking, including project plans, hand tools, hardwoods, finishing products and the instruction you need to develop and expand your woodworking skills. We're the premier Woodworking Company.

From our humble beginning, we have grown and established ourselves as the leader in home woodworking. We have a growing network of more than 40 retail stores conveniently located across the U.S., U.K., and Canada. And we're opening more. Our stores are unique in the woodworking industry. They educate woodworkers of all abilities through classes and seminars taught by our own expert instructors. Plus, our other educational resources – such as books and video training tapes – provide a complete woodworking education. We also keep you abreast of the latest innovations and techniques of interest to woodworking enthusiasts.

In addition to our outstanding educational programs, we also offer our customers the most comprehensive warranty offered by any power tool manufacturer – The Shopsmith Gold Medal Buyer Protection Plan. And our FREE Service Hotline is always just a toll-free phone call away, should you ever have questions or need assistance. Our Customer Service Representatives and store personnel undergo extensive training on woodworking and Shopsmith equipment, so they can provide the answers to your questions.

If you have any questions about woodworking or Shopsmith equipment, please call our toll-free number (**1-800-543-7586**). We can also direct you to the store nearest you.

All this and more – it's just part of the Shopsmith commitment. So come join the Shopsmith family of woodworkers and find out how fun, safe and rewarding woodworking can be.

Sincerely,

John R. Folkerth
Chairman, Shopsmith, Inc.

Popular Science®
Woodworking Projects Yearbook

10th Anniversary Edition

Edited by Al Gutierrez

Meredith® Press
New York

Cover Photo: Jonathan Press

For Meredith® Press
    Vice President, Editorial Director: Elizabeth P. Rice
    Assistant: Ruth Weadock
    Editorial Project Manager: Gene Schnaser
    Editorial Assistant: Carolyn Mitchell
    Production Manager: Bill Rose
    Coordinator: Connie Schrader
    Assistant Coordinator: G. B. Anderau

For Jonathan Press
    Produced by Jonathan Press, Cannon Falls, MN
    Producer/Executive Director: Al Gutierrez
    Copy Editor: Berit Strand
    Copy Editor: Cheryl Clark
    Technical Consultant: Gary Branson
    Illustrator: Geri Klug
    Draftsman: Joe Horch
    Woodworking Technician: Jeremy Irrthum
    Woodworking Technician: Pat Manion
    Photo Stylist: Sharon Doucette
    Photo Stylist: Gladys Clark

Book Design: Jonathan Press

Preface

We are pleased with this year's 10th anniversary edition of woodworking projects and techniques. There is a project to suit everyone. Many of the projects have been specially designed for this book, whereas many past projects were reprints of those that first appeared in *Popular Science*® magazine.

The *Popular Science*® *Book Club* and *Popular Science*® magazine have been operated separately, but were owned by Times Mirror. Recently, the *Popular Science*® *Book Club* changed ownership and is now owned by Meredith Publishing Co., the same publishers who bring you *Better Homes and Gardens* magazine.

Meredith is determined to make every book in its woodworking series one that all woodworkers will be proud to own. As an example, note our brand-new appearance. This book has been redesigned to make it easier to read and more attractive.

Even though the book is improved, the basic fundamental information that you have come to expect is still there. Detailed stories continue to give you descriptive construction information and are presented along with helpful step-by-step construction photography. The concise, technical illustrations give you accurate assembly information as well.

Woodworking as a Hobby

Most of us became interested in woodworking at an early age. We either began hammering blocks of wood on our own or had the loving guidance of a parent to lead us in this captivating hobby. With growth, we gained the basic woodworking skills and interest to carry us into adulthood. With this in mind, we have created many projects that are ideal for the young woodworker. The "Easy-To-Build Sawhorse" project is a fine example. This project is challenging enough, yet teaches the young woodworker how to lay out a project, form a simple mortise and cut angles with the aid of basic hand tools. (Of course, use only the tools that are appropriate for the age of your child.) With every project comes construction photography that shows how to cut or lay out the work in simple terms. Drawings help youngsters recognize the project dimensionally.

Learning alongside Mom or Dad can lead to a life-long hobby. Use this book so that children may reap the benefits of a rewarding hobby and the problem-solving skills needed to repair or construct projects around the home! In a day of high technology and busy lives, it is easy to overlook the companionship and the unceasing interest young people have in their parents' hobbies.

Even if you don't have children around, there are many exciting projects that will attract your interest. Take a look at the "Charming Occasional Table" — it's not only a challenging project, but one that any woodworker would appreciate owning.

Last, but not least, the range of projects cover every room in your house, and even fulfill your needs for outdoor items. You'll find projects like "Make Your Own Media Center" for the living room; "Contemporary Entertainment Center" for the family room; "Fold-Up Play Center/Bed" for the bedroom; "Trestle Table And Bench" for the dining room; "Oak Drafting Table" for the shop or study; and "Build a Bathroom Caddy" for the bathroom. For the great outdoors we've included "Garden Table/Bench" and "Build Your Own Bass Boat" plus many more.

Plant a Tree

Dwindling lumber resources are now a reality. To insure that the future has both clean air and trees, we need to actively support the efforts of replanting burned and cut forests. It will take a lifetime before our efforts are realized, but our children will be guaranteed lumber and cleaner air only if we begin to do our part now. Contact your local county extension agent about reforestation efforts, and begin planting trees in your neighborhood.

Al Gutierrez

Table of Contents

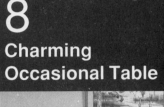

8
Charming Occasional Table

45
Rustic Bird Feeder

72
Vegetable Bin

4

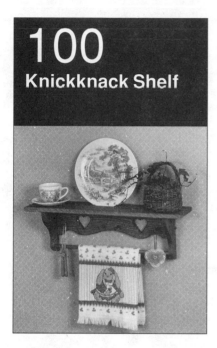

100
Knickknack Shelf

164
**Clamping
Know-How**

133
Magical Carousel

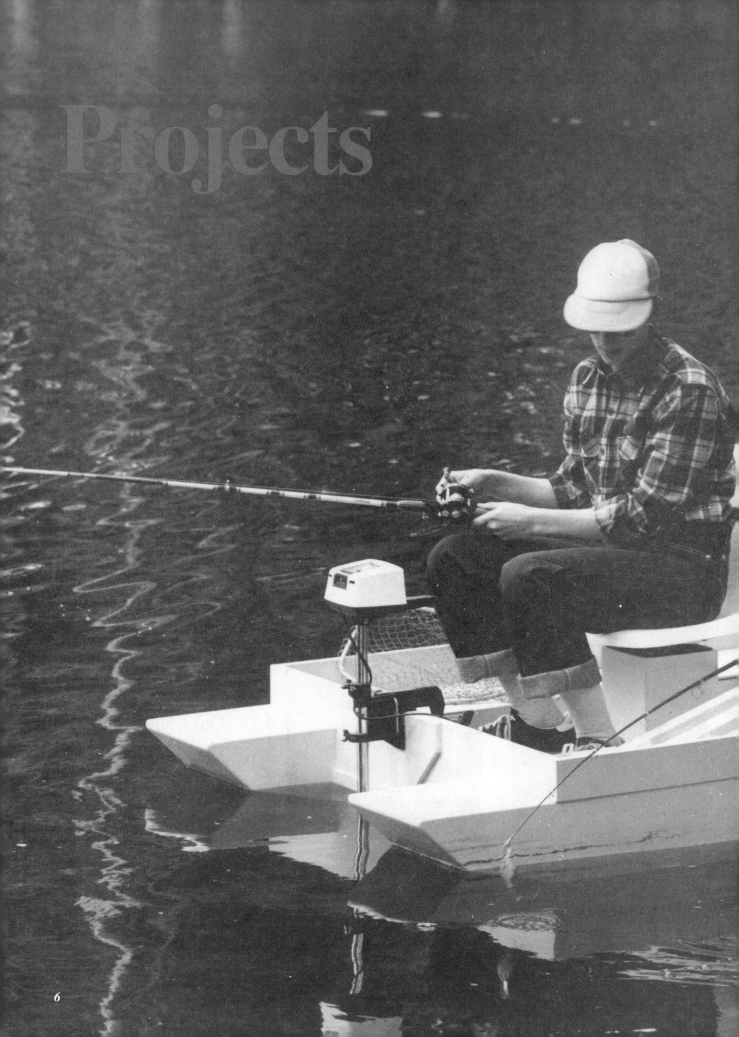

Charming Occasional Table

The simple yet elegant lines of this table give it plenty of eye appeal.

Build this country-style table and add charm to any room in the house.

This country-style occasional table will add charm to any room. Its simple lines, compact size and handy drawer make it a perfect addition to a living room, bedroom, kitchen or hall. Constructed of ash, its interesting grain pattern and appealing design are sure to bring compliments from your guests.

TIPS
Use ash to add visual interest to the table. The wood's prominent grain gives the overall project a very distinctive look. Even if you do not use ash lumber, select clear, straight material that will give the project character. Try to stay away from the more neutral materials such as maple.

CONSTRUCTION
Begin by cutting all of the project parts to their overall widths and lengths. Notice that the top (D) must be cut slightly oversize, as well as the drawer face (H). Also, do not cut the hold downs (G) to length at this time. Joint and then edge-glue the workpieces that will form the top. Securely clamp the workpieces with bar clamps.

After the glue has dried, scrape off any hardened glue with a paint scraper.

It is a good idea to sand both surfaces of the table top with a belt sander. Start with a medium grit sandpaper, working down to a fine grit. Afterwards, trim the table top to its proper width and length, and carefully sand all edges.

Now rout a ¼ in. cove all around the top and bottom edge of the table top. Follow this up by routing the edges of the four legs (A).

Now mark the contours for the front/back (C) and side rails (B). Then cut out the contours on your band saw. For such tight contours, first generate a rough shape with your band saw by working up to the cutting line. Then install a drum sander in your drill press and smooth out these rough-cut contour areas.

Carefully mark the cutout in the front (C) workpiece. Draw this layout on the inside facing surface. Now drill a ¾ in. starter hole in the middle of the cutout area, making sure to use a backup board to minimize wood splintering. Cut out this rectangular area using a saber saw equipped with a sharp, fine-tooth cutting blade. Before cutting, make sure that the blade is square

Figure 1. *A portable jointer is an ideal power tool for surfacing the workpieces that make up the top (D). It is much less expensive than a stationary jointer and offers you more control and accuracy than a hand plane.*

Figure 2. *After edge-gluing the top (D), use a paint scraper to remove the dried glue that has oozed out between the joints. Then cut the top to its proper size.*

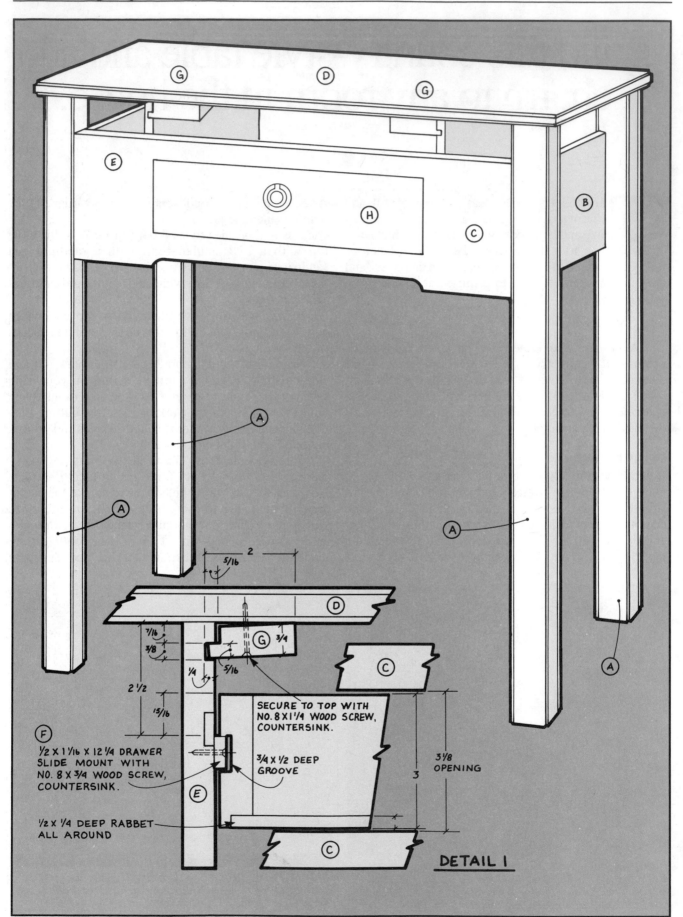

2

5/16

Ⓖ Ⓓ Ⓖ

Ⓔ

Ⓗ Ⓒ

Ⓑ

Ⓐ

Ⓐ Ⓐ

Ⓐ

Ⓓ

7/16

3/8

Ⓖ 3/4

1/4

5/16

Ⓒ

2 1/2

15/16

SECURE TO TOP WITH
NO. 8 X 1 1/4 WOOD SCREW,
COUNTERSINK.

Ⓕ
1/2 X 1 1/16 X 12 1/4 DRAWER
SLIDE MOUNT WITH
NO. 8 X 3/4 WOOD SCREW,
COUNTERSINK.

Ⓔ

3/4 X 1/2 DEEP
GROOVE

1/2 X 1/4 DEEP RABBET
ALL AROUND

3 1/8
OPENING

3

Ⓒ

DETAIL I

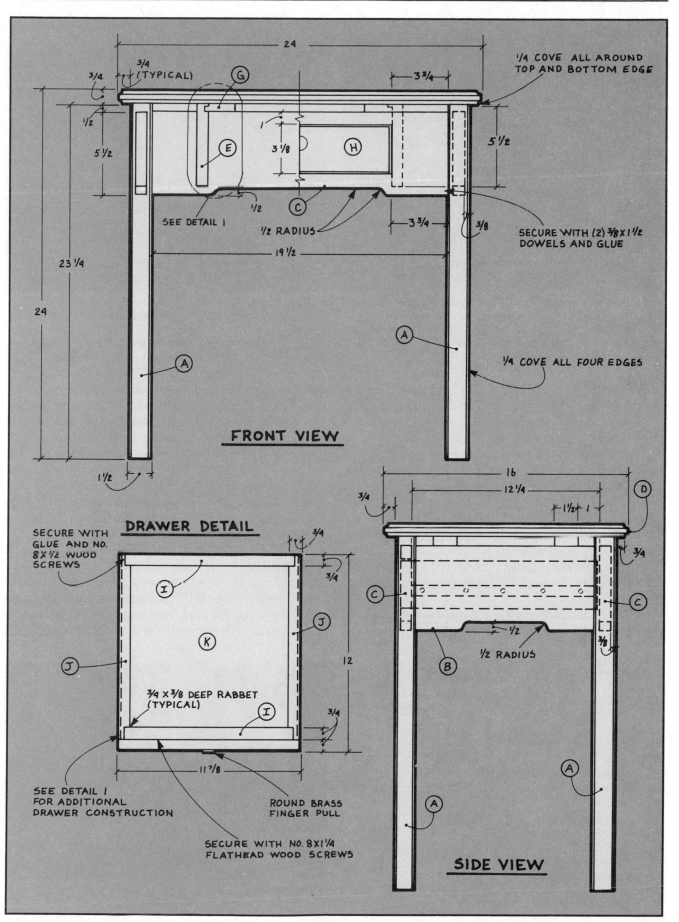

FRONT VIEW

DRAWER DETAIL

SIDE VIEW

24

3/4 (TYPICAL)

3/4

1/4 COVE ALL AROUND
TOP AND BOTTOM EDGE

3 3/4

1/2

5 1/2

3 1/8

5 1/2

23 1/4

24

SEE DETAIL 1

1/2

19 1/2

1/2 RADIUS

3 3/4

3/8

SECURE WITH (2) 3/8 X 1 1/2
DOWELS AND GLUE

1/4 COVE ALL FOUR EDGES

1 1/2

SECURE WITH
GLUE AND NO.
8 X 1/2 WOOD
SCREWS

3/4

3/4

12

3/4 X 3/8 DEEP RABBET
(TYPICAL)

11 7/8

3/4

SEE DETAIL 1
FOR ADDITIONAL
DRAWER CONSTRUCTION

ROUND BRASS
FINGER PULL

SECURE WITH NO. 8 X 1 1/4
FLATHEAD WOOD SCREWS

16

12 1/4

3/4

1 1/2

1

3/4

1/2

1/2 RADIUS

3/8

Figure 3. *Cut a cove into all four exposed edges of the legs (A), using a router equipped with a Roman ogee bit. This bit should have a pilot guide installed. Notice that the bottom part of a Roman ogee bit is curved and forms a cove on the edge of the wood.*

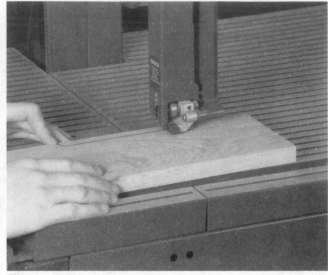

Figure 4. *Lay out the contour design for the side rails (B) and cut out the design with a band saw. Shown here is a band saw with a $1/2$ in. blade. To shape the radius of the design, cut in with the blade, working up to the cutting line.*

to the saber saw's pad. Make your cut slowly, keeping the saw blade right up to the edge of the cutting line. The workpiece should be securely clamped to a workbench to minimize vibrations.

After cutting the front workpiece, clamp it in a bench vise and use a flat wood file to smooth out the cut. Make long strokes and work from one corner to the other. Always file away from the good surface area, again to minimize wood splitting. When you are satisfied with the filing results, follow this up by sanding the edges with a sanding block.

Cut a groove into the two guides (E) with your table saw. If you do not want the groove to show, cut a stopped groove.

Now cut the rabbets in the four hold downs (G) from one long piece of material. In other words, don't cut

these workpieces to their proper lengths yet; instead, rabbet them first on your table saw. Make sure that they will draw down the table top when they are inserted into the guides (E). After rabbeting the hold downs from a longer piece of material, cut them to their proper lengths.

Next, cut a groove along the lengths of the drawer sides (J) with a dado blade installed in your table saw. Use pushsticks to move the workpieces over the dado blade. Then cut rabbets into the drawer sides to accommodate the drawer front and back (I).

ASSEMBLY
Assemble the drawer front and back (I) to the drawer sides (J) with No. 8 by $1\frac{1}{2}$ in. flathead wood screws and carpenter's glue. Do not place screws close to the bottom edge, because after assembly this area will be rabbeted

BILL OF MATERIALS — Charming Occasional Table

Finished Dimensions in Inches

A	Leg	$1\frac{1}{2}$ x $1\frac{1}{2}$ x $23\frac{1}{4}$ ash	4
B	Side Rail	$\frac{3}{4}$ x $5\frac{1}{2}$ x $11\frac{1}{2}$ ash	2
C	Front/Back	$\frac{3}{4}$ x $5\frac{1}{2}$ x $19\frac{1}{2}$ ash	2
D	Top	$\frac{3}{4}$ x 16 x 24 ash	1
E	Guide	$\frac{3}{4}$ x $5\frac{1}{2}$ x $12\frac{1}{4}$ ash	2
F	Drawer Guide	$\frac{1}{2}$ x $11/16$ x $12\frac{1}{4}$ ash	2
G	Hold Down	$\frac{1}{2}$ x $1\frac{1}{2}$ x 2 ash	4
H	Drawer Face	$\frac{3}{4}$ x 3 x $11\frac{7}{8}$ ash	1
I	Drawer Front/Back	$\frac{3}{4}$ x 3 x $11\frac{1}{8}$ ash	2
J	Drawer Side	$\frac{3}{4}$ x 3 x 12 ash	2
K	Drawer Bottom	$\frac{1}{2}$ x $11\frac{3}{8}$ x $11\frac{1}{2}$ plywood	1

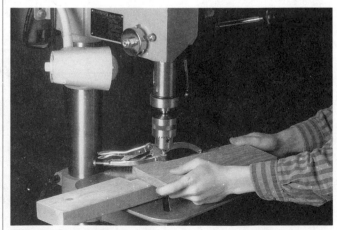

Figure 5. *Equip your drill press with a small drum sander, and finish sand the contours of the side rails.*

Figure 6. *Cut out the opening for the drawer in the front workpiece (C). Drill a starter hole, and use a saber saw equipped with a plywood cutting blade to cut out the hole. Work with the good side down, and cut up to the cutting line. Make sure the blade is perpendicular to the pad.*

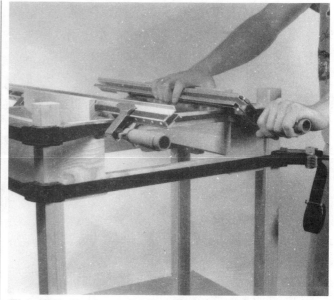

Figure 7. *Use band clamps in combination with bar clamps to secure the project during assembly. Make sure everything is square before gluing.*

to accept the drawer bottom (K). Square the assembly and allow the glue to dry. Once the glue has dried, rabbet the bottom of the drawer to precisely fit it with the rest of the drawer assembly. Secure the bottom with carpenter's glue and 1 in. brads.

Now finish sand all of the project parts, being careful not to round over surfaces that will be joined together. Particular problem areas are the legs, the drawer face and the opening in the front. It is best to sand these areas using sandpaper wrapped around a small block of wood. Make long strokes when sanding.

The next step involves assembling the table. You will need to position the workpieces and then drill dowel holes for securing the side rails (B) and the front and back (C) to the legs. Take your time to guarantee a smooth, accurate assembly. Dry-assemble the rails to the legs, wrap a band clamp around the legs to keep the joints tight and then square the assembly. Insert the guides (E) in position and mark them. They should be positioned flush with the left and right opening cut into the front rail. After the guides are positioned, mark their locations and dismantle the assembly. Drill dowel holes for securing the guides to the rails.

Now assemble the rails, guides and legs using carpenter's glue and dowels. Wrap several band clamps around the legs to snug up the leg joints. Then use several bar clamps to insure that the guides are snug to the front and back rails. After the glue has dried, remove the clamps and scrape off any glue that has oozed up from the joints. Now trim the drawer face (H) to suit the opening in the front rail.

Mount the drawer guides (F) to the guides (E) with

three or four No. 8 by ¾ in. flathead wood screws. Make sure you countersink the screw holes. Position the drawer guides to suit the groove in the drawer. Slide the drawer in to make sure there is no binding. If there is binding, you will have to readjust the position of the drawer guides.

Once you are satisfied with the drawer's installation, attach the drawer face (H) to the drawer front (I) with No. 8 by 1¼ in. flathead wood screws, countersunk. Do not glue the drawer face. Reinstall the drawer to check alignment. Notice that the drawer face stops against the drawer guides.

We used a round brass finger pull. This hardware required mortising out an area to accommodate the base of the pull. Whatever your situation calls for, install the pull at this time and then remove it so that the project can be finished.

FINISHING
Finish sand the entire project, making sure to slightly dull all sharp corners. Round over or bevel the leg bottoms to prevent them from splintering when the table is moved. We applied four coats of ZAR semi-gloss wipe-on tung oil to enhance the ash's grain pattern. When applying tung oil, use a rag or a brush, and carefully follow the manufacturer's instructions for application and safety recommendations.

Finally, secure the top to the table by attaching the four hold downs (G) with countersunk No. 8 by 1¼ in. flathead wood screws. You must predrill the holes so that the wood screws turn freely in the hold downs. Now reinstall the brass finger pull to complete your project.□

Country-Style Corner Shelf

This country-style corner shelf features decorative spindles, a heart cutout and contoured front. Coved edges give it a polished, professional look.

Build this corner shelf and you'll get requests for more. Its multiple uses and country charm make it an instant favorite.

Liven up your walls with this delightful corner shelf. The project is fun to build, and there's virtually no limit to its possible uses. Make two shelves to frame in a dining nook, or hang one or more in your child's bedroom for displaying knickknacks and toys. The rail also makes it a great shelf for showcasing plates and other collectibles. With its heart cutout, decorative spindles and contoured front, this shelf will bring country charm to any room.

TIPS
Look for decorative spindles at home centers or in mail order catalogs. The holes in the rail (C) and the top (A) must be drilled to suit the size of your particular spindles. Be sure to buy spindles made from the same type of wood used for the rest of the project. We used oak for our project.

CONSTRUCTION
Carefully lay out the top (A) using a protractor to determine the 45 degree angles (see diagram). Then cut out the top workpiece (A) on your table saw, using a miter gauge set to 45 degrees. Make sure that the workpiece is held securely as you feed it through the saw blade, because at this angle it will have a tendency to slip and bind. Use a plywood cutting blade to minimize wood splintering. After forming the basic triangular shape of the top workpiece, notch the back corner as specified in the illustration. This allows the shelf to fit snugly into the corner of a wall.

Lay out the decorative front (B) using graph paper with ½ in. squares. Begin with laying out the center of

Figure 1. *Transfer the design for the front (B) onto graph paper. Mark each of the points where the design intersects the square. Then connect these dots with a French curve or a flexible curve. Trace this design onto the workpiece.*

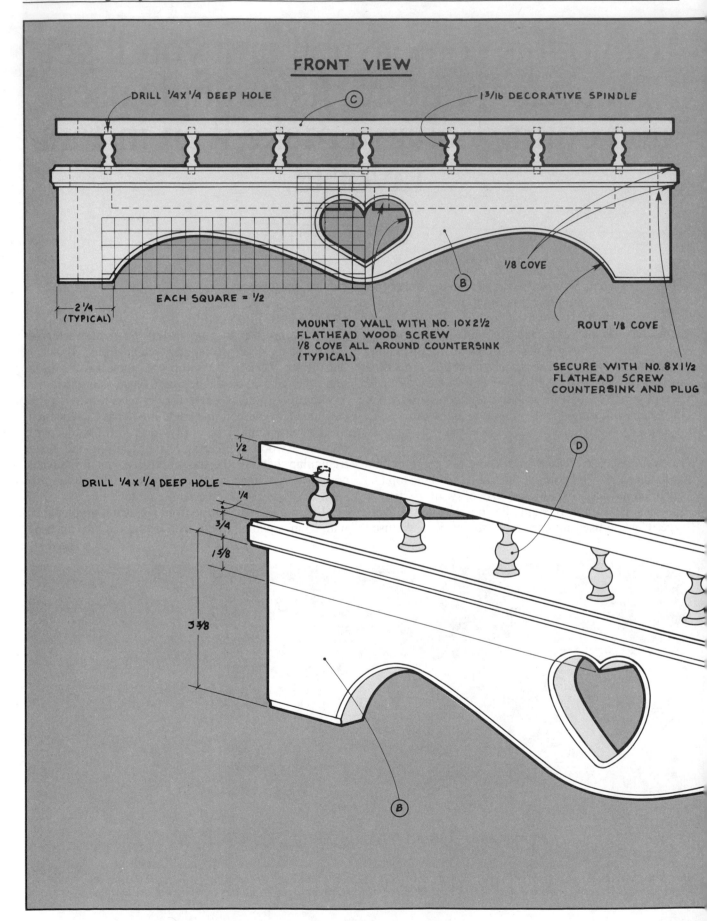

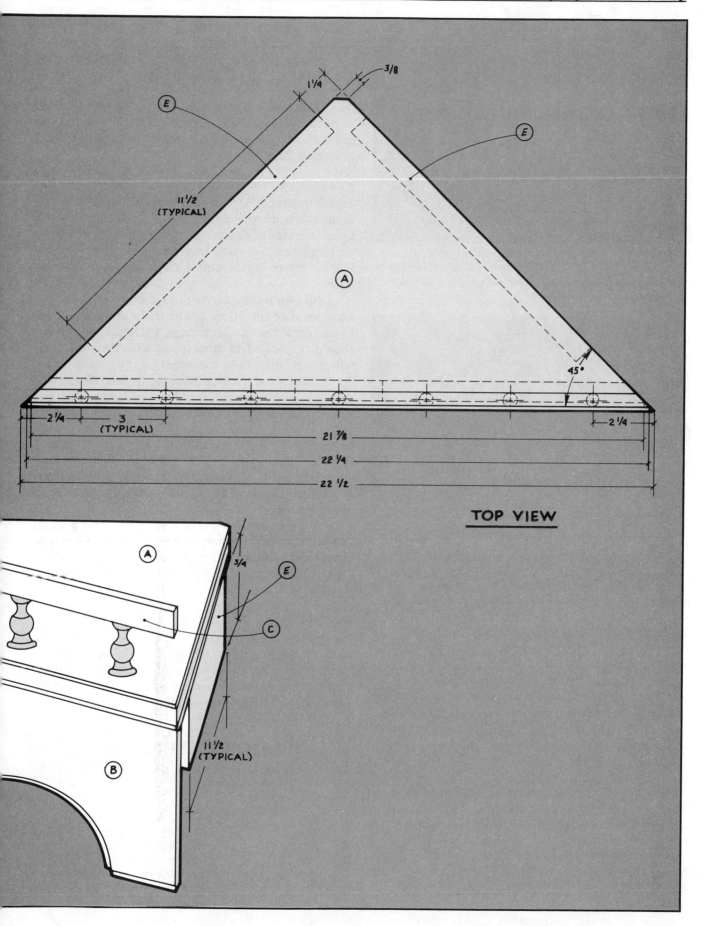

3/8

1¼

E

E

11½
(TYPICAL)

A

45°

2¼

3
(TYPICAL)

21 ⅞

22 ¼

22 ½

2¼

TOP VIEW

A

3/4

E

C

11½
(TYPICAL)

B

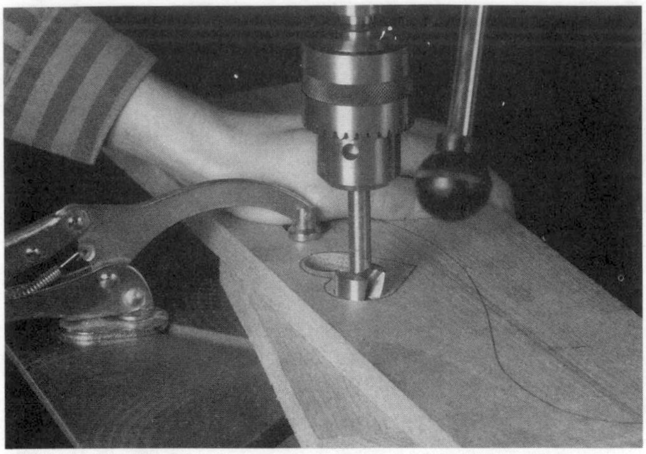

Figure 2. *Form the heart shape by drilling two 1 in. diameter starter holes with a Forstner bit. Use a backup board to prevent splintering. Then cut out the waste area with a sharp saber saw blade.*

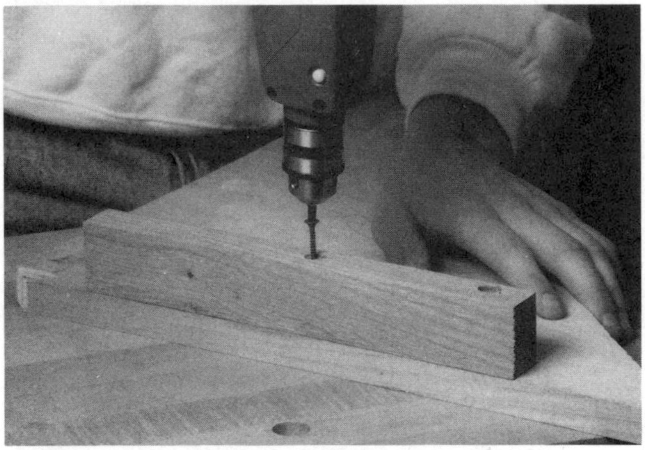

Figure 3. *Lay out the triangular shape of the top (A) with a carpenter's square. Notice that the point is to be notched to insure that the back corner will fit properly. Secure the two cleats (E) with wood screws driven in from the top (A). Counterbore these holes and plug with oak.*

the heart so it corresponds to a vertical line on the graph paper. Then cut out the pattern and trace it onto the front workpiece.

Next, cut out the heart shape in the contour in the shelf front (B). Drill starter holes for the heart and cut out the waste area with a saber saw. Again, use a fine-tooth blade to minimize wood splintering. Then cut the remaining decorative front design.

Now cut the rail (C) and cleats (E) to their overall lengths and widths.

Rout a 1/8 in. cove around the bottom of the front workpiece, inside the heart, and around the edges of the top. Notice that only the showing edges of the top workpiece are routed.

Miter the front (B) and the rail (C) on your table saw. Notice that the rail in the front is not cut to the same length and therefore is not recessed equally.

Sand the edges of the top (A) and the front (B). Wrap sandpaper around a dowel to sand the heart cutout.

Position the rail on the top, and use a pencil to draw a line along both sides of the rail. Then use these reference lines to locate the center of the rail and lay out the spindle holes, both for the top and for the rail. Drill stopped holes into these workpieces to suit your specific spindle sizes. Finally, finish sand all of the workpieces to prepare them for assembly.

ASSEMBLY

Secure the front (B) to the top (A) with No. 8 by 1½ in. flathead wood screws. Countersink and plug the screw holes. Similarly, attach the cleats (E) to the top by drilling holes and using fasteners through the top and into the cleats. Again, counterbore and plug the screw holes.

Drill two mounting holes in each of the cleats to accommodate No. 10 by 2½ in. flathead wood screws. Countersink the hole openings. Preferably, the holes should be located to correspond with the wall studs where the shelf will be mounted.

Now glue the spindles to the top (A) and the rail (C). After the glue has cured, sand the wood plugs flush and smooth out any irregularities in the wood.

FINISHING

Apply a suitable stain with a brush. After you have coated the entire area, wipe off the excess with a clean cotton cloth. Wipe in the direction of the wood grain to eliminate streaking.

Once the stain has thoroughly dried, apply a sealer coat with a brush. Follow this up by lightly sanding with either steel wool or a fine grit sandpaper. Apply a final coat of satin varnish, and your corner shelf is ready to be hung.

MOUNTING

Mount the shelf to a corner wall with No. 10 by 2½ in. flathead wood screws. Check to make sure that the inside point is not in contact with the corner, otherwise you will have to remove more of the point so that the sides of the shelf conform to the wall. ❒

BILL OF MATERIALS — Country-Style Corner Shelf

Finished Dimensions in Inches

A	Top	¾ x 22½ x 11½ oak	1
B	Front	¾ x 3⅜ x 21⅞ oak	1
C	Rail	½ x ½ x 22¼ oak	1
D	Spindle	¼ x 13/16 decorative spindle oak	7
E	Cleat	¾ x ¾ x 11½ oak	2

All-Purpose Work Table

The table is nearly 5 ft. long, yet its streamlined construction gives it a clean, uncluttered look. Special knockdown fittings allow for easy disassembly.

Solve workspace problems with this streamlined table.

For the seamstress, student or hobbyist, finding enough space to spread out and work is always a problem. This table is designed to be at a comfortable working height and provides a large, flat work surface that is nearly 5 ft. long. Best of all, the table is assembled with knockdown fittings so it can be taken apart easily for moving or storage.

TIPS
Select only solid, knot-free material.

Note that the table is assembled with knockdown fittings. These fittings make a strong joint while allowing easy disassembly.

CONSTRUCTION
Cut all but the top front/back (B) workpieces to their overall widths and lengths. Make sure that your saw is cutting square. A planer blade is ideal for making smooth cuts. Note that the top (A) must be cut with a circular saw blade. Again, make sure that the blade is perpendicular to the saw's pad. Cut with the good side of the wood facing down to minimize splintering on the good side.

Edge-glue the top ends (C) to the top (A) with bar clamps. If your bar clamps are not long enough, counterbore three to four screw holes in the top ends, then glue the workpieces and secure them to the top with 3 in. screws. Fill in the hole recesses with wood plugs cut with a plug cutter.

Now cut the top front/back (B) to fit the top assembly and glue in place. To insure strong joints, secure the top front/back to the table assembly with dowels and glue. Clamp the assembly with bar clamps until the glue dries.

Figure 1. Edge-glue the top ends (C) to the top (A) with carpenter's glue. Secure the assembly with bar clamps. If you do not have bar clamps, use wood screws. Make sure that you counterbore the screws and fill in the hole recesses with wood plugs.

Figure 2. Round over the edges of the lower rail (D) with a rounding over bit. Use a pilot guide with your router. Be sure to wear safety goggles and clamp the workpiece while routing.

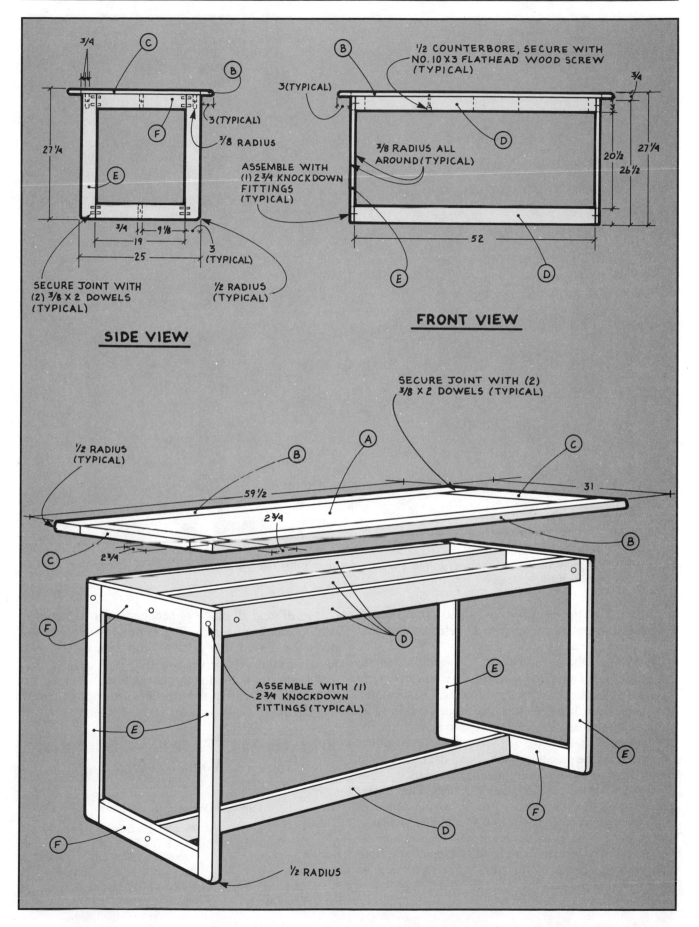

3/4

Ⓒ

Ⓑ

3(TYPICAL)

Ⓕ

3/8 RADIUS

27 1/4

Ⓔ

ASSEMBLE WITH
(1) 2 3/4 KNOCKDOWN
FITTINGS
(TYPICAL)

3/4   9 1/8

19

3 (TYPICAL)

25

SECURE JOINT WITH
(2) 3/8 X 2 DOWELS
(TYPICAL)

1/2 RADIUS
(TYPICAL)

SIDE VIEW

Ⓑ

1/2 COUNTERBORE, SECURE WITH
NO. 10 X 3 FLATHEAD WOOD SCREW
(TYPICAL)

3(TYPICAL)

3/4

3

Ⓓ

3/8 RADIUS ALL
AROUND (TYPICAL)

27 1/4

20 1/2

26 1/2

52

Ⓔ

Ⓓ

FRONT VIEW

SECURE JOINT WITH (2)
3/8 X 2 DOWELS (TYPICAL)

1/2 RADIUS
(TYPICAL)

Ⓑ

Ⓐ

Ⓒ

59 1/2

31

2 3/4

Ⓒ

2 3/4

Ⓑ

Ⓓ

Ⓕ

Ⓔ

ASSEMBLE WITH (1)
2 3/4 KNOCKDOWN
FITTINGS (TYPICAL)

Ⓔ

Ⓔ

Ⓕ

Ⓓ

Ⓕ

1/2 RADIUS

Figure 3. *Drill holes for the knockdown fittings. The manufacturer's instructions should describe how to locate the holes and install the fittings.*

Next, round the corners of the top assembly to a ½ in. radius. Lay out the radius with a circle template, and then cut out the radius with a saber saw.

Each leg consists of two stiles (E) attached to the end rails (F). Secure these workpieces with carpenter's glue and ⅜ in. diameter by 2 in. dowels. Locate all the dowel holes and then drill. It is a good idea to drill ⅛ in. deeper into each adjoining workpiece to allow room for excess glue. Assemble the leg sets and secure with bar clamps. Once the glue has dried, round over the bottom corners of the leg assemblies to a ½ in. radius.

Sand all of the project edges carefully. Then round over the top's showing edges with a ⅜ in. rounding over bit, using a router equipped with a pilot guide. Similarly, rout the inside edges of the leg pairs. You also should rout both the outside and the inside facing edges. Rout all but the outside edges where the leg assembly adjoins the top. Be sure to rout the rails (D) where indicated in the illustration.

Finish sand all of the project parts. A pad sander is ideal for sanding the rails. Be careful not to remove too much wood from the plywood top (A), or you will quickly go through the veneer.

Locate the holes for the knockdown fittings. (Information on locating these fittings is supplied by the manufacturer.) Drill the holes to the diameter specified

BILL OF MATERIALS — All-Purpose Work Table

Finished Dimensions in Inches

A	Top	¾ x 25½ x 54 oak plywood	1
B	Top Front/Back	¾ x 2¾ x 59½ oak	2
C	Top Ends	¾ x 2¾ x 25½ oak	2
D	Rail	¾ x 3 x 52 oak	4
E	Stile	¾ x 3 x 26½ oak	4
F	End Rail	¾ x 3 x 19 oak	4

Figure 4. *Counterbore holes into the top rail (D) and secure the rail to the top assembly with wood screws. Test to make sure that you haven't bored the holes too deeply, or the screws will punch through the table top.*

by the manufacturer. Make sure that you use a backup board to avoid excessive wood splintering.

The top is secured to the rails (D) with No. 10 by 3 in. flathead wood screws. Drill a ½ in. deep counterbore in the bottom of the rail to accommodate the screws. Before driving the screws, doublecheck to make sure that the screws will lie below the surface of the plywood top.

Finally, secure the leg assemblies to the rails with the knockdown fittings. If you do not plan on ever disassembling the table, you can also coat the joints with carpenter's glue.

FINISHING
Give the entire project a final sanding. If you want to leave the work table natural, apply a coat of sealer followed by several coats of a satin finish polyurethane.

We used a stain and then applied a sealer and several coats of a satin finish polyurethane. Make sure that you sand lightly between coats. ❐

Figure 5. *Locate and drill mating dowel holes to connect the stiles (E) to the end rails (F). Drill the holes 1/8 in. deeper than the dowel lengths to allow for glue expansion.*

Fold-Up Play Center/Bed

This cleverly designed unit offers play space and sleeping space all wrapped up in one.

Give your children extra play and sleeping space by building this inexpensive unit.

Whether it is a sleep-over or an afternoon of fun, this unit gives your children plenty of room for entertainment. By day the unit becomes a full-fledged play center, complete with a desk and chair, chalkboard, bulletin board and book rack. And, of course, there's also plenty of pigeonholes for storing toys, games and other important "things." By night the unit folds down to provide a comfortable single bed. Built from ¾ in. plywood, this wall-hugging, space-saving unit is an inexpensive answer to that crowded bedroom or play area.

TIPS

Plan your cuts carefully, and use a straightedge in combination with a circular saw. You should also use a plywood cutting blade to minimize wood splintering.

Also, buy the mattress before constructing the project and change the dimensions accordingly.

CONSTRUCTION

Carefully lay out and then cut all of the project parts to the shapes shown in the illustrations.

When drilling the holes in the desk top (M), remember to use a backup board to prevent excessive wood

Figure 1. *Cut out the silhouette for the two desk holders (E) with a saber saw. Cut with the good side of the wood facing down.*

BILL OF MATERIALS — Fold-Up Play Center/Bed

Finished Dimensions in Inches

A	Bed Rail	¾ x 4½ x 75½ plywood	1
B	Bed Rail	¾ x 12½ x 75½ plywood	1
C	End	¾ x 12½ x 41 plywood	2
D	Divider	¾ x 6 x 41 plywood	2
E	Desk Holder	¾ x 6 x 16 plywood	2
F	Box Top	¾ x 3¾ x 24 plywood	1
G	Upper Horizontal Divider	¾ x 4⁹⁄₁₆ x 24 plywood	1
H	Lower Horizontal Divider	¾ x 5¼ x 24 plywood	1
I	Vertical Divider	¾ x 6 x 22⅜ plywood	2
J	Tray Front	¾ x 4 x 76½ plywood	1
K	Box Front	¾ x 10⅜ x 25½ plywood	1
L	Box Front	¾ x 3⅞ x 25½ plywood	2
M	Desk Top	¾ x 22⅛ x 25⅜ plywood	1
N	Desk Support	¾ x 6 x 18 plywood	2
O	Brace	¾ x 4 x 4½ plywood	2
P	Leg	¾ x 4 x 6⅜ plywood	2
Q	Leg	¾ x 4 x 8⅛ plywood	2
R	Leg Brace	¾ x 3 x 4 plywood	4
S	Leg Pivot	¾ x 3 x 3 plywood	2
T	Desk Retainer	¾ x 1½ x 4 plywood	2
U	Wall Cleat	¾ x 5¼ x 75½ plywood	1
V	Seat Top	¾ x 12⅜ x 12⅜ plywood	1
W	Seat Bottom	¾ x 11⅜ x 11⅜ plywood	1
X	Seat Side	¾ x 11⅜ x 14½ plywood	2
Y	Seat Front/Back	¾ x 12⅜ x 14½ plywood	2
Z	Seat Divider	¾ x 11⅜ x 11⅜ plywood	1
AA	Deck	¾ x 40 x 75½ plywood	1

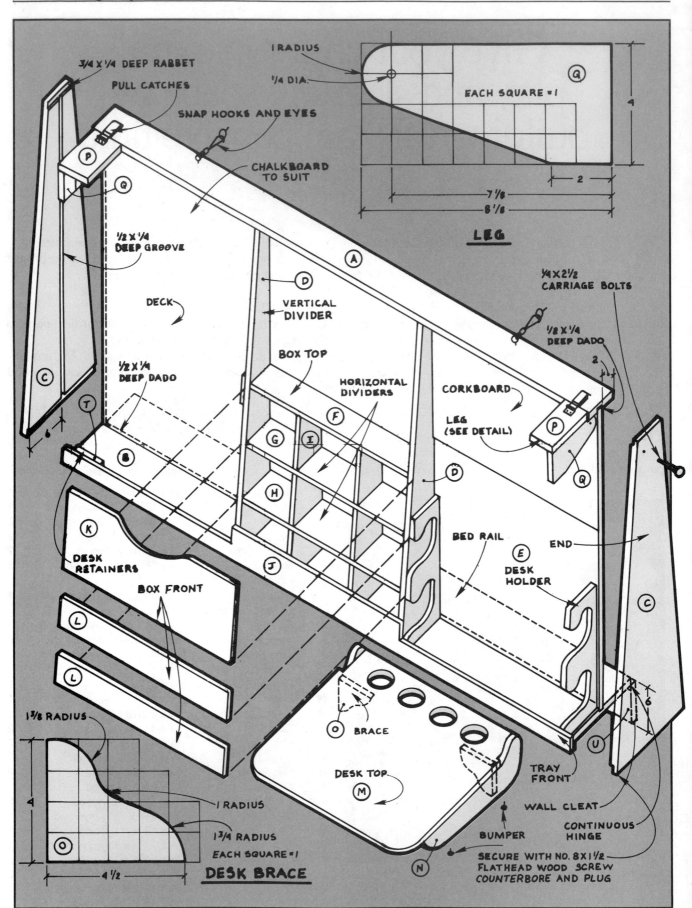

3/4 X 1/4 DEEP RABBET

PULL CATCHES

SNAP HOOKS AND EYES

1 RADIUS

1/4 DIA.

EACH SQUARE = 1

4

7 1/8

8 1/8

LEG

CHALKBOARD TO SUIT

1/2 X 1/4 DEEP GROOVE

DECK

VERTICAL DIVIDER

1/4 X 2 1/2 CARRIAGE BOLTS

1/8 X 1/4 DEEP DADO

2

BOX TOP

HORIZONTAL DIVIDERS

CORKBOARD

LEG (SEE DETAIL)

1/2 X 1/4 DEEP DADO

DESK RETAINERS

BOX FRONT

BED RAIL

END

DESK HOLDER

1 3/8 RADIUS

4

1 RADIUS

1 3/4 RADIUS

EACH SQUARE = 1

4 1/2

DESK BRACE

BRACE

DESK TOP

TRAY FRONT

WALL CLEAT

CONTINUOUS HINGE

BUMPER

6

SECURE WITH NO. 8 X 1 1/2 FLATHEAD WOOD SCREW COUNTERBORE AND PLUG

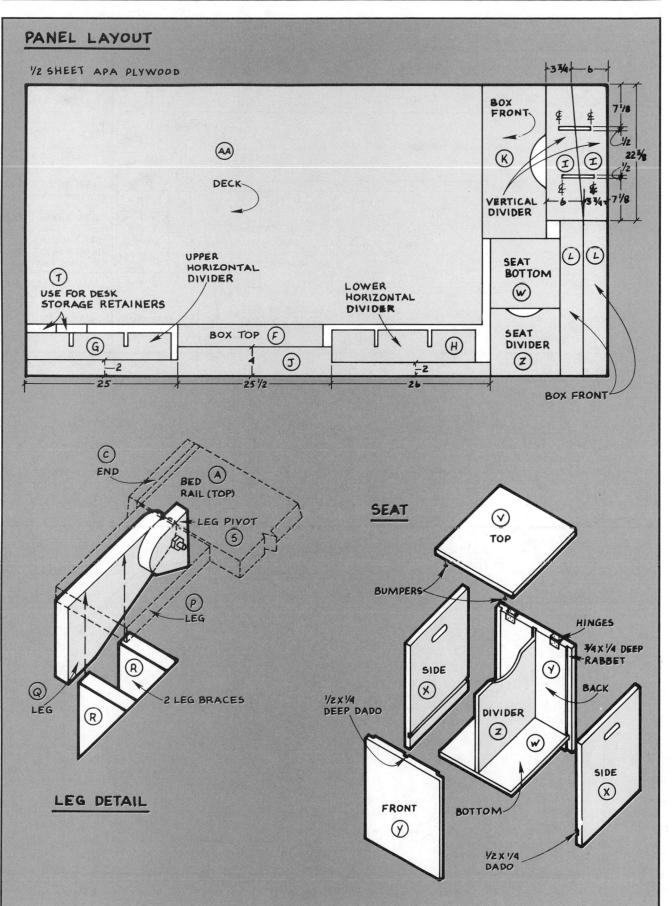

PANEL LAYOUT

1/2 SHEET APA PLYWOOD

AA

DECK

BOX FRONT

K

VERTICAL DIVIDER

3¾ 6

7⅛

½

22⅜

½

6 3¾ 7⅛

Ⓘ Ⓘ

SEAT BOTTOM Ⓦ

Ⓛ Ⓛ

UPPER HORIZONTAL DIVIDER

LOWER HORIZONTAL DIVIDER

SEAT DIVIDER Ⓩ

T

USE FOR DESK STORAGE RETAINERS

BOX TOP Ⓕ

Ⓖ

Ⓙ

Ⓗ

2

25

25½

26

BOX FRONT

LEG DETAIL

Ⓒ END

BED RAIL (TOP) Ⓐ

LEG PIVOT

Ⓢ

Ⓟ LEG

Ⓠ LEG

Ⓡ

Ⓡ

2 LEG BRACES

SEAT

TOP Ⓥ

BUMPERS

HINGES

¾ X ¼ DEEP RABBET

SIDE Ⓧ

Ⓨ

BACK

½ X ¼ DEEP DADO

DIVIDER Ⓩ

Ⓦ

FRONT Ⓨ

BOTTOM

SIDE Ⓧ

½ X ¼ DADO

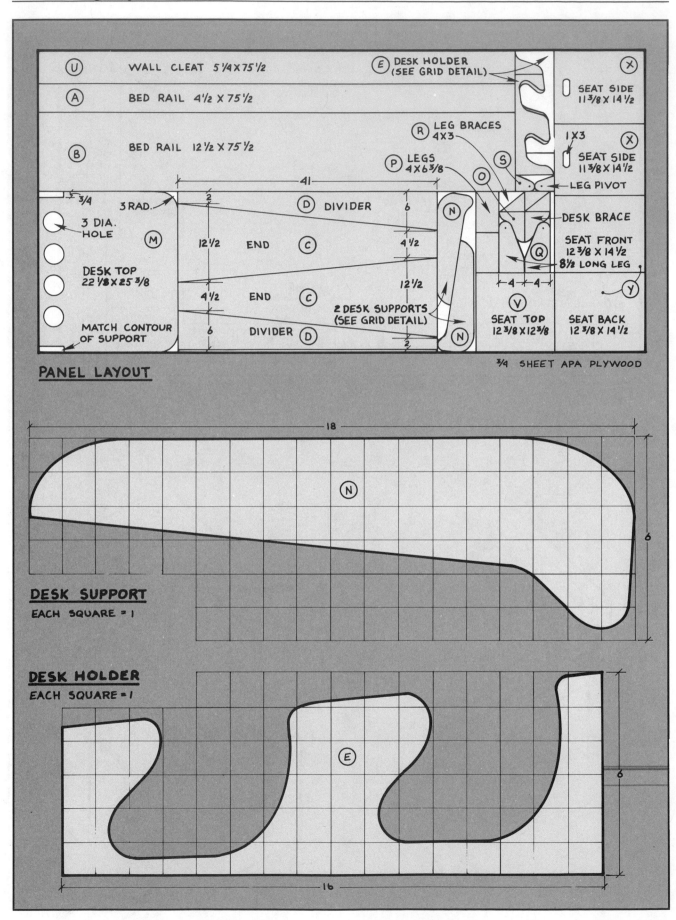

(U) WALL CLEAT 5 1/4 X 75 1/2

(E) DESK HOLDER (SEE GRID DETAIL)

(X) SEAT SIDE 11 3/8 X 14 1/2

(A) BED RAIL 4 1/2 X 75 1/2

(B) BED RAIL 12 1/2 X 75 1/2

(R) LEG BRACES 4X3

1 X 3

(X) SEAT SIDE 11 3/8 X 14 1/2

LEG PIVOT

(P) LEGS 4 X 6 3/8

(S)

(O)

3/4

3 RAD.

41

(D) DIVIDER

6

DESK BRACE

3 DIA. HOLE

(M)

12 1/2

END

(C)

4 1/2

(N)

SEAT FRONT 12 3/8 X 14 1/2

8 1/2 LONG LEG

DESK TOP 22 1/8 X 25 3/8

4 1/2

END

(C)

12 1/2

(Q)

MATCH CONTOUR OF SUPPORT

6

DIVIDER

(D)

2

2 DESK SUPPORTS (SEE GRID DETAIL)

(N)

2

4 4

(V)

SEAT TOP 12 3/8 X 12 3/8

SEAT BACK 12 3/8 X 14 1/2

(Y)

PANEL LAYOUT

3/4 SHEET APA PLYWOOD

18

(N)

DESK SUPPORT

EACH SQUARE = 1

6

DESK HOLDER

EACH SQUARE = 1

(E)

6

16

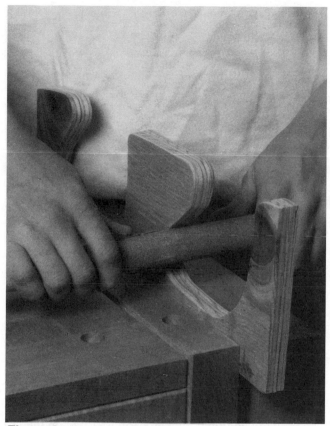

Figure 2. *Sand both the inside and outside curves of the desk holders using sandpaper wrapped around a dowel. Start with a medium grit sandpaper and work to a fine grit sandpaper.*

splintering. Follow this same technique for cutting the handles in the seat sides (X).

Note the slots in the vertical dividers (I), upper horizontal divider (G) and lower horizontal divider (H). Cut these slots deep enough so that they will adequately overlap the workpieces to which they will be adjoined.

Rabbet both ends of the end workpieces (C). Use a dado blade installed in your table saw. Next, groove the end workpieces as well as the bed rails (A, B).

Now attach the rails and the end workpieces to the deck (AA). Secure the joints with carpenter's glue and No. 8 by 1½ in. flathead wood screws. Predrill all of the holes and counterbore them slightly. Later you will fill in the blemishes and hole recesses with wood filler. Be careful not to counterbore too deeply, or you will not have enough holding power.

Now install the vertical dividers (D) along with the box top (F), horizontal dividers (G, H) and vertical dividers (I). Secure the assembly with carpenter's glue and 4d finishing nails.

Sand the inside and outside curves of the desk holders (E), and then install the desk holders using

This story is courtesy of the American Plywood Association, P.O. Box 11700, Tacoma, WA 98411.

carpenter's glue. Clamp the desk holders in place until the glue has cured. Form the desk unit by securing the desk top (M) to the desk supports (N) with carpenter's glue and 4d finishing nails. Also install the braces (O).

Now form the two legs by attaching the legs (P, Q) to the leg braces (R) with carpenter's glue and 4d finishing nails. Predrill for the nails that go into the leg braces (R). You will need two leg braces for each leg assembly.

Attach the two leg pivots (S) to the deck (AA) with No. 8 by 1½ in. flathead wood screws and carpenter's glue. Countersink the screw heads. Next, position one of the leg assemblies in place and drill a 5/16 in. diameter hole through the end workpiece (C), leg (Q) and leg pivot (S). Use a backup board to eliminate wood splintering. Then install a carriage bolt so that the nut and flat washer is on the inside of the unit. Check to make sure that the leg folds down easily. Follow this same procedure for installing the second leg assembly.

Next, form the seat by rabbeting and dadoing the workpieces indicated in the illustration. Secure the assembly with carpenter's glue and 4d finishing nails.

FINISHING

Finish sand all of the project parts and remove all dust particles before painting. Apply a good coat of paint sealer and then lightly sand when dry. Follow this up by applying two coats of nontoxic paint, again sanding between coats.

Figure 3. *Use a power hand planer to joint the plywood edges. Make light passes, and use the tool's edge guide.*

Figure 4. *Fill in all wood blemishes and screw holes with a nontoxic wood filler.*

Figure 5. *Dado and rabbet the end workpieces (C) on your radial arm saw or table saw. Equip the saw with a dado blade. Then smooth the dado with a wood chisel.*

MOUNTING

Attach the bed rail (B) to the wall cleat (U) with a continuous hinge. With the aid of a helper, secure the wall cleat to the wall by driving two No. 10 by 2½ in. flathead wood screws into each wall stud. Install two heavy-duty eye hooks at two stud locations and connect a set of snap hooks and eyes to the bed rail (A). Then snap the unit to the wall's eye hooks.

Now install two pull catches to both legs (P). The pull catches prevent the legs from being kicked out when the unit is folded down into the bed position. When the unit is being used as a play center, however, undo the pull catches to prevent children from bumping their heads on the legs.

Next, cut and install cork board above the desk top and install the chalkboard. Then attach the box fronts (K, L) with 4d finishing nails. Similarly, attach the tray front (J).

The assembled desk top fits into the special desk holders (E) when the center is being used. When the play center is folded down, the desk top is stored on the left side of the play center and held in place by two desk retainers (T). Secure the desk retainers with carpenter's glue, clamping them until the glue is dry. Now hinge the seat top (V), then install bumpers underneath the seat top and the desk top, as indicated in the illustrations. ❑

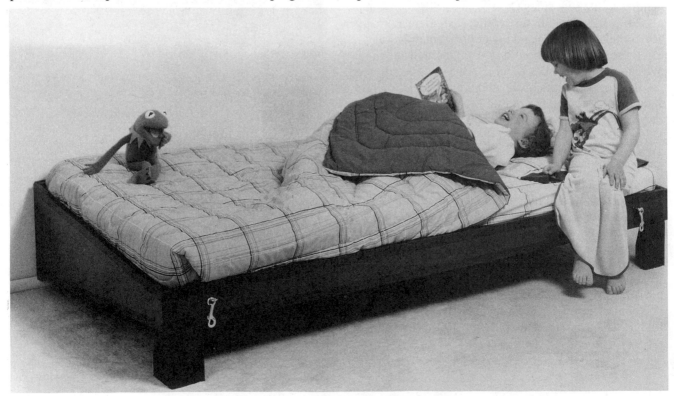

Old-Fashioned Display Cupboard

A nail set and a hammer are all you need to produce the design in the tin door front. Our full-size pattern makes duplicating the design easy.

Recall the past with this nostalgic pierced-tin cabinet.

This project offers something a little different, both in terms of its look and the techniques used to make it. The pierced-tin door gives the compact cupboard lots of appeal, while duplicating the design in the tin is fun and challenging. Built from pine and plywood, it is easily customized by simply giving it a couple of coats of an antique paint. Or, you may want to try your hand at rosemaling or stenciling. Even the type of knobs used for the door and the drawer offers an opportunity to stylize the cupboard to suit your tastes. Use your imagination, and you'll find that this cupboard can go just about anywhere, from bedroom or bathroom to dining room or kitchen.

TIPS

Built from pine, this project will look better if it is painted, rather than stained. So look around to find the paint that will both go with your room decor and make the project look its best.

Figure 1. *Cut the half laps in the door rails (E) and door stiles (F) with a dado blade installed in your radial arm saw. You must doublecheck to make sure that the saw is square with the fence and is cutting to a depth of 1/4 inch.*

You may be able to purchase the tin for the cabinet door at a grocery store. A large cookie sheet or jelly roll pan can be used to make your tin design. Try to stay away from aluminum flashing that is purchased in a roll. Getting the bend out of the rolled flashing is a job in itself.

CONSTRUCTION

Cut out all of the project parts to their overall widths and lengths. Notice that most of the parts are cut from 3/4 in. pine. However, the door rails (E) and stiles (F) are made up of 1/2 in. pine. Obtain this thickness by running the stock through a planer or on your jointer.

Finish sand all of the project parts at this time. A stationary belt sander is ideal for working with these small pieces. Be careful and try not to round over the edges. Keep the workpieces absolutely flat as you sand.

Install a 3/8 in. cove bit equipped with pilot guide in your router. Then rout a design on the showing edges of the top workpieces (J, K). Next, install a 1/2 in. rounding over bit with pilot guide and rout the base (D).

Attach the top (K) and the base (D) to the two sides (A) with 4d finishing nails and carpenter's glue. Be sure to sink all nailheads. Square the assembly and allow to dry. Then rout a 1/2 in. by 1/4 in. deep rabbet all around the back of the cabinet assembly, as indicated in the Side

BILL OF MATERIALS — Old-Fashioned Display Cupboard

Finished Dimensions in Inches

A	Side	3/4 x 6 x 20 pine	2
B	Upper Shelf	3/4 x 5 1/4 x 10 1/2 pine	1
C	Lower Shelf	3/4 x 5 3/4 x 10 1/2 pine	1
D	Base	3/4 x 6 x 10 1/2 pine	2
E	Door Rail	1/2 x 1 5/8 x 10 1/4 pine	2
F	Door Stile	1/2 x 1 5/8 x 13 pine	2
G	Drawer Front/Back	3/4 x 3 5/8 x 10 3/8 pine	2
H	Drawer Side	3/4 x 3 5/8 x 5 pine	2
I	Drawer Bottom	1/4 x 4 3/4 x 9 3/8 plywood	1
J	Top	3/4 x 7 1/2 x 15 pine	1
K	Top	3/4 x 6 3/4 x 13 1/2 pine	1
L	Tin	1/16 x 7 7/8 x 10 3/4 tin	1
M	Back	1/4 x 11 1/2 x 18 3/4 plywood	1

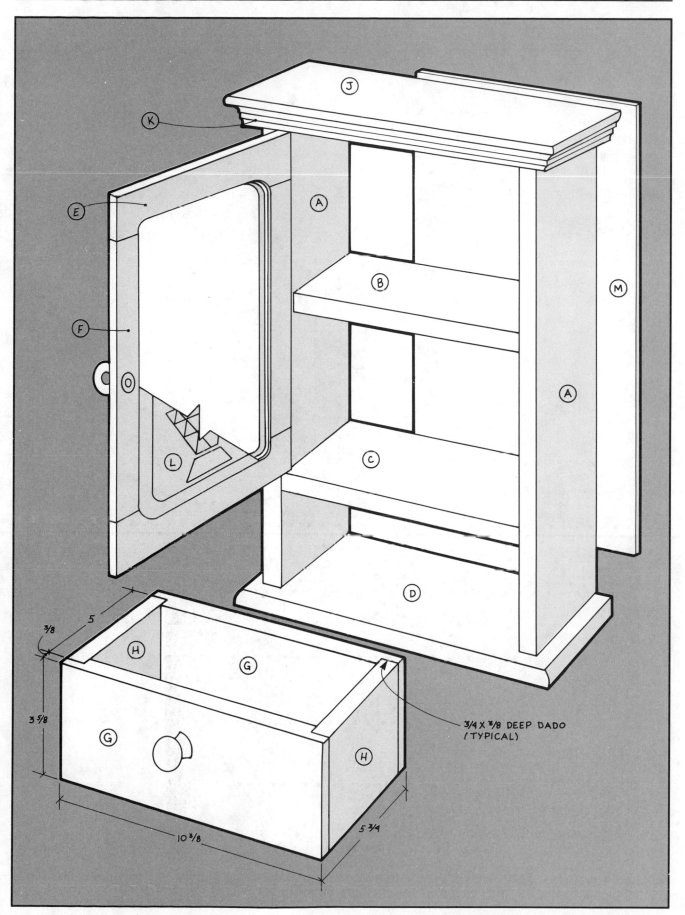

3/8

5

3 5/8

10 3/8

5 3/4

3/4 X 3/8 DEEP DADO
(TYPICAL)

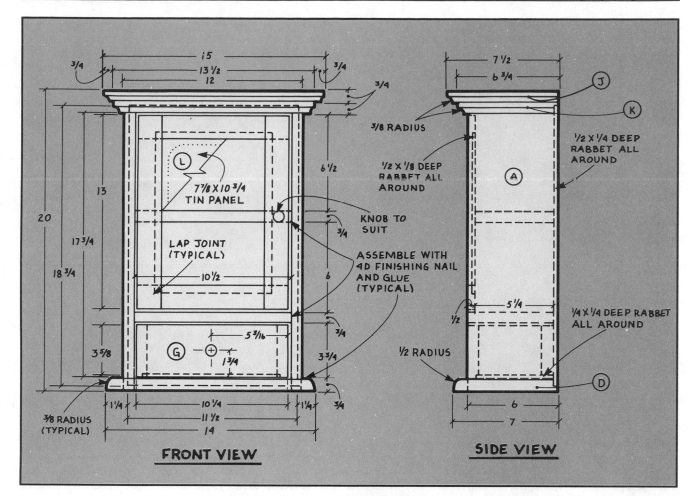

FRONT VIEW

SIDE VIEW

View illustration. Square the corners with a sharp wood chisel.

Now install the plywood back (M), upper shelf (B), lower shelf (C) and top (J) with 4d finishing nails and carpenter's glue. Note that the upper shelf (B) is ½ in. short of the front edges of the side workpieces (A). This allows clearance for the door.

With a dado blade installed in your radial arm saw, cut the half-lap joints in the door rails (E) and stiles (F). It is always a good idea to test cut the half-lap cuts on scrap material first to make sure that you do not cut the lap joints too deeply. Afterwards, smooth the half-lap cuts with a sharp wood chisel. Clamp the workpieces so that both hands are free to do the chiseling.

As an alternative to cutting half-lap joints, substitute with butt joints. If you choose this alternative, cut the door stiles (F) to the same length as specified in the bill of materials. However, cut the two door rails (E) shorter, so they fit between the stiles.

Drill two dowel holes into the areas to be joined to accommodate a ¼ in. by 1 in. dowel.

Cut dadoes into the drawer front/back workpieces (G) with your radial arm saw.

Attach the drawer front/back workpieces to the drawer sides (H) with 4d finishing nails and carpenter's

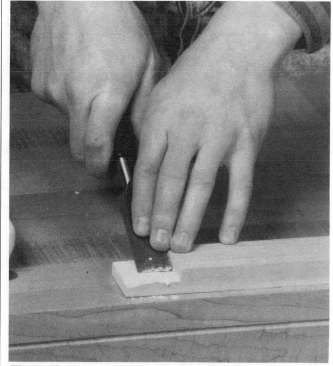

Figure 2. *Clean out the half-lap areas with a sharp wood chisel to remove the ridges caused by your dado blade. Clamp the workpiece so you can use both hands.*

Figure 3. *Rout a ³/8 in. radius along three sides of the top (K) with your router. The router must have a pilot guide installed.*

Figure 4. *As an alternative to taping and then punching the door design, tape the pattern for the pierced tin design onto the tin along with carbon paper. Reproduce each dot in the pattern. Remove the pattern and create the design by driving a nailset into each dot location with your hammer.*

glue. Square the assembly and allow the glue to cure overnight.

Next, rout a ¼ in. by ¼ in. deep rabbet along the bottom inside edges of the drawer, and square the rabbeted corners with a wood chisel. Then install the drawer bottom (I) using 4d finishing nails and carpenter's glue.

Assemble the door by gluing and clamping the door rails and door stiles together. Do not drive any nails in the half-lap areas. After the glue has dried, rout a ½ in. by ⅛ in. deep rabbet around the inside of the door opening to accommodate the tin panel.

Finish sand all of the project parts, and make sure that the door has enough clearance to open and close properly. Similarly, check the drawer for fit. It should easily slide into the cabinet.

Now form the design in the tin using our full-size design pattern. Remove the page from the book and tape it onto the tin. Then position the tin on a flat plywood surface. Use scrap plywood, since the pattern's indentations will be left in the wood. Select a nailset with a small point. Then align the nailset with a dot, and use a hammer to drive the nailset in the tin. You can either

Figure 5. *Install the pierced tin (L) to the door using dabs of hot glue.*

tap the nailset lightly to form a slight indentation or you can drive it all the way through to the plywood so the tin is completely pierced. Practice in a waste area of the tin first to help you get a feel for the operation, and to decide on which technique you want to use.

Once you are comfortable with the procedure, follow the bottom half of the pattern and work your way upward. When you are finished, the pattern will be almost completely decimated, so make sure that the pattern is taped all the way around and that you work systematically from the bottom up.

FINISHING

Sink all nailheads and fill in with a good wood filler. Finish sand where necessary and apply a coat of paint sealer. After the sealer has dried thoroughly, sand lightly. Follow this up with an application of paint. Once again, after the paint has dried, sand lightly and apply a second coat.

Drill holes into the drawer and the door to accommodate knobs. Remember to use a backup board to eliminate wood splintering. Then install the knobs. Attach a ½ in. wide brass hinge to the door so it corresponds to the door's thickness. There is no need to mortise out the door. Then install a magnetic catch on the inside of the cabinet.

Finally, install the door tin with hot glue. ❐

Build Your Own Bass Boat

This bass boat may be small, but it will get you to where the big fish are.

Add mobility to your angling with this plywood bass boat.

If the high cost of fishing boats has you dry-docked, then this mini bass boat is for you. With only a couple weekends of your time and a minimum of materials, you can build a boat that's perfect for reaching those out-of-the-way fish haunts. The pontoons make it easy to propel the boat with an electric trolling motor, while providing a stable platform for casting. Hinged doors in the tops of the pontoons offer easy access to storage wells for holding tackle, gear and other fishing necessities. Compact and lightweight, this is a boat that's ready to go whenever you are.

TIPS

You should buy only APA marine grade plywood or, if available, APA trademarked Medium Density Overlay (MDO), overlaid both sides.

Secure all joints with brass wood screws and a suitable waterproof wood adhesive. After you have assembled the basic pontoon, thoroughly caulk the inside seams, including the bulkheads (K), with a good waterproof caulk. Before applying the caulk, make sure you thoroughly clean the inside seams with a dry cloth.

CONSTRUCTION

Cut out all of the plywood parts to the widths, lengths and shapes indicated in the diagrams for the three plywood panels. Use a circular saw equipped with a plywood cutting blade. Guide the saw along the edges with a straightedge clamped to the plywood panel. Cut the pontoon tops (C) from a full-length section of plywood that is 11⅞ in. wide. Then cut out the hinged doors from that section of plywood. Cut these doors with your circular saw. The inside cuts will have to be made by making a plunge cut with a saw. Then cut to the inside corners with a handsaw or saber saw. When cutting the two pontoon tops, make sure that the best surface will be facing up and that the door locations are mirror images of one another.

Assemble the pontoon bottoms (B) to the pontoon sides (A), and then secure the pontoon backs (D) with waterproof glue and No. 6 by 1¼ in. brass flathead wood

This story is courtesy of the American Plywood Association, P.O. Box 11700, Tacoma, WA 98411.

screws, countersunk. Make sure that you predrill for the screws.

Position the two pontoon fronts (E) onto the assembly and determine the bevel angle that must be cut into the fronts in order for them to be adjoined to the edge of the pontoon bottom. Then cut the taper into the pontoon fronts with a circular saw. The top edges of the fronts should be flush with the tops of the pontoon sides. After cutting the pontoon fronts, attach them to the pontoon assembly with waterproof glue and brass wood screws.

The inside of the pontoon must be reinforced with 1 x 2 framing (M). Custom cut the framing to suit the inside dimensions of the pontoon assembly. Notice that the 1 x 2 cross braces are positioned to suit the door openings in the pontoon top (C), so make sure you position them accordingly. Secure the 1 x 2 framing with waterproof glue and 1 in. stainless steel finishing nails. You can secure the 1 x 2 framing to the ¼ in. plywood skin by driving the nails directly from the outside. When

BILL OF MATERIALS — Build Your Own Bass Boat

Finished Dimensions in Inches

A	Pontoon Side	¼ x 11⅞ x 96 marine plywood	4
B	Pontoon Bottom	¼ x 11⅞ x 84 marine plywood	2
C	Pontoon Top	¼ x 11⅞ x 96 marine plywood	2
D	Pontoon Back	¼ x 11⅞ x 12⅜ marine plywood	2
E	Pontoon Front	¼ x 11⅞ x 17⅜ marine plywood	2
F	Transom	¾ x 7¼ x 47¾ pine	2
G	Transom Pad	¼ x 7¼ x 11⅞ marine plywood	4
H	Splash Rail	¾ x 3½ x 82¼ pine	2
I	Floor	¼ x 24 x 84 marine plywood	1
J	Center Support	¾ x 3½ x 82½ pine	1
K	Bulkhead	¼ x 9⅞ x 11⅞ marine plywood	4
L	Floor Support	¼ x 5½ x 22½ marine plywood	4
M	Framing	¾ x 1½ x 96 pine	16
N	Seat Sides	¼ x 7 x 10 marine plywood	8
O	Seat Top/Bottom	1½ x 6½ x 6½ pine	4

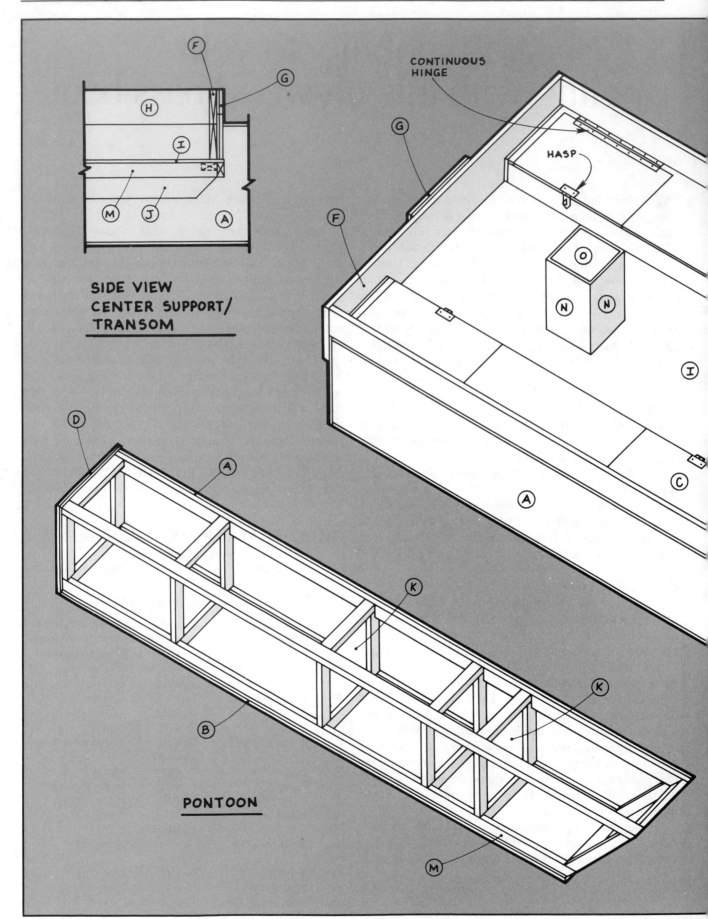

SIDE VIEW
CENTER SUPPORT/
TRANSOM

CONTINUOUS HINGE

HASP

PONTOON

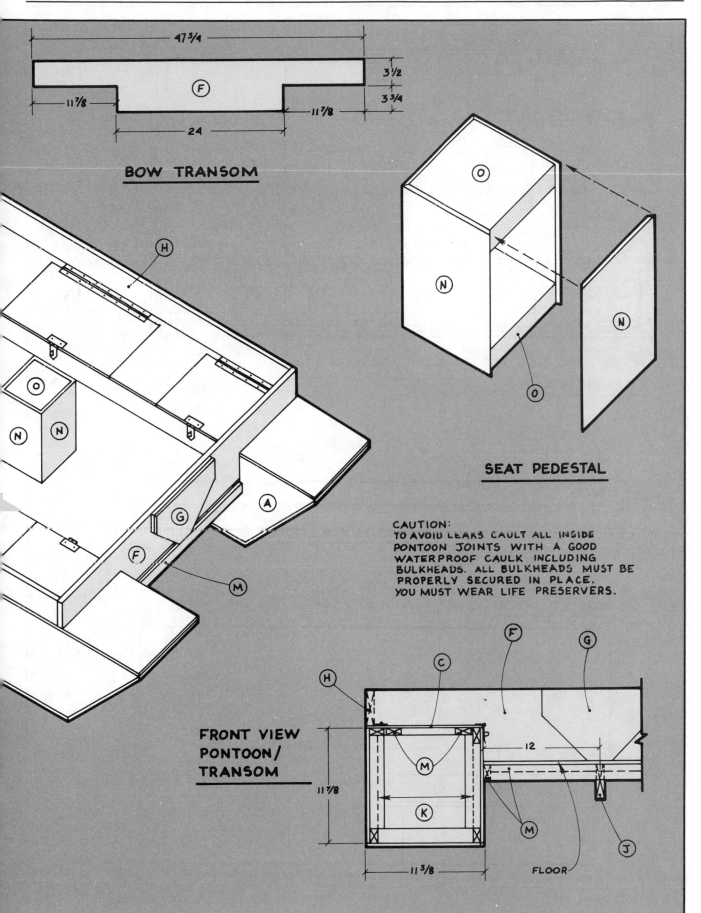

47¾

3½

3¾

11⅞   11⅞

24

F

BOW TRANSOM

H

O

N   N

A

G

F

M

O

N

N

SEAT PEDESTAL

CAUTION:
TO AVOID LEAKS CAULT ALL INSIDE
PONTOON JOINTS WITH A GOOD
WATERPROOF CAULK INCLUDING
BULKHEADS. ALL BULKHEADS MUST BE
PROPERLY SECURED IN PLACE.
YOU MUST WEAR LIFE PRESERVERS.

FRONT VIEW PONTOON / TRANSOM

H   C   F   G

M

12

11⅞

K

M

J

11⅜

FLOOR

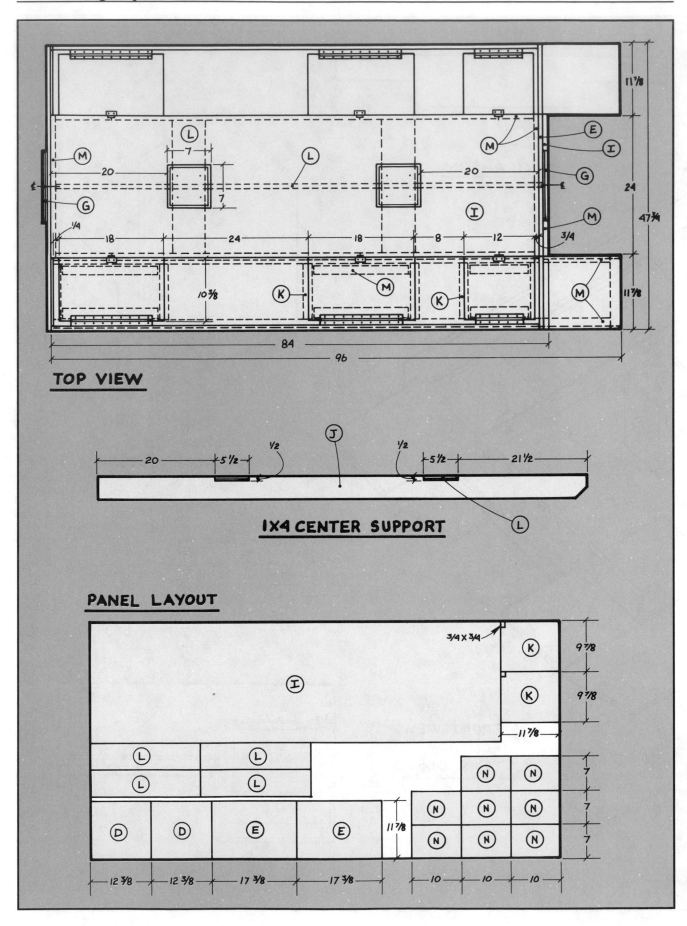

TOP VIEW

1X4 CENTER SUPPORT

PANEL LAYOUT

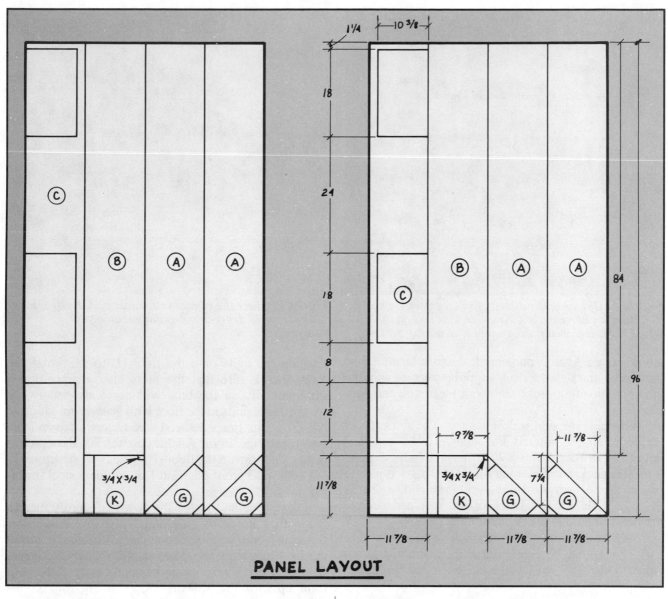

PANEL LAYOUT

you are finished driving the nails, make sure you sink all nailheads.

Cut 1 x 2 framing for each of the doors, and secure the framing to each door. Use waterproof glue and 1 in. stainless steel finishing nails driven from the good side of the plywood. The positions of the framing are arbitrary; however, make sure that the framing does not interfere with the inside pontoon structure.

Now install the bulkheads (K) with 1 in. stainless steel finishing nails and waterproof glue.

After the glue has dried, apply a coat of marine epoxy resin to the inside of the pontoon as well as to the bottom of the pontoon top (C). (Marine epoxy resin is available at businesses that do marine repair.) This involves mixing two solvents together, and then brushing on the mixed epoxy resin. It is important that you wear adequate eye protection, a good respirator and gloves. Follow the manufacturer's instructions for safe applica-

tion. It is best to apply this toxic resin outdoors.

After the resin has dried thoroughly, caulk all inside corners with a good waterproof caulk. Complete the basic pontoon by securing the pontoon top with waterproof glue and 1 in. stainless steel finishing nails.

The next phase of construction consists of building the deck structure. Begin by cutting all of the 1 x 2 deck framing (M). Secure the framing along with the center support (J) and floor supports (L). Note that each floor support is comprised of two pieces of plywood glued together.

Assemble the deck structure with waterproof glue and No. 6 by 2 in. brass flathead wood screws. Countersink all screw heads. Make sure that the unit is square, and then allow the glue to cure before proceeding to the next step.

Now secure the deck assembly to both pontoons with waterproof glue and No. 6 by 2 in. brass flathead

Figure 1. *Cut the doors directly from the pontoon tops (C). Make a plunge cut with your circular saw on the inside edges and then finish the cut with a saber saw.*

Figure 2. *Miter the edges of each seat side (N) by setting your saw to 45 degrees and guiding it along a straightedge.*

wood screws. Again, countersink all screw heads. Drive the screws through the deck support structure and into the corresponding cross members located in the pontoons.

Assemble the seat pedestals next. The sides (N) of the pedestals are mitered and secured to the tops and bottoms (O). Then secure with waterproof adhesive and 1 in. stainless steel finishing nails. It is a good idea to insert some sort of buoyancy material, such as Styrofoam, into the cavities of the seat pedestals to provide flotation in the event of an accident.

Now install two swivel chairs to suit these pedestals. Swivel seats can be purchased at most sporting goods stores. Once the seats are attached to the pedestals,

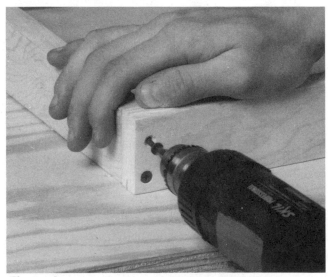

Figure 3. *Assemble the floor framing (M) before attaching the assembly to the pontoons.*

position the units onto the floor (I) to maximize leg room. Make sure that the units also are positioned symmetrically so the boat will not lean. Secure the seat/pedestal units to the floor with waterproof glue and No. 6 by 2 in. brass flathead wood screws driven from underneath the floor. Again, countersink these screw heads. Then attach the floor (I) to the floor structure (L, M) with waterproof glue and 1 in. stainless steel finishing nails.

Next, glue and fasten the bow and stern transoms (F) with waterproof glue and No. 6 by 2 in. brass flathead wood screws, countersunk. Similarly, install the 1 x 4 splash rail (H). Then install No. 6 by 2 in. brass flathead wood screws from the open cavity of the pontoon up into the splash rails, spacing the screws approximately every 8 to 12 inches. Finally, glue and secure the transom pads (G) to the transoms with waterproof glue and No. 6 by 2 in. brass flathead wood screws, countersunk.

FINISHING

Finish sand the entire project, including the unhinged doors. Round over all edges slightly and check the pontoons for any gaps. Apply a waterproof wood filler to all nail holes and sand flush.

Wipe all the dust away with a clean cloth and spray a good marine sealer to the entire project. After the sealer has dried thoroughly, lightly sand the project. Follow this up by applying two coats of marine paint.

Complete the project by hinging the doors and adding hasps. Cut the hinges from a 6 ft. long section of continuous piano hinge. Six hinge hasps are also needed.

To power your new mini bass boat, simply install an electric motor at either the front or rear of the boat. ❏

Rustic Bird Feeder

Rough-sawn cedar makes this rustic bird feeder a natural for the backyard, and for the birds.

Build a project that's for the birds — and your watching enjoyment!

The age-old pastime of bird-watching has been revived, thanks to the increasing interest in outdoor activities and concern for our environment. This bird feeder will let you enjoy nature from your own backyard, and do your part in helping our feathered friends. Constructed of lightweight, yet weather-resistant cedar, the feeder can be hung just about anywhere for the best possible vantage.

TIPS
Use a weather-resistant wood, such as cedar, to insure long-lasting use. We used rough-sawn cedar, leaving the rough surface visible for a rustic look. We also left the feeder unfinished to weather naturally.

CONSTRUCTION
Cut the workpieces for the roof (A) and sides (B) to their overall widths and lengths. Then cut the 45 degree miters as shown in the diagram, using your table saw. Also cut the bottom (C) to size.

Readjust your table saw to cut a ⅛ in. by ¼ in. deep groove into the two side pieces (B). This will accommodate the Plexiglas front (G) and back (H).

Now cut the front and back using a saber saw equipped with a plastic or laminate cutting blade. Work carefully, and remember to wear safety goggles. Before cutting, run a strip of masking tape along the center of the cutting area, then mark the cutting line on the tape. The tape will minimize chipping of the Plexiglas.

Stack the front and back workpieces on top of each other, and drill the two holes through them at the same time. On your drill press, drill the ⁷⁄₁₆ in. diameter hole with a twist drill bit; drill the 1½ in. diameter hole with a spur bit or hole saw. Use a backup board to prevent the

Figure 1. *We left the rough surface of the rough-sawn cedar showing. If you choose to do the same, keep this in mind when planning your miter cuts for the sides (B) and roof (A).*

Figure 2. *Cut a groove along the full length of the side workpieces (B) with a table saw or on a router table. Two grooves are required for each side piece to accommodate the Plexiglas.*

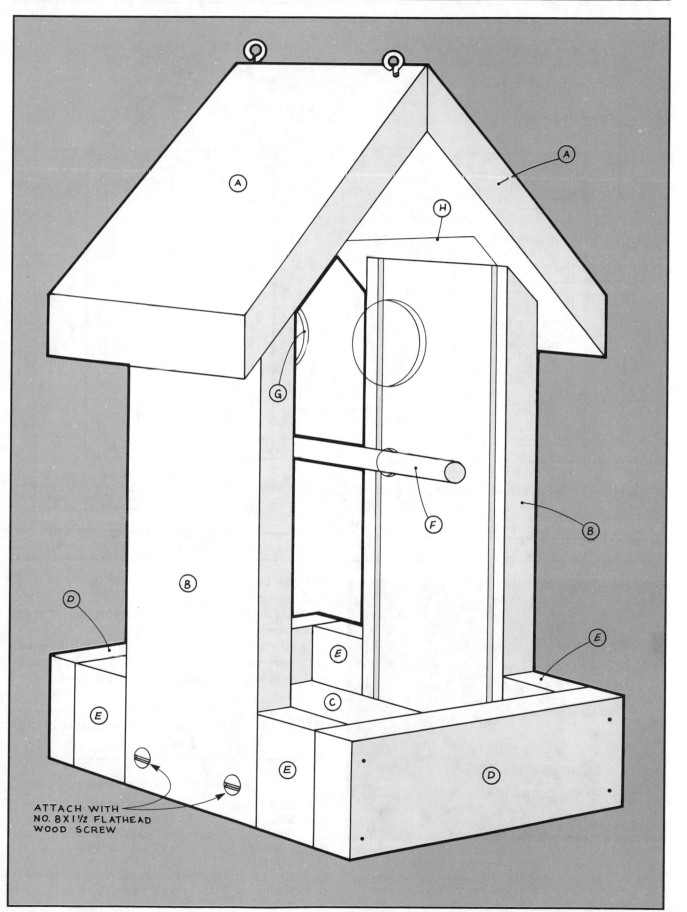

ATTACH WITH
NO. 8 X 1½ FLATHEAD
WOOD SCREW

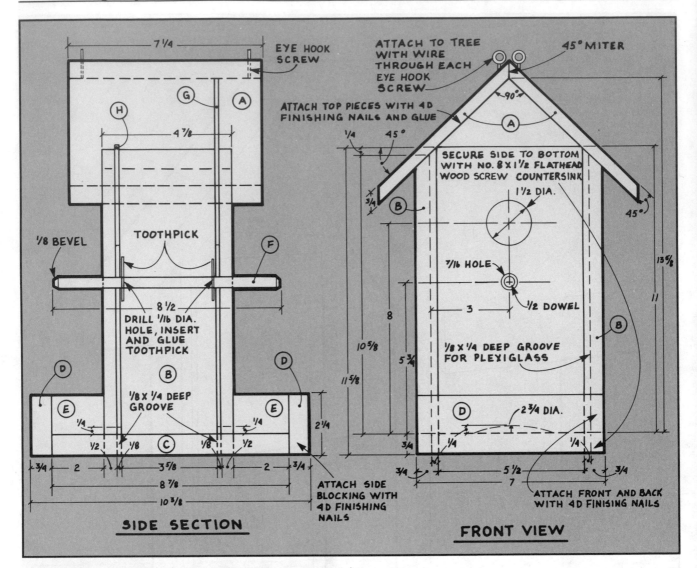

SIDE SECTION

7 1/4

EYE HOOK SCREW

ATTACH TO TREE WITH WIRE THROUGH EACH EYE HOOK SCREW

45° MITER

G

A

H

90°

ATTACH TOP PIECES WITH 4D FINISHING NAILS AND GLUE

4 7/8

45°

A

1/4

SECURE SIDE TO BOTTOM WITH NO. 8 X 1 1/2 FLATHEAD WOOD SCREW COUNTERSINK

1/8 BEVEL

TOOTHPICK

F

3/4

B

1 1/2 DIA.

45°

7/16 HOLE

1/2 DOWEL

13 5/8

8 1/2

DRILL 1/16 DIA. HOLE, INSERT AND GLUE TOOTHPICK

8

3

11

10 5/8

5 3/4

1/8 X 1/4 DEEP GROOVE FOR PLEXIGLASS

B

D

B

11 5/8

E

E

1/4

1/8 X 1/4 DEEP GROOVE

1/4

D

2 1/4

1/2

1/8

C

1/8

1/2

2 3/4 DIA.

1/4

1/4

3/4

2

3 5/8

2

3/4

3/4

1/4

5 1/2

1/4

3/4

8 7/8

3/4

7

10 3/8

ATTACH SIDE BLOCKING WITH 4D FINISHING NAILS

ATTACH FRONT AND BACK WITH 4D FINISING NAILS

FRONT VIEW

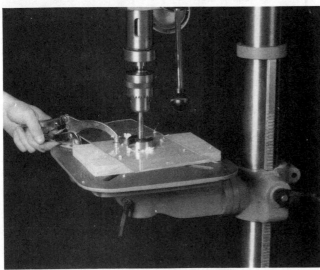

Figure 3. *Drill the 1 1/2 in. diameter hole required for the front (G) and back (H) with a spur bit mounted on a drill press. Notice the use of a hold-down clamp to keep the workpieces stationary while drilling. Work slowly and wear eye protection.*

Plexiglas from shattering, and work slowly to avoid cracking the workpieces.

Form the feeder opening in the Plexiglas front and back using a stationary belt sander.

Assemble the roof to the sides with 4d finishing nails and waterproof glue. You will need to slip the Plexiglas in place to help position the roof and the sides.

BILL OF MATERIALS — Rustic Bird Feeder

Finished Dimensions in Inches

A	Roof	3/4 x 7 1/4 x 7 3/8 cedar	2
B	Side	3/4 x 4 7/8 x 11 5/8 cedar	2
C	Bottom	3/4 x 5 1/2 x 8 7/8 cedar	1
D	Front Rail	3/4 x 2 1/4 x 7 cedar	2
E	Side Rail	3/4 x 2 x 2 1/4 cedar	4
F	Perch	1/2 dia. x 8 1/2 hardwood dowel	1
G	Front	1/8 x 6 x 13 5/8 Plexiglas	1
H	Back	1/8 x 6 x 11 Plexiglas	1

Cut the dowel for the perch (F) to length, and bevel the ends by sanding them on a flat sheet of sandpaper. Move and slowly turn the dowel on the sandpaper to produce this bevel.

Drill two $\frac{1}{16}$ in. diameter holes in the dowel so that the perch can be pinned with toothpicks from the inside, next to the Plexiglas. Run the perch through the holes in the Plexiglas, and insert half a toothpick through one of the perch holes and the other half through the remaining perch hole.

Secure the sides (B) to the bottom (C) with No. 8 by $1\frac{1}{2}$ in. flathead wood screws. Predrill the holes and countersink. Do not glue this joint.

Next, cut the front rails (D) and the side rails (E) to fit. Secure these to the bottom and to one another using 4d finishing nails and waterproof glue. Predrill the holes to prevent the wood from splitting.

Attach two eye hooks to the roof as shown in the illustration, and your bird feeder is complete.

Fill the feeder from the back by pouring the seed through the space created by the shorter Plexiglas back (H). Thread wire through the hooks, and the feeder is ready for the birds. ❑

Figure 4. *Form the feeder opening required at the bottom of the front (G) and back (H) on a stationary belt sander. Hold the workpiece firmly as you shape.*

Figure 5. *Secure the sides (B) to the bottom (C) with wood screws. In the event that you have to replace the Plexiglas or the perch, you can disassemble the unit to make your repairs.*

Colonial Bench

This attractive bench goes anyplace where extra seating space is needed. We built the bench with ash, but you can also use pine for a more rustic look.

Add a touch of country — and more seating space — to your home with this Colonial bench.

You can add a touch of country to any room with this Colonial-style bench. It is the perfect complement to a kitchen, foyer, hall or bedroom while providing a practical place to sit down and take off your shoes. Built with a minimum of materials, the bench is an inexpensive, attractive answer to the ever-present problem of not enough seating space.

TIPS
Purchase select-grade ash. Stay away from any warped or bowed material.

CONSTRUCTION
Begin by cutting the back (C) and seat (B) to length. You will need to edge-glue several narrower pieces to come up with the appropriate width for these workpieces. Cut

Figure 1. Cut, joint and edge-glue the workpieces for the sides (A). Clamp firmly, but do not overtighten.

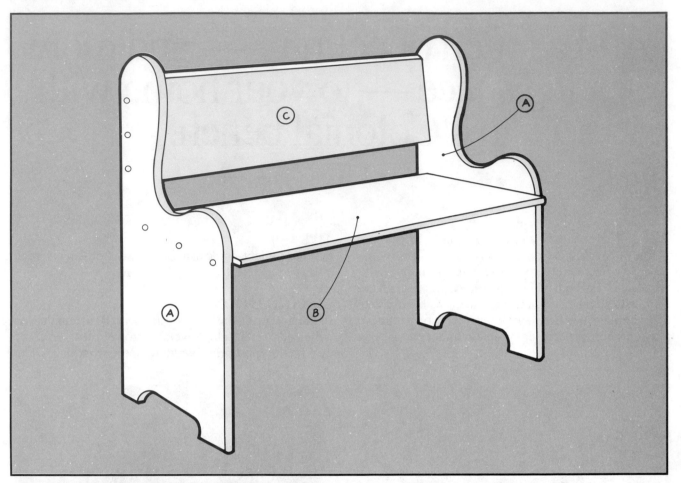

Figure 2. *Notch the seat (B) as shown to fit into the side's (A) dado. Use a plywood cutting blade or other fine-tooth blade, and stay to the outside of the cutting line.*

the material to its exact length, but make it about $1/16$ in. to $1/8$ in. wider. Then joint the edges until you achieve the final width. Joint the edges to be edge-glued on your jointer or with a hand planer. Glue and clamp in place with bar clamps. Allow the glue to cure for at least 24 hours before removing the bar clamps.

Next, cut the two workpieces for the sides (A). Lay out the pattern for the sides on newspaper or cardboard. Then cut lengths of material and place the side pieces in position on the pattern. This will produce less waste because you do not need to cut them all to the same length. Again, cut each side piece slightly wider. Then joint the edges and glue up each of the side sections.

Trace the side pattern onto the wood and cut out the design with a saber saw equipped with a fine-tooth blade. Cut carefully and stay to the outside of the cutting

BILL OF MATERIALS — Colonial Bench

Finished Dimensions in Inches

A	Side	¾ x 20¾ x 32½ ash	2
B	Seat	¾ x 16¾ x 36½ ash	1
C	Back	¾ x 10 x 36½ ash	1

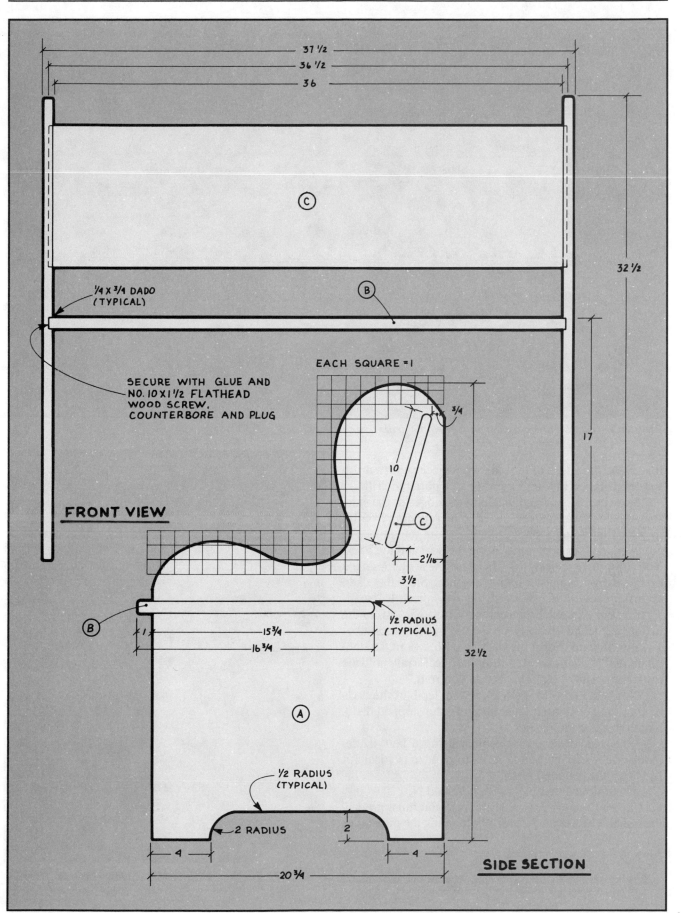

EACH SQUARE = 1

FRONT VIEW

SIDE SECTION

¼ X ¾ DADO
(TYPICAL)

SECURE WITH GLUE AND
NO. 10 X 1½ FLATHEAD
WOOD SCREW.
COUNTERBORE AND PLUG

½ RADIUS
(TYPICAL)

2 RADIUS

Figure 3. *Install a drum sander in a portable drill to sand the contours of the sides.*

line. Sand the edges of the side workpieces with a drum sander installed in a drill press or in a portable drill.

Now rout a ½ in. radius along the edges of the side, seat and back workpieces. Use a ½ in. rounding over bit in your router and a pilot guide. Lay out the dadoes in the two sides for accommodating the seat and the back. You must measure carefully because these dadoes need to be mirror images of one another. Stop the dado approximately 1 in. short of the workpiece to be inserted. For example, the seat is located 15¾ in. to the inside of the side workpiece, so the dado is located at 14¾ in. inward. Form the dadoes with a ¾ in. straight bit guided along a clamped straightedge. Firmly hold the router against the straightedge as you rout.

Notch the ends of the back to the depth of the dado so that the back can be inserted into the stopped dado. Notch the seat similarly.

Finish sand the entire project using a belt sander along the wider surfaces. A palm sander is ideal for finishing the rounded areas.

The unit is assembled with glue and No. 10 by 1½ in. flathead wood screws. However, you must predrill the holes. This requires carefully locating the pilot holes

Figure 4. *Round over the side's (A) edges with a ¹/2 in. rounding over bit. Use a pilot guide installed in your router.*

SOURCES
Minwax Pastels Wood Stain (Slate Blue): Minwax Company, Inc., 15 Mercedes Drive, Montvale, NJ 07645-1575.

Figure 5. *Assemble the seat (B) and back (C) to the two sides (A) with carpenter's glue and flathead wood screws. Here we are predrilling the holes and counterboring at the same time using a Stanley Screw-Mate. Cover the holes with wood plugs or buttons.*

before you begin drilling. First test-fit the unit, and secure it with long bar clamps. You may need to trim the legs of the sides so the bench will rest flat on the floor. Disassemble the unit, then reassemble using glue and bar clamps to secure the project.

Predrill at least three holes through each side and into the seat area. Drill at least three more holes in each side to secure the back workpiece. Counterbore the screw holes to accommodate wood plugs. You have to be careful not to counterbore too deeply, otherwise you will not have much thickness remaining for driving the screws. Assemble the bench with No. 10 by 1½ in. flathead wood screws. Then install wood plugs and glue in place.

FINISHING

Finish sand the entire project, making sure to remove any excess glue with a wood chisel. We finished the project with Minwax Pastels Wood Stain (Slate Blue). When staining, it is important that you work on one flat area at a time. Using a clean cloth, apply a generous amount of stain to one portion of the project, and then allow it to stay on for a few minutes. Remove the excess stain with another clean, lint-free cloth. As you remove the stain, wipe in the direction of the wood grain. After the stain has dried, give the project several coats of a satin polyurethane finish. ❒

Figure 6. *We applied a Minwax Pastels Wood Stain (Slate Blue) to the bench. Apply a generous amount of stain to one area at a time, then remove the excess with another clean cloth. Remember to wipe off the stain in the direction of the wood grain.*

Easy-To-Build Sawhorse

This sawhorse is designed to be built in a few hours, but it will take years of abuse.

Building your own sawhorses is a great rainy-day project — for you and the kids!

As every woodworker knows, sawhorses really take a beating. If your sawhorses have become rickety, this project is for you. The easy-to-build design makes constructing one or more of these sawhorses a great rainy-day project. It's also a great parent-child project. It is simple enough to be built with hand tools, while offering some basic woodworking challenges.

TIPS

If this will be a parent-child project, use hand tools instead of dangerous power tools. Use pine and plywood for sturdy, cost-saving construction.

CONSTRUCTION

Cut out all of the project parts to their overall widths and lengths. Carefully lay out the areas to be mortised in the top workpiece (A) to accommodate the legs. Then make a series of saw kerfs, spaced at ½ in. intervals, and remove the waste area with a sharp wood chisel. Follow this technique for mortising the remaining areas.

Mark the legs (B) for cutting. Notice that both ends of the legs must be cut at compound angles. Next, lay out the end workpiece (C) for cutting. Notice that the top surface of the end workpiece is beveled so that it will create a flush joint when positioned next to the top workpiece (A). Now cut the workpiece.

Secure each leg to the top with three No. 10 by 1¾ in. flathead wood screws. Countersink these holes so that the screw heads are flush with the wood's sur-

This story is courtesy of The Stanley Works, New Britain, CT 06050.

Figure 1. *Lay out the areas to be mortised onto the top workpiece (A).*

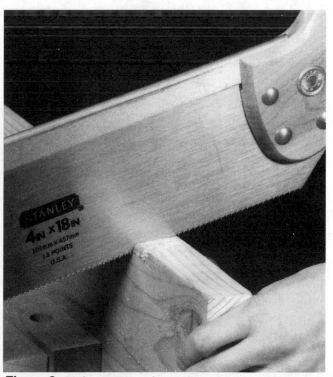

Figure 2. *Make a series of cuts that coincide with the areas to be mortised.*

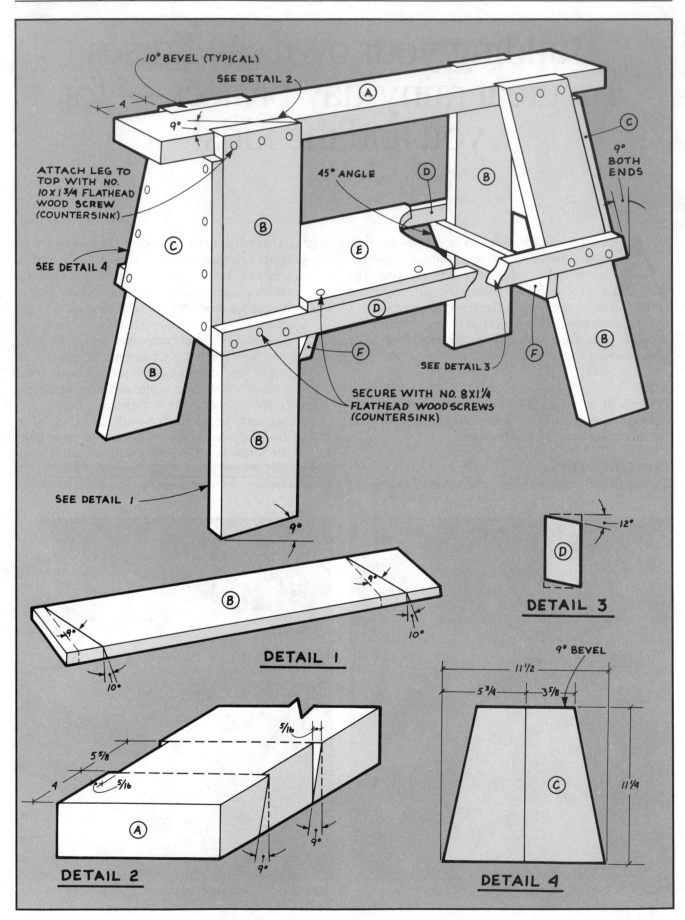

10° BEVEL (TYPICAL)

SEE DETAIL 2

Ⓐ

4

9°

ATTACH LEG TO
TOP WITH NO.
10 X 1¾ FLATHEAD
WOOD SCREW
(COUNTERSINK)

Ⓒ

SEE DETAIL 4

Ⓑ

45° ANGLE

Ⓓ

Ⓑ

Ⓒ

9°
BOTH
ENDS

Ⓔ

Ⓓ

Ⓕ

Ⓑ

SEE DETAIL 3

Ⓕ

Ⓑ

SECURE WITH NO. 8 X 1¼
FLATHEAD WOODSCREWS
(COUNTERSINK)

Ⓑ

SEE DETAIL 1

9°

Ⓑ

9°

9°

Ⓑ

10°

10°

DETAIL 1

12°

Ⓓ

DETAIL 3

9° BEVEL

11½

5¾

3⅝

5⅝

5/16

5/16

4

5/16

9°

9°

9°

Ⓐ

DETAIL 2

Ⓒ

11¼

DETAIL 4

Figure 3. *Clean out the mortised areas with a wide wood chisel.*

Figure 4. *Use a hand plane to form the top and bottom bevels in the cleats (D). Take long strokes, and carefully check your work.*

face. Attach the end workpieces (C) to the legs with No. 10 by 1¾ in. flathead wood screws. Again, countersink the screw heads.

Create a top and bottom bevel on the two cleats (D) with a hand plane. Securely clamp the workpieces while planing. Then cut the end angles so they will be flush with the end workpieces (C). Notice that the bottom of each cleat is also flush with the end workpiece. Now secure the cleats to the legs with No. 8 by 1¼ in. flathead wood screws. Countersink all screw heads.

Cut 45 degree angles in both cross braces (F), and secure the braces to the legs with No. 8 by 1¼ in. flathead wood screws. Then countersink.

Finally, secure the shelf (E) to the cleats with No. 8 by 1¼ in. flathead wood screws. Countersink these screw heads as well.

FINISHING

It is not necessary to apply any sort of finish to the sawhorse. However, if the sawhorse will be kept outside, it is a good idea to apply several coats of weather preservative. Or, if you prefer, paint the sawhorse with an exterior paint. ❏

SOURCES

A VHS videotape is available from The Stanley Works for constructing this sawhorse and includes an adult-size workbench and a child-size workbench. To order the tape, send a check or money order for $14.95 to The Stanley Works, Advertising Services, Box 1800, Dept. WBB, New Britain, CT 06050.

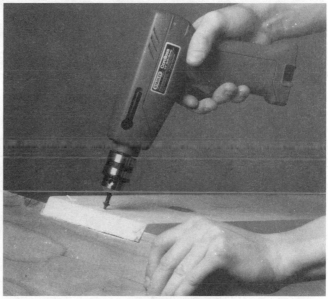

Figure 5. *Secure the legs (B) to the top (A) with No. 10 by 1³/4 in. flathead wood screws.*

BILL OF MATERIALS — Easy-To-Build Sawhorse

Finished Dimensions in Inches

A	Top	1½ x 5½ x 36 pine	1
B	Leg	¾ x 5½ pine	4
C	End	¾ x 11¼ x 11½ plywood	2
D	Cleat	¾ x 1½ x 29½ pine	2
E	Shelf	¾ x 13 x 23½ plywood	1
F	Cross Brace	¾ x 1½ x 13 pine	2

Trestle Table And Bench

The height and generally ... make this a project that will suit just about any purpose, in any room.

Save money and space by building this economical, go-anywhere table and bench set.

Trestle furniture has long been admired for its clean, simple lines, sturdy construction and space-saving design. This trestle table and bench set is no exception. The table is 4 ft. long, making it the perfect size for a breakfast nook or eat-in kitchen. It also can serve as a desk in the student's bedroom, a game table in the family room or an extra work table in the den. The separate bench provides nearly 3 ft. of seating space, and it can be tucked under the table and out of the way when not in use.

Constructed of plywood, the project is relatively inexpensive to build and can be painted to match any decor. Personalize the table and bench by stenciling the edges of the tops or painting appliqués on the legs. The possibilities are virtually unlimited!

TIPS

Use only a good quality APA trademark plywood such as A-B plywood. This will reduce blemishes and save you lots of sanding time. When assembling the workpieces, use a good carpenter's glue and make sure that you have enough C-clamps on hand.

Because food may come in contact with the surfaces of the project, apply only nontoxic wood fillers and finishes. To reduce wood splintering and insure cutting accuracy, make sure you have a sharp plywood cutting blade before you begin the project.

CONSTRUCTION

The project calls for material for one table and one bench. With suitable planning, two sheets of ¾ in. plywood should be enough.

The top is comprised of two pieces of ¾ in. plywood secured together. The top workpiece (A1) is cut shorter and narrower than the bottom (A2) so that ¾ in. quarter-round edging (A3) can be placed along the edge of A1. For detailed information on this, refer to the Top Edge Detail.

This story is courtesy of the American Plywood Association, P.O. Box 11700, Tacoma, WA 98411.

Begin by cutting the plywood. Use a circular saw or table saw equipped with a plywood cutting blade, and test to make sure that it is cutting square to avoid unsightly gaps in the project.

The next step is to glue up the top workpieces (A1, A2). First, however, decide if you are going to secure the workpieces with finishing nails or screws. If you opt for screws, select No. 8 by 1¼ in. flathead wood screws. Then drill pilot holes under workpiece A2 to make sure you countersink for the screw heads. Apply carpenter's glue to one of the plywood workpieces, smoothing out the glue with a brush or a piece of wood. After the glue has been distributed evenly, center A1 onto A2. Then begin securing the top workpieces. Make sure the workpieces stay centered as you work to insure that the edging (A3) will fit.

BILL OF MATERIALS — Trestle Table And Bench

Finished Dimensions in Inches

A1	Top	¾ x 28½ x 46½ plywood	1
A2	Top	¾ x 30 x 48 plywood	1
A3	Top Edge	¾ x 156 quarter round pine	1
B	Leg	¾ x 6 x 29 plywood	4
C	Stretcher	¾ x 3 x 43 plywood	2
D	Top Stretcher	¾ x 6 x 34½ plywood	1
E	Foot	¾ x 4½ x 16 plywood	4
F	Foot Blocking	¾ x 3 x 5 plywood	8
G	Stretcher Spacer	¾ x 1 x 5 plywood	4
H	Spacer	¾ x 2 x 4 plywood	1
I1	Top (Upper)	¾ x 16 x 34 plywood	1
I2	Top (Lower)	¾ x 17½ x 35½ plywood	1
I3	Top Edge	¾ x 106 quarter round pine	1
J	Leg	¾ x 6 x 16 plywood	4
K	Stretcher	¾ x 3 x 31 plywood	2
L	Top Stretcher	¾ x 6 x 23 plywood	1
M	Foot	¾ x 3 x 14 plywood	4
N	Foot Blocking	¾ x 2 x 4 plywood	8
O	Stretcher Spacer	¾ x 1 x 5 plywood	4
P	Spacer	¾ x 2 x 4 plywood	1

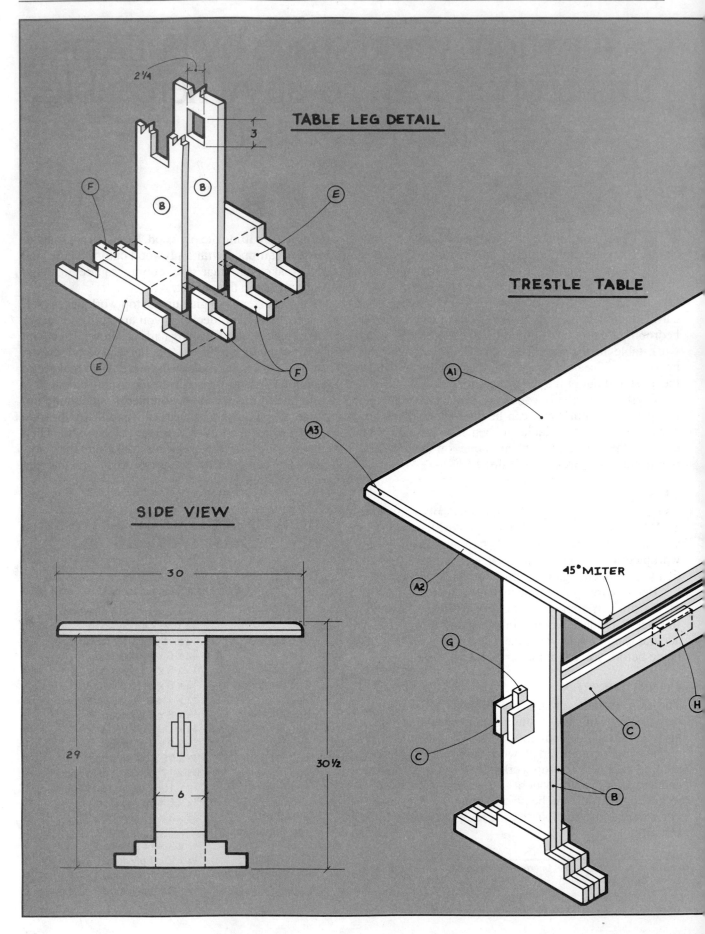

TABLE LEG DETAIL

2 ¼

3

F

B

B

E

E

F

TRESTLE TABLE

A1

A3

A2

45°MITER

G

C

C

H

B

SIDE VIEW

30

29

6

30 ½

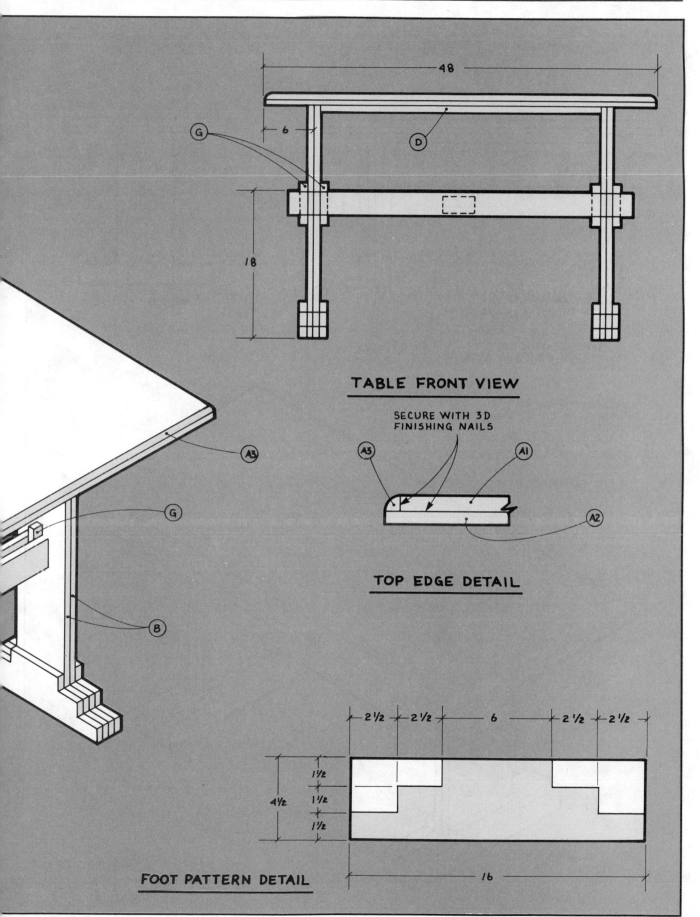

TABLE FRONT VIEW

SECURE WITH 3D
FINISHING NAILS

TOP EDGE DETAIL

FOOT PATTERN DETAIL

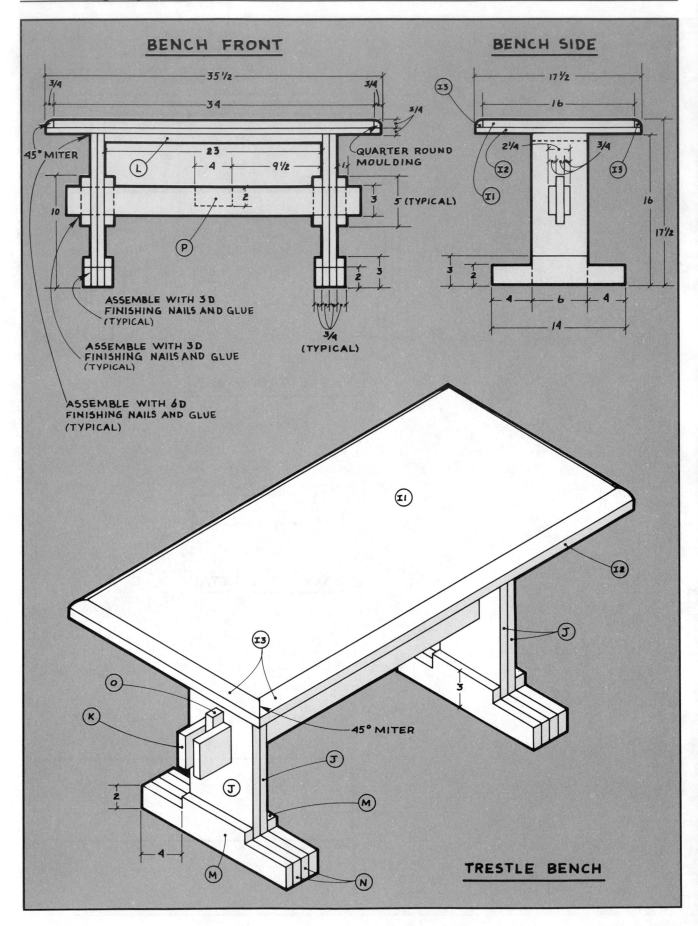

BENCH FRONT

35 1/2
3/4
34
3/4
3/4
45° MITER
L
23
4
9 1/2
QUARTER ROUND MOULDING
P
10
2
1
3
5 (TYPICAL)
2
3
ASSEMBLE WITH 3D FINISHING NAILS AND GLUE (TYPICAL)
3/4
(TYPICAL)
ASSEMBLE WITH 3D FINISHING NAILS AND GLUE (TYPICAL)
ASSEMBLE WITH 6D FINISHING NAILS AND GLUE (TYPICAL)

BENCH SIDE

I3
17 1/2
16
2 1/4
3/4
I2
I1
I3
16
17 1/2
3
2
4
6
4
14

I1
I2
I3
O
J
K
J
J
3
45° MITER
M
2
M
N
4

TRESTLE BENCH

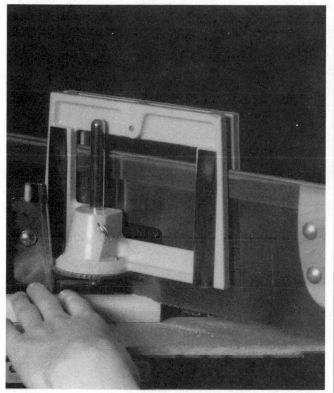

Figure 1. *Secure the top edge (A3) of the table to the other two top workpieces (A1, A2) with carpenter's glue and finishing nails. Predrill the nail holes and miter the corners as shown.*

Figure 2. *Assemble and glue the bench legs (J), then joint the edges to make them square. Take light passes with your jointer.*

Now measure and miter the edges of A3 to fit the top's ledge. Refer to the Top Edge Detail. Secure A3 to the top's ledge with 3d finishing nails. Make sure you predrill for the nails to avoid splitting the edging.

Now cut and glue up the bench top (I1, I2, I3) following the same procedures.

Cut out the table and bench legs (B, J) next. Cut the workpieces slightly oversize so they can be trimmed later. Then glue up the leg pairs. Spread the glue evenly with a brush or a small block of wood, and then clamp the assemblies with C-clamps. Use plenty of C-clamps to insure a tight bond. Before gluing, make sure you have plenty of newspaper or wax paper beneath the workpieces.

Once the leg assemblies have dried (usually 24 hours), joint the edges of the legs and trim the legs to length on your radial arm saw. Now carefully lay out the rectangular holes to be cut in the legs for the stretchers. Drill a starter hole, making sure you use a backup board underneath the leg to prevent wood splintering. Then cut out the waste area with a saber saw. Make sure you work carefully to avoid mistakes. When finished, check the hole size on both surfaces of the leg and use a sharp wood chisel to square up the hole.

Now cut the table and bench stretchers (C, K) to their appropriate lengths, but cut them slightly wider (about ⅛ in.) to allow for jointing. Then joint the edges

Figure 3. *Lay out the rectangular holes to be cut in the bench legs. Drill a starter hole and cut out the mortise with a saber saw. Check to make sure that the blade is cutting accurately.*

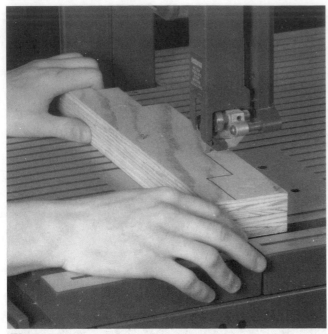

Figure 4. *Cut out the table feet (E) with a band saw. Gang saw these pieces by driving two finishing nails partway into the foot blanks. Position the nails well away from the cutting line. The nails will prevent the wood from slipping while cutting.*

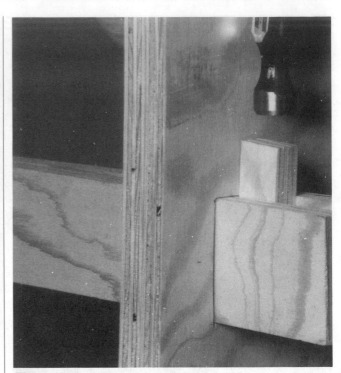

Figure 5. *Insert the two stretchers (K) into the rectangular holes in the legs. Then install the stretcher spacer (O).*

of the stretchers, being careful to joint just enough so that the stretchers fit into the rectangular leg holes.

Next, mark and cut the stretchers and the feet for both the table and the bench. These workpieces include the top stretchers (D, L), the stretcher spacers (G, O) and the spacers (H, P). The workpieces making up the feet include parts E, F for the table and parts M, N for the bench. Use a saber saw or a band saw to cut out the silhouettes.

Assemble the feet workpieces to the legs with carpenter's glue and 3d finishing nails. Do this for both the table and the bench. Assemble on a flat work area, and use a carpenter's square to adjust the legs perpendicular to the feet.

After the glue on these project parts has dried, finish sand all of the table and bench workpieces. For flat areas, such as the table and bench tops, use a belt sander equipped with a fine grit belt. Use a pad or palm sander for medium-sized workpieces such as the legs and feet, and use a stationary belt sander to sand small pieces such as the spacers. Be careful when sanding the spacers and the stretchers. If you sand off too much of the surface area, the spacers and stretchers will not fit snugly into the rectangular holes in the legs. Also, fill in all blemishes with a nontoxic wood filler.

ASSEMBLY

Assemble the table and the bench on a flat surface. Start assembling the table by inserting the two stretchers (C)

into the legs, along with the spacers (G, H). The fit should be snug. If not, you may have to cut thicker spacers. Now secure the top stretcher (D) to the table top with glue and 3d finishing nails. The stretcher needs to be perfectly centered on the bottom of the table top. Now place the table top on the leg assembly. When everything is perfectly aligned, disassemble the stretchers and spacers and apply glue to the joining surfaces of the appropriate workpieces.

Reassemble the table and secure the joints with 3d finishing nails. Use a carpenter's square as you work to guarantee the project's squareness. Then sink all nailheads and fill in the holes with a nontoxic wood filler.

Allow the glue to cure before moving the project, and then finish sand the surfaces as necessary.

Follow this same procedure for assembling the bench, using parts K, L, O and P.

FINISHING

A spray gun is ideal for painting your project. Start by applying a good sealer coat. If you do not use a sealing coat, the plywood will absorb the paint unevenly, and you'll need several more coats of paint to cover this uneven absorption. After the sealer has dried, give it a light sanding. A palm sander is ideal for getting at many of those hard-to-reach areas. Now give the project a coat of paint. An additional coat may be necessary. If it is, make sure you sand the first coat lightly. ❒

Hall Table

This compact table is easy to build and is assembled with dowels and glue. Only the sides and back are attached to the top with screws.

Greet guests with charm by building this elegant hall table.

This simple yet elegant table is 32½ in. high, 20 in. wide and 12 in. deep, making it the perfect size for a hall or foyer. It also could be used as a telephone stand in a kitchen or bedroom. The curved back and sides add interest to the table without overwhelming its straightforward lines. You can customize the table by designing your own pattern for the decorative back and sides.

TIPS

This table can be made from virtually any type of wood. We used maple, but pine, oak or ash are other options. When assembling this project, you will need a good doweling jig or a good set of doweling centers along with a drill press.

CONSTRUCTION

Begin by cutting all of the project parts, with the exception of the back (F), to their overall widths and lengths. Make sure that your radial arm saw or table saw is cutting square; otherwise the table will not be square

Figure 1. *Rip the legs (A) from 1¹/2 in. thick material on your band saw. Cut the legs approximately ¹/4 in. wider to allow for jointing.*

at assembly, and this problem is virtually impossible to correct. Also, cut the legs (A) ¼ in. wider to allow for jointing.

You will probably have to glue up the top (D) from two or more pieces of material. If so, joint the edges to be joined on your stationary jointer. Then edge-glue with carpenter's glue and clamp the workpieces with bar clamps. After the glue has dried, cut the top to its precise width and length. Now draw the contours for the two sides (E) and cut them out on a band saw or saber saw.

We designed the back (F) with a slight arc. You can do the same by striking an arc with the aid of trammels attached to a wooden yardstick. However, you may wish to come up with your own design. Whatever shape you choose, cut the back's contour about ¹⁄₁₆ in. short of the cutting line. Then carefully sand the edges of the back and the sides, periodically checking to make sure that the workpieces will join properly at assembly.

Now finish sand all of the project parts. A stationary sander is ideal for this. If you opt to use a palm sander, be careful not to round over or taper the surface areas to be joined. Palm sanders are great tools, but they have a tendency to remove material rather quickly and to round narrow workpieces like the legs.

ASSEMBLY

The legs (A) are affixed to the rails with two ¼ in. diameter by 1½ in. dowels and carpenter's glue. The sides (E) are secured to the back (F) with dowels and glue as well. Likewise, the top (D) is secured to the leg assembly with dowels and glue. Notice that the assembled sides/back are secured to the top with No. 6 by 1½ in. flathead wood screws, countersunk.

BILL OF MATERIALS — Hall Table

Finished Dimensions in Inches

A	Leg	1½ x 1½ x 27½ maple	4
B	Front/Back Rail	¾ x 2½ x 15 maple	2
C	Side Rail	¾ x 2½ x 8 maple	2
D	Top	¾ x 12 x 20 maple	1
E	Side	¾ x 3¼ x 11 maple	2
F	Back	¾ x 4¼ x 16½ maple	1

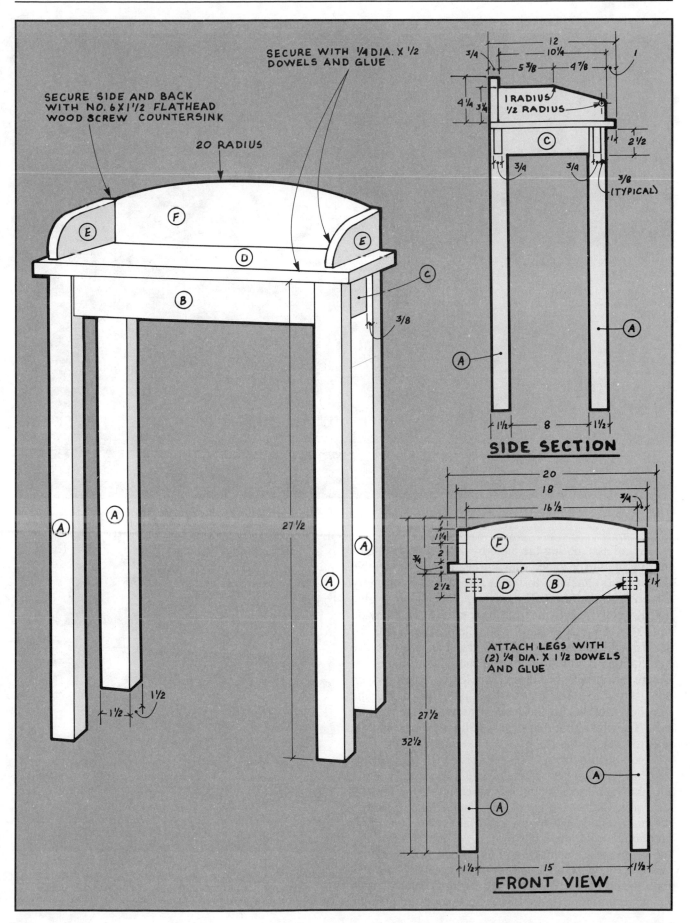

SECURE WITH ¼ DIA. X ½
DOWELS AND GLUE

SECURE SIDE AND BACK
WITH NO. 6 X 1½ FLATHEAD
WOOD SCREW COUNTERSINK

20 RADIUS

1 RADIUS
½ RADIUS

12
10¼
5⅜   4⅞
¾
1
4¼   3¾

3/8
(TYPICAL)

3/4   3/4

C

2½

A

A

SIDE SECTION

E   F   E

D

B

C

3/8

27½

A

A

A

A

A

1½

1½

20
18
16½
¾

1¼
2
¾
2½

F

D   B

ATTACH LEGS WITH
(2) ¼ DIA. X 1½ DOWELS
AND GLUE

27½

32½

A

A

1½   15   1½

FRONT VIEW

Figure 2. *Use pushsticks to joint the rough-cut surface of the legs (A) on your jointer. Make light passes.*

Begin assembling the table by drilling dowel holes into the areas to be joined with dowels. Then dry-assemble the project, checking to make sure that it is properly aligned and that the holes are deep enough. Now glue and dowel the legs to the front/back rails (B) and the side rails (C). Several sets of band clamps are ideal for securing the joints. If you do not have band clamps, use bar clamps. If you do not have enough bar clamps to secure the entire assembly, assemble two leg sets which consist of gluing two legs to one rail (B). Then after the glue has dried, secure these two leg sets to the remaining rails (C). Make sure that the assembly is square and the legs rest flat on the floor.

Now secure the sides (E) to the back (F) with dowels and carpenter's glue. Again, square the assembly. After the glue has dried, secure this assembly to the top (D) with glue and No. 6 by 1½ in. flathead wood screws driven from underneath the top. Make sure you predrill and countersink the screw holes. Position the finished top on the leg assembly, and use a pencil to mark the positioning on the underside of the top. Remove the top, then locate and drill a hole into the top center of each leg to accommodate a dowel. Install dowel centers,

Figure 3. *Lay out the back (F) by locating the positions where the back adjoins the two sides (E). Then draw the circular back with a bar compass, made from trammels attached to a wooden rule.*

Figure 4. *Form the top (D) by jointing and then edge-gluing two or three boards cut slightly oversize. Check for gaps before you apply the glue.*

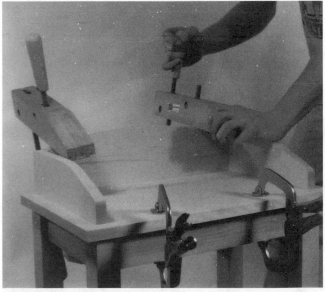

Figure 5. *Glue and clamp the top assembly to the leg assembly. Remove the clamps only after the glue has cured for at least 24 hours.*

reposition the top on the legs and press down. This will result in a corresponding mark on the underside of the top for drilling the dowel hole. Follow this procedure for drilling the remaining dowel holes.

Finally, secure the top assembly to the leg assembly with dowels and carpenter's glue. Use wood clamps to hold the assembly until the glue dries.

FINISHING
Finish sand the entire project and slightly round over any sharp edges. Use an old wood chisel to remove glue that has oozed out from the joints. It is a good idea to bevel the bottom of the legs where they come in contact with the floor. Otherwise, the legs will have a tendency to splinter as you move the table about, particularly if the legs are made of a soft wood.

We applied tung oil to the table for a natural look. If you use tung oil, apply at least two coats and quickly dispose of the soiled rags. Carefully follow the manufacturer's safety and application instructions. ❏

Vegetable Bin

The contour in the bottom rail, cove moulding around the top, and wire mesh in the doors, make this vegetable bin an authentic replica.

The vegetable bin is back — and better than ever before.

This replica of the antique vegetable bin is popular for its nostalgic looks and its versatile uses. It can be used to store dry goods or cookbooks in the kitchen, or towels and linens in the bathroom. It can be used as a telephone stand in the hall, or as a display cabinet in the family room. It even can be used as a plant stand or a lamp table. The antique charm of the project, coupled with its practical uses, makes this a cabinet that will be a welcome addition to just about any room in the house.

TIPS
Purchase wire mesh or screen from a hardware store or from a specialty catalog. Typically, these vegetable bins are made out of either pine or oak. We used No. 2 pine to best replicate the project.

CONSTRUCTION
Cut out all of the project parts to their overall widths and lengths, with the exception of the front and side trim (L, M). You may have to edge-glue several narrower pieces in order to form the wider top (G).

Cut dadoes into the sides (A) to accommodate the two shelves (F). Now cut a ¼ in. wide by ¼ in. deep rabbet along the inside back edges of the side workpieces (A). Use a router or a table saw to cut these rabbets. Note

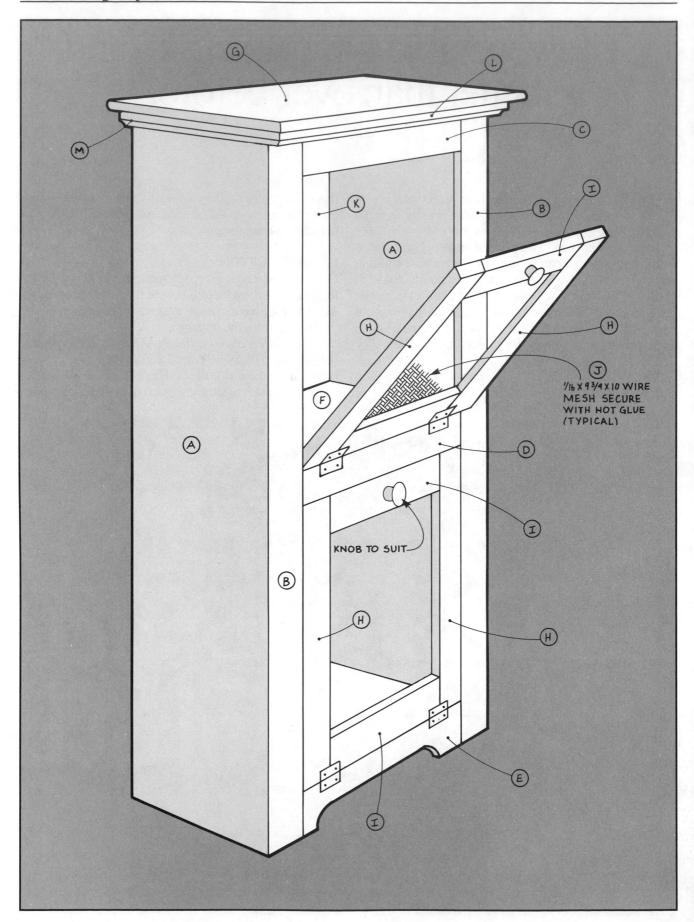

1/16 X 9 3/4 X 10 WIRE
MESH SECURE
WITH HOT GLUE
(TYPICAL)

KNOB TO SUIT

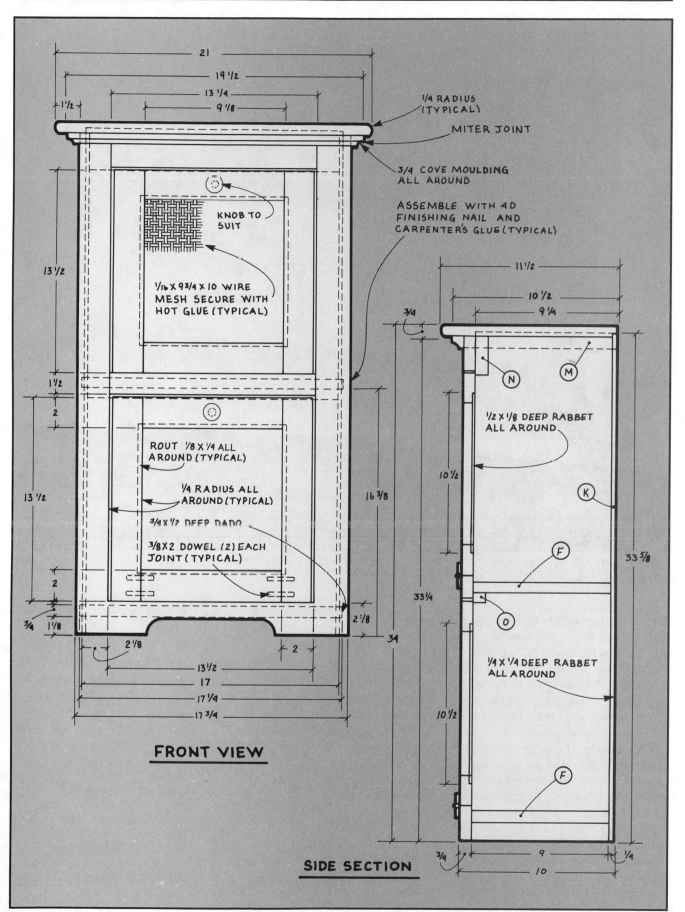

21

19 1/2

13 1/4

9 1/8

1 1/2

1/4 RADIUS
(TYPICAL)

MITER JOINT

3/4 COVE MOULDING
ALL AROUND

ASSEMBLE WITH 4D
FINISHING NAIL AND
CARPENTER'S GLUE (TYPICAL)

13 1/2

KNOB TO
SUIT

1/16 X 9 3/4 X 10 WIRE
MESH SECURE WITH
HOT GLUE (TYPICAL)

1 1/2

2

ROUT 1/8 X 1/4 ALL
AROUND (TYPICAL)

1/4 RADIUS ALL
AROUND (TYPICAL)

3/4 X 1/2 DEEP DADO

13 1/2

3/8 X 2 DOWEL (2) EACH
JOINT (TYPICAL)

16 3/8

2

3/4 1 1/8

2 1/8

2 1/8

2

2 1/8

34

13 1/2

17

17 1/4

17 3/4

FRONT VIEW

11 1/2

10 1/2

9 1/4

3/4

N

M

1/2 X 1/8 DEEP RABBET
ALL AROUND

10 1/2

K

F

O

33 1/4

10 1/2

33 5/8

1/4 X 1/4 DEEP RABBET
ALL AROUND

F

3/4

9

10

1/4

SIDE SECTION

Figure 1. *Attach the door rails (I) to the door stiles (H) with dowels and carpenter's glue. Secure the assembly with bar clamps, making sure the workpieces are kept absolutely flat.*

that it is important to cut the rabbets at this stage. If you wait until the time of assembly, the two shelves will prevent you from making a complete cut.

Next, lay out the rabbet location for the top workpiece (G). Then use your router equipped with a rabbeting bit and pilot guide to rout this area. Use a wood chisel to square the corner cuts. Then rout a ¼ in. radius around the top's showing edges.

Assemble the sides to the two shelves with carpenter's glue and 4d finishing nails. Be careful to avoid leaving hammer marks on the project. Similarly, secure the back (K) to the assembly. Make sure the assembly is square before you nail the back. Now secure the top (G) with finishing nails and carpenter's glue. Attach the stiles (B) in the same fashion. Then secure the top, middle and bottom rails (C, D, E) and back stops (N, O).

Lay out the decorative design for the bottom rail (E), and cut out the workpiece with a saber saw. Use a

BILL OF MATERIALS — Vegetable Bin

Finished Dimensions in Inches

A	Side	¾ x 9¼ x 33⅝ pine	2
B	Stile	¾ x 2⅛ x 33¼ pine	2
C	Top Rail	¾ x 2⅛ x 13½ pine	1
D	Middle Rail	¾ x 1½ x 13½ pine	1
E	Bottom Rail	¾ x 2⅛ x 13½ pine	1
F	Shelf	¾ x 9 x 17¼ pine	2
G	Top	¾ x 11½ x 21 pine	1
H	Door Stile	¾ x 2 x 13½ pine	4
I	Door Rail	¾ x 2 x 9¼ pine	4
J	Wire Mesh	1/16 x 9¾ x 10 wire	2
K	Back	¼ x 17¼ x 33⅝ plywood	1
L	Front Trim	¾ x ¾ x 19½ cove moulding	1
M	Side Trim	¾ x ¾ x 10½ cove moulding	2
N	Top Back Stop	¾ x 2½ x 16⅜ pine	1
O	Bottom Back Stop	¾ x ¾ x 16⅜ pine	1

Figure 2. *To make your own cove moulding for the front and side trim (L, M), rout a ³/4 in. cove into the edges of a long and wide workpiece. Then rip the ³/4 in. cove to width on your table saw.*

fine-tooth blade to minimize wood splintering. Then sand the edges with a drum sander installed in your drill.

Attach the door stiles (H) to the door rails (I), using two ⅜ in. diameter by 2 in. long dowels at each joint. Use a doweling jig to help insure accuracy. Secure the door frames with carpenter's glue and the dowels. Use bar clamps to firmly hold the doors until the glue has dried.

Remove the bar clamps from the doors, and mill ½ in. wide by ⅛ in. deep rabbets along the inside back edges of the doors to accommodate the wire mesh (J). Use a rabbeting bit equipped with a pilot guide in your router to cut the rabbets. Then square the corners with a sharp wood chisel. Place each door in its proper location in the cabinet assembly, and determine how much has to be trimmed off the doors to fit properly. Use a jointer to trim each door. The doors should fit snugly but should not bind.

Remove the doors and rout a ¼ in. radius around the edges. Now cut the front and side trim (L, M). Miter the edges to be joined. Then attach the trim to the cabinet with 4d finishing nails and carpenter's glue.

Finish sand the entire project. A palm sander is ideal for sanding this project. Make sure you sink all nailheads and fill in with a suitable wood filler.

FINISHING

Apply an antique stain to the project with a clean cloth. Remove any excess stain with another clean cloth. Use tung oil to help bring out a deep, warm finish on the wood. We applied two coats of ZAR tung oil satin finish.

Now cut the wire mesh (J) to fit the rabbeted door area, and secure the mesh with hot glue. Drill holes in the door rails to accommodate knobs. Install the knobs, hinge the doors and add two magnetic latches to complete your project. ❏

Figure 3. *Mill a rabbet into the inside back edge of each door. Use a rabbeting bit equipped with a pilot guide. Move the router counterclockwise, and make sure that one end of the workpiece is securely clamped to your workbench.*

Figure 4. *Install the wire mesh (J) in the doors with hot glue. Use enough hot glue to cover up any sharp areas that may cause injuries.*

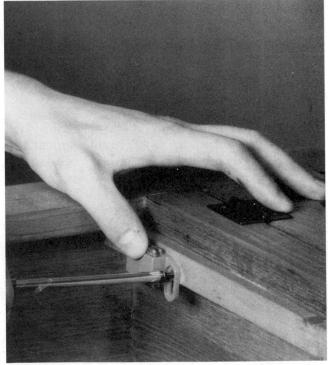

Figure 5. *Secure magnetic latches to the back stops (N, O). It is best to position these latches off to the side of the door opening.*

Garden Table/Bench

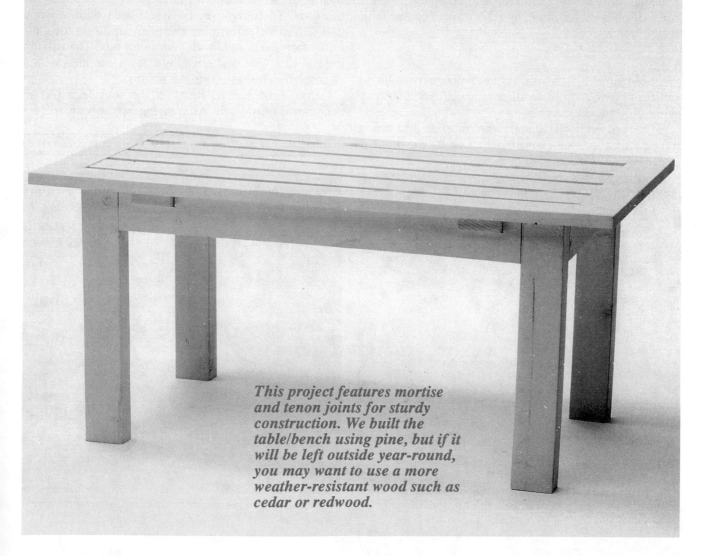

This project features mortise and tenon joints for sturdy construction. We built the table/bench using pine, but if it will be left outside year-round, you may want to use a more weather-resistant wood such as cedar or redwood.

Sturdy construction and a clever design make this a great outdoor project.

Whether it is used on a deck, patio or in the garden, this table/bench can fit many needs — from seating space to a serving table. Or maybe you just need a place for displaying your favorite plants? The clever design of the project offers interchangeable use. The top is 3 ft. long to provide ample seating space. At 16 in. high, the project also rests at a comfortable coffee-table height. The slat construction of the top will complement most types of outdoor furniture, and the project can be built easily in one weekend.

TIPS
We used pine for the project, but you may want to substitute with a more weather-resistant wood such as cedar or redwood.

The project is designed with mortise and tenon joints. However, you can use doweling for the joints if you are uncomfortable with making mortise and tenon joints.

CONSTRUCTION
Cut out all of the project parts to their appropriate widths and lengths. Then lay out the tenons in the front/back rails (B) as well as the mortise areas that will accommodate the top assembly. Use a mechanical miter box to cut the front/back rail areas to the depth of the mortises. Then remove the waste area with a wood chisel. Similarly, form the shoulder depths on the ends of the front/back rails with your miter box. Then clamp the rail in a vise, and chisel out the waste area with a wide, sharp chisel to form the tenons.

Now form the mortises in the four legs (A) to accommodate the rails. After laying out the basic rectan-

This story is courtesy of The Stanley Works, New Britain, CT 06050.

Figure 1. *Carefully lay out the tenons in the side rails (C).*

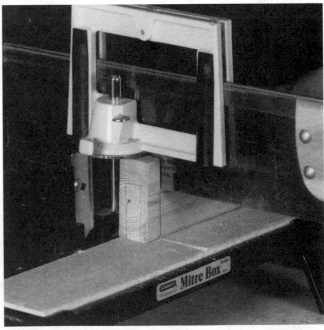

Figure 2. *Cut to the shoulder depths of the tenons using a miter box.*

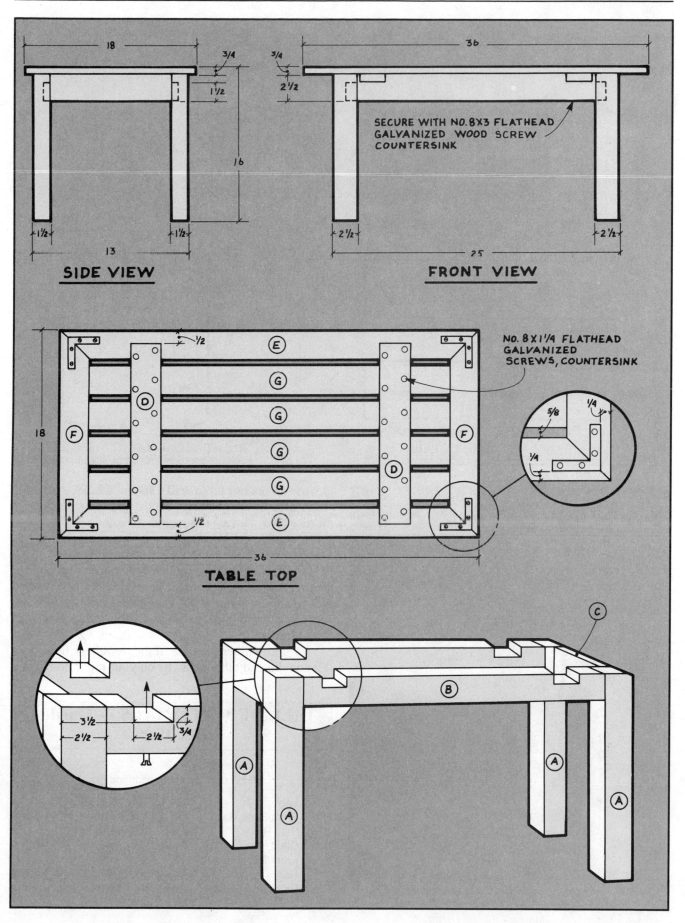

18

3/4

3/4

2 1/2

1 1/2

16

1 1/2

1 1/2

13

SIDE VIEW

36

25

2 1/2

2 1/2

SECURE WITH NO. 8X3 FLATHEAD
GALVANIZED WOOD SCREW
COUNTERSINK

FRONT VIEW

1/2

E

NO. 8 X 1 1/4 FLATHEAD
GALVANIZED
SCREWS, COUNTERSINK

G

G

D

G

1/4

18

F

G

5/8

F

D

1/4

E

1/2

36

TABLE TOP

C

B

3 1/2

2 1/2

2 1/2

3/4

A

A

A

A

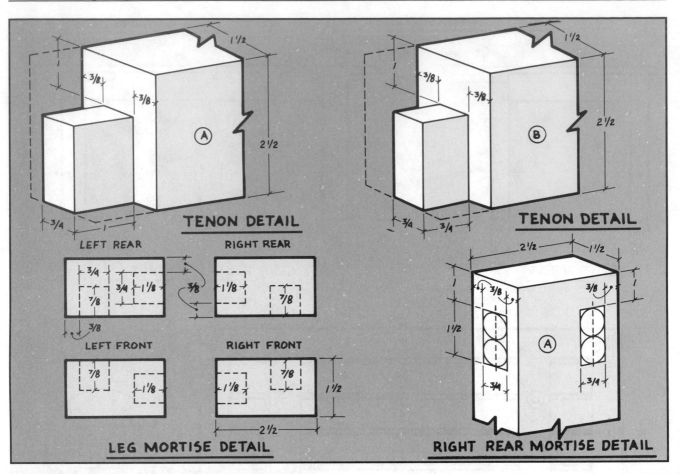

TENON DETAIL

LEFT REAR   RIGHT REAR

LEFT FRONT   RIGHT FRONT

LEG MORTISE DETAIL

TENON DETAIL

RIGHT REAR MORTISE DETAIL

Figure 3. *Clamp the side rail (C) in your bench vise, and use a wide wood chisel to form the tenon.*

gle, use a Forstner bit to drill a series of holes inside the waste area to the required depth. Then square out the mortise area with a ¾ in. wood chisel.

Assemble the legs to the rails, and test-fit all joints. Make sure they are snug, but not overly tight.

Now reassemble the rails to the legs using waterproof glue to secure all joints. Place a band clamp around all four legs and draw the band clamp tight. Make sure the assembly is square, and allow the glue to cure for 24 hours.

Carefully miter the ends of the front/back table rails (E) and the end table rails (F) on your miter box. Then

BILL OF MATERIALS — Garden Table/Bench

Finished Dimensions in Inches

A	Leg	1½ x 2½ x 16 pine	4
B	Front/Back Rail	1½ x 2½ x 27 pine	2
C	Side Rail	1½ x 2½ x 14½ pine	2
D	Cleat	¾ x 2½ x 17 pine	2
E	Front/Back Table Rail	¾ x 2½ x 36 pine	2
F	End Table Rail	¾ x 2½ x 18 pine	2
G	Table Slat	¾ x 2½ x 31 pine	4

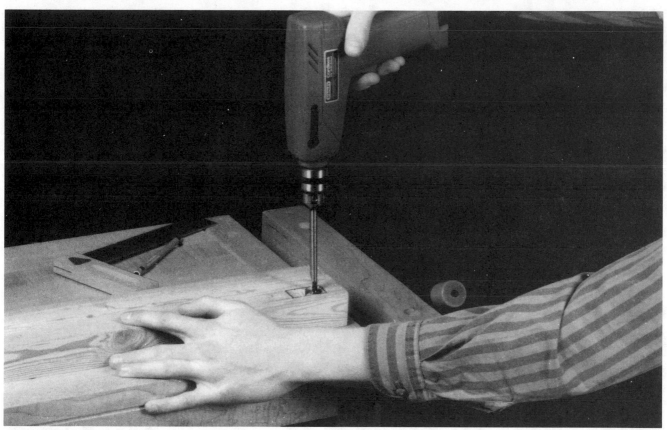

Figure 4. *Carefully lay out the leg mortises. Remove the waste area by using a Forstner bit to drill two ³⁄4 in. diameter holes to the required depth.*

assemble the table rails along with the cleats (D) and table slats (G). Use waterproof glue and No. 8 by 1¼ in. flathead galvanized screws to secure the workpieces. Predrill holes and then drive the screws through the cleats (D). Make sure you sink all screw heads. Now install 3 in. flat corner braces underneath each table rail joint. Again, allow the glue to cure for 24 hours before proceeding.

Now attach the top assembly to the bottom leg assembly with waterproof glue and No. 8 by 3 in. flathead galvanized screws. Drive the screws up through the mortised areas of the front/back rails (B) so they pass through the cleats (D) and through the front/back table rails (E). Remember to countersink the screw heads.

FINISHING
Finish sand the entire project, making sure to dull all sharp edges. Before applying any finish, keep in mind that food will come in contact with the project. Therefore, be sure to apply a finish that is nontoxic once

dry. Carefully check the label before applying the finish. If you opt to paint the project, first apply a good coat of exterior grade paint sealer. A paint sprayer is ideal for covering all of those hard-to-reach areas. ❏

SOURCES
A VHS videocassette, available from The Stanley Works, offers good tips for constructing outdoor furniture. To order a cassette, send a check or money order for $14.95 to The Stanley Works, Advertising Services, Box 1800 Outdoor Projects, Dept. OPB, New Britain, CT 06050.

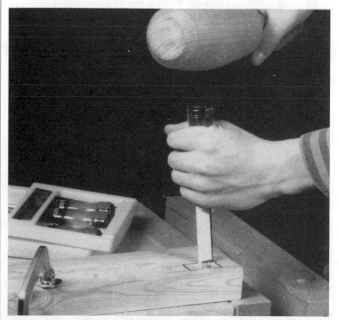

Figure 5. *Finish the mortise by chiseling out the remaining waste area with a ³⁄4 in. wood chisel.*

Colonial Sofa Table

This sofa table features slim, sleek lines and is designed to be placed against a sofa or wall. If it will be used as a freestanding unit, you may want to shorten the table and widen its sides for better stability.

Build this sofa table, and win the heart of someone special!

With today's open floor plans, sofa tables are back in style. This sofa table is perfect for any room where the sofa is used as a space divider. It also makes a great hall table. With its heart-shaped cutouts and Colonial charm, it is sure to win the heart of someone special.

TIPS

This table is designed to fit up against a wall or a sofa where it is less likely to be tipped over. If the table will be placed on a carpeted floor and will be freestanding, we suggest that you shorten the unit and widen its sides to provide greater stability.

We used No. 2 pine to construct the sofa table, giving

Figure 1. *Carefully lay out the grid pattern for the rail (A) on graph paper. Place dots where the pattern crosses each square, making sure that your grid pattern corresponds with the one illustrated. We are doing a half pattern here.*

it a rustic look. For a more refined look, you may want to use a select hardwood or pine.

CONSTRUCTION

Use your table saw to cut all of the components to their overall widths and lengths. Your saw should be equipped with a combination blade or a plywood cutting blade.

The challenging part about this project is transferring the design for the rails (A) and sides (B). This is one of those occasions when a pantograph is quite useful for enlarging the grid. However, we suggest that you draw a half grid. This means that instead of drawing the whole side (B), you draw half the side. Similarly, instead of drawing the grid for the entire rail (A), draw half the rail. This calls for taping or pasting pieces of graph paper together until you have enough paper to accommodate each half pattern. For the side, you will need to locate the appropriate half width and draw an edge to represent the centerline that passes through the heart shape.

Make sure that your grid lines correspond to those shown in the illustration. Now locate the points where your grid design passes through any one square, and place a dot at this point. Continue doing this for all of the locations where the grid design passes through the line of a square. Then use a French curve to connect all the points into one smooth curve or, if you prefer, draw the curve freehand.

Cut out the pattern, then position it onto the actual workpiece and trace the half pattern. Now flip the template over to draw the remaining half.

Once you have transferred the patterns to the rails and sides, cut out the workpieces with a saber saw

BILL OF MATERIALS — Colonial Sofa Table

Finished Dimensions in Inches

A	Rail	¾ x 6 x 38½ pine	2
B	Side	¾ x 10 x 30¼ pine	2
C	Top	¾ x 12 x 42 pine	1
D	Shelf	¾ x 9½ x 36½ pine	1

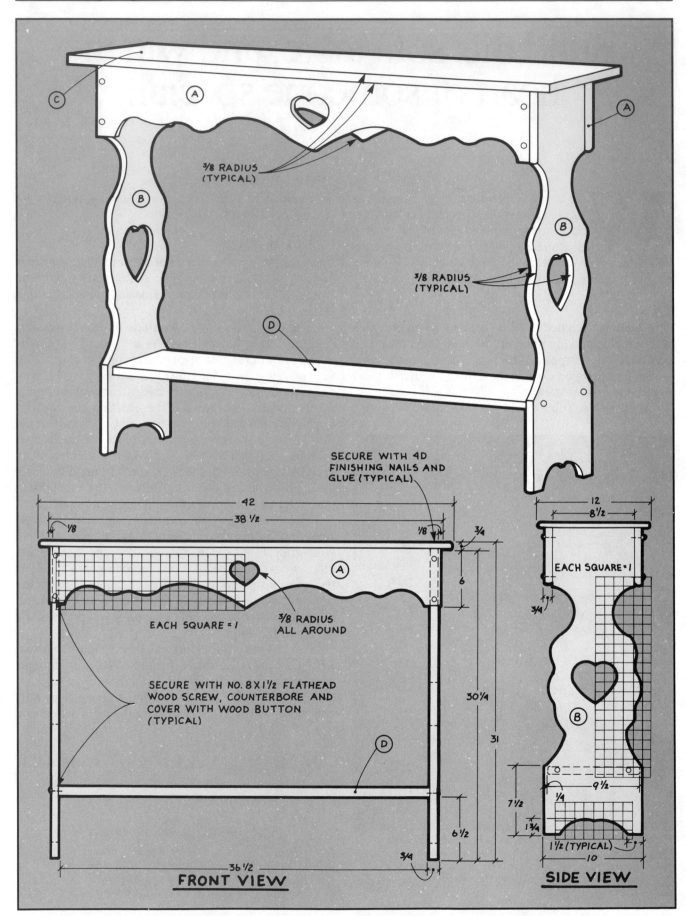

3/8 RADIUS (TYPICAL)

3/8 RADIUS (TYPICAL)

SECURE WITH 4D FINISHING NAILS AND GLUE (TYPICAL)

42

38 1/2

1/8

1/8

3/4

6

EACH SQUARE = 1

3/8 RADIUS ALL AROUND

SECURE WITH NO. 8 X 1 1/2 FLATHEAD WOOD SCREW, COUNTERBORE AND COVER WITH WOOD BUTTON (TYPICAL)

30 1/4

31

6 1/2

36 1/2

3/4

FRONT VIEW

12

8 1/2

EACH SQUARE = 1

3/4

9 1/2

7 1/2

1/4

1 3/4

1 1/2 (TYPICAL)

10

SIDE VIEW

Figure 2. *Use a flexible curve (available from art or drafting supply stores) to connect the dots in a smooth curve.*

equipped with a fine-tooth blade. Cut with the good side of the wood facing down to minimize visible wood splinters.

Cut out the heart shapes by drilling a starter hole and then finishing the cut with your saber saw.

Finish sand all of the edges and surfaces of the project parts. Now rout a ⅜ in. radius in the rails, sides, top (C) and shelf (D), as indicated in the illustration.

Begin assembly by securing the shelf to the sides with glue and dowels. Predrill the shelf and install with two No. 8 by 1½ in. flathead wood screws. Counterbore and then cover the hole recesses with wood buttons.

Now attach the rails, using glue and two No. 8 by

1½ in. flathead wood screws at each joint. Again, counterbore these holes and cover them with wood buttons. Use a carpenter's square during assembly to insure that the unit is perfectly square.

Complete the assembly by securing the top with glue and 4d finishing nails. Sink all nailheads, and fill in the recesses with an appropriate wood filler.

FINISHING

Finish sand the entire project, and wipe dry with a clean, damp cloth. Now apply a stain of your choice. Follow this up by applying tung oil. The tung oil will bring out the wood's grain and enhance its rustic appearance. ❏

Figure 3. *Cut out the pattern and trace it onto the rail (A). Complete the design by flipping the pattern over and tracing it onto the other half of the rail.*

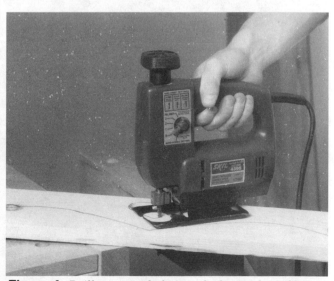

Figure 4. *Drill a starter hole into the heart-shaped area, and cut out the shape with a saber saw.*

Build a Bathroom Caddy

This deluxe bathroom caddy has several handy features, plus a decorative back and a display shelf. The one shown here is built of pine, but you can use any wood to best suit your decor.

This bathroom caddy is fun to build and much nicer than anything you can buy.

Storage and space-saving units have never been more popular, yet the retail prices for such items can be out of this world. This bathroom caddy is fun and economical to build, and its decorative back and contoured sides really set it apart from the department-store versions. It features a handy magazine rack and tissue holder, plus a display shelf. Its compact size and low profile make it ideal for the smallest of bathrooms, and it can be designed to enhance any decor.

TIPS
A nice feature of this project is that it can be constructed from any type of wood, so you can match it to your bathroom's decor. We used pine for the caddy shown here, but oak, maple or cedar are just a few of your choices. It can be left unfinished, or it can be stained or painted to complement your bathroom's color scheme. Choose a wood that best suits your style and pocketbook.

CONSTRUCTION
Begin by cutting all of the project parts to their overall widths and lengths. In other words, cut the basic rectangles for the sides (A), back (B), rail (C), shelves (D, G) and divider (E). Then cut to length the dowels for the bars (F) and the tissue holder (H).

Carefully lay out the design for the sides and back using graph paper with ½ in. squares. Tape two 8½ by

Figure 1. *Mark the grid points for the sides (A) using graph paper. Mark dots where the contour crosses each square, and then connect these dots with a French curve.*

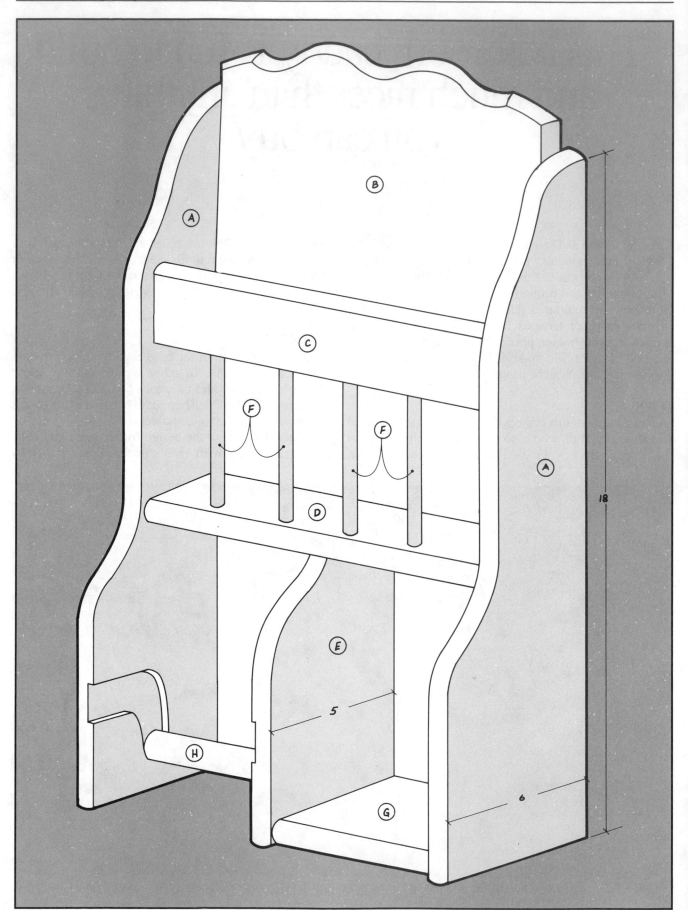

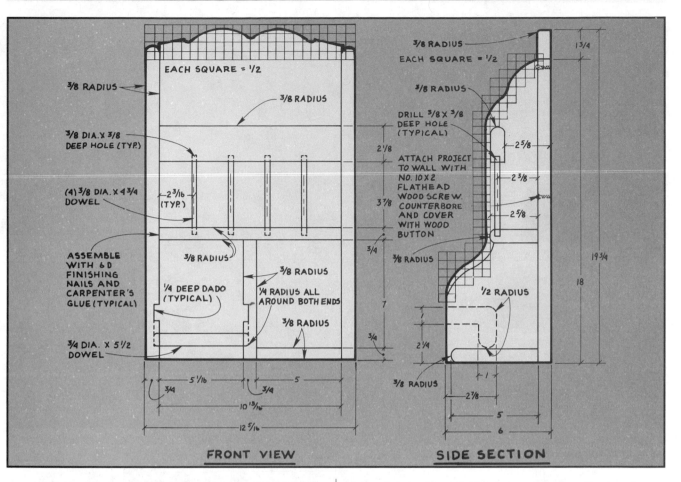

FRONT VIEW

EACH SQUARE = 1/2

3/8 RADIUS

3/8 RADIUS

3/8 DIA. X 3/8 DEEP HOLE (TYP.)

(4) 3/8 DIA. X 4 3/4 DOWEL

ASSEMBLE WITH 6 D FINISHING NAILS AND CARPENTER'S GLUE (TYPICAL)

3/4 DIA. X 5 1/2 DOWEL

3/8 RADIUS

1/4 DEEP DADO (TYPICAL)

1/4 RADIUS ALL AROUND BOTH ENDS

3/8 RADIUS

2 3/16 (TYP.)

5 1/16

3/4

5

3/4

10 13/16

12 5/16

SIDE SECTION

3/8 RADIUS

EACH SQUARE = 1/2

3/8 RADIUS

DRILL 3/8 X 3/8 DEEP HOLE (TYPICAL)

ATTACH PROJECT TO WALL WITH NO. 10 X 2 FLATHEAD WOOD SCREW. COUNTERBORE AND COVER WITH WOOD BUTTON

3/8 RADIUS

3/8 RADIUS

1/2 RADIUS

1 3/4

2 5/8

2 3/8

2 5/8

2 1/8

3 7/8

3/4

7

3/4

2 1/4

1

2 7/8

5

6

19 3/4

18

11 in. sheets of graph paper together lengthwise so you will have enough room to draw the contours for the side workpieces. Make dots where the curved line passes through each square on the graph paper. Then connect the lines using a French curve. If you do not have a French curve, connect the dots freehand. Carefully cut out the design and trace it onto one of the side workpieces. Use a coping saw, saber saw or band saw to cut out the side. Then use this workpiece as a pattern to cut the other side workpiece.

Draw the back's contour using the same techniques as you did for the side. After you have traced the pattern onto the wood, carefully cut it out.

Figure 2. *Sand the side workpieces (A) using a drum sander equipped in a drill press, drill or flexible chucked shaft.*

BILL OF MATERIALS — Build a Bathroom Caddy

Finished Dimensions in Inches

A	Side	3/4 x 6 x 18 pine	2
B	Back	3/4 x 10 13/16 x 19 3/4 pine	1
C	Rail	3/4 x 2 1/8 x 10 13/16 pine	1
D	Shelf	3/4 x 2 5/8 x 10 13/16 pine	1
E	Divider	3/4 x 6 x 7 pine	1
F	Bar	3/8 dia. x 4 3/4 birch	4
G	Lower Shelf	3/4 x 5 x 5 pine	1
H	Tissue Holder	3/4 dia. x 5 1/2 birch	1

Figure 3. *Form the L-shaped dado for the tissue holder (H) with a straight bit. Draw the area to be routed and use an edge guide to guide the router.*

Now use one of the sides to help trace out the middle divider (E). Notice that the top of the divider is curved at a sharper angle in order to fit underneath the shelf (D). Use a straightedge or a French curve to draw the pattern, and then trace and cut the contour.

It is important that you thoroughly sand all of the edges of any contoured pieces. Make sure that these edges are free of any indentations or conspicuous blemishes. Now equip your router with a ⅜ in. rounding over bit with pilot guide, and round over all edges with a ⅜ in. radius as specified in the drawing. These areas include parts of the sides, back, rail, shelf, divider and lower shelf.

The next step requires cutting a 1 in. wide by ¼ in. deep dado into the left side workpiece (A) to accommodate the tissue holder (H). You will need a ¾ in. straight bit and an edge guide for your router. Lay out the L-shaped dado on one of the side workpieces and set up your router's edge guide to follow the cutting line. Set the depth of cut to ¼ inch. You will be able to cut only one of the lengths of the L-shaped dado at one time. Since most consumer-grade straight bits don't come any larger than ¾ in. diameter, you also will not be able to make the full 1 in. wide swath. Before routing, clamp the workpiece securely to your workbench. Complete one of the lengths of the L-shape by readjusting the edge guide and cutting the side. Then rout the divider work-

piece (E) using the same technique.

Test the dowel (H) to insure that it slides in the dado. If it does not slide freely, you will have to make some slight modifications in the dado with your router.

Locate the center points for the bars (F) on the rail (C) and shelf (D). Use a drill press to drill ⅜ in. diameter by ⅜ in. deep holes. Preferably, use a Forstner bit so the bottoms of the holes are flat.

Slightly bevel the ends of the dowel (H) on a stationary belt sander or disk sander. Carefully hold onto the dowel while turning the dowel's edge into the belt sander. You should turn the dowel so it rotates against the sanding belt and not with it.

Thoroughly sand all of the project parts, including the dowel.

ASSEMBLY

Assemble the sides (A) to the back (B) with carpenter's glue and 6d finishing nails. Now install the shelf (D), making sure that it is square. You should also install the divider and the lower shelf at this time to allow you to drive nails into the top shelf (D). If instead you install the top rail and the bars, you will not be able to drive nails through the shelf and into the divider. Finally, install the rail along with the four bars. There is no need to glue the bars in place. When the rail is perfectly aligned, secure it to the assembly with nails and glue.

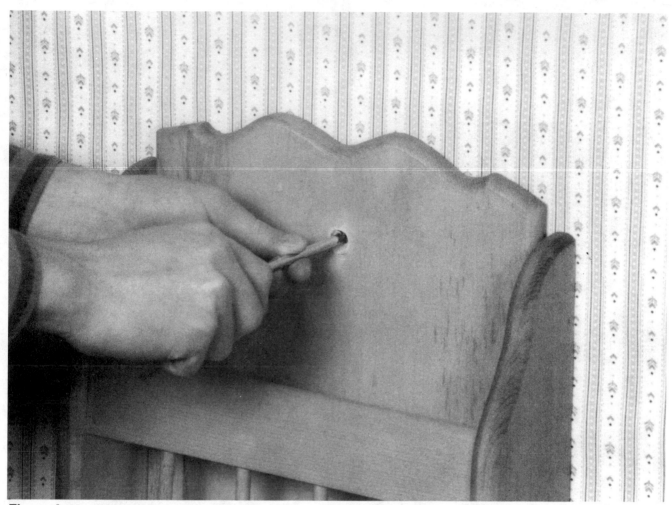

Figure 4 *Mount the caddy to the wall with wood screws. Counterbore the screw holes and cover the recesses with wood plugs. Do not glue the plugs.*

Set all nailheads and allow the glue to cure for 24 hours.

Ideally, you should mount the bathroom caddy to a wall stud. Locate a wall stud and drill two holes in the back workpiece for inserting No. 10 by 2 in. flathead wood screws. Counterbore the holes so they will accommodate a wood button or removable wood plug. One of the mounting holes should be at the upper portion of the back workpiece. The other hole should be in the middle of the back workpiece, located between the two center bars.

If you are not able to mount the caddy directly to a stud, then drill a total of three holes; two in the upper portion of the back, located symmetrically off-center, and one between the two center bars as mentioned above. Again, counterbore to suit three wood plugs or buttons.

Now fill in all nail recesses with an appropriate wood filler and finish sand the project.

FINISHING

If you plan on staining the project, use a clean, soft cloth to apply the stain evenly. Cut down on cleanup by wearing disposable plastic gloves. Immediately after applying the stain, use a clean, soft cloth to wipe off any excess stain and to create an even finish. Then apply a satin finish polyurethane. Some manufacturers sell polyurethanes in spray cans. On a small project like this, a spray varnish is ideal for covering those hard-to-reach areas. Anytime you use a spray-on varnish, make sure the area is well ventilated and that you wear a respiratory mask. You will need to apply three or four coats of a spray-on varnish to get the desired effect. If you brush on the polyurethane finish, it will probably take about two applications. No matter which method you use for applying the polyurethane finish, sand lightly between coats. Don't forget to finish the wood plugs or buttons as well.

MOUNTING

Attach the finished bath caddy to the wall with at least two No. 10 by 2 in. flathead wood screws. Again, these should be secured to a wall stud if possible. If not, then use a good wall anchor to mount your caddy to the wall.□

Covered Shadow Box

The contoured rails and glass panels make this project a real standout. Built from oak, the shadow box can be finished with a clear sealer for a natural look, or stained to match your decor.

Build a shadow box that's a step above the rest!

Shadow boxes are popular wall display units, but this version will prove to be more popular than most. Rather than the pine shadow boxes seen so commonly in stores, this one is built of quality oak for beauty and long life. The shadow-box design is further refined by adding a decorative door and antique-brass hinges.

The scalloped door features glass panels to not only keep out dust, but also to protect your collectibles from curious fingers. The three interior shelves are a little more than 1½ ft. long, providing much more space for knickknacks than similar units. Simple butt joints make assembly easy, and the project can be stained to match just about any decor.

TIPS

Buy solid, straight-grain oak for the project. Select the best material for the rails (C, D) and stiles (E, F).

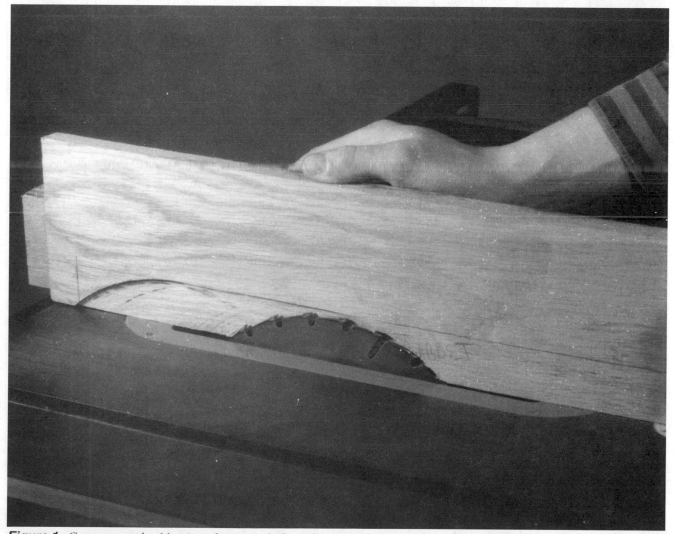

Figure 1. *Cut a stopped rabbet into the top rail (C) with your table saw. As shown here, the contours in the rail are not cut until after you have formed the rabbet.*

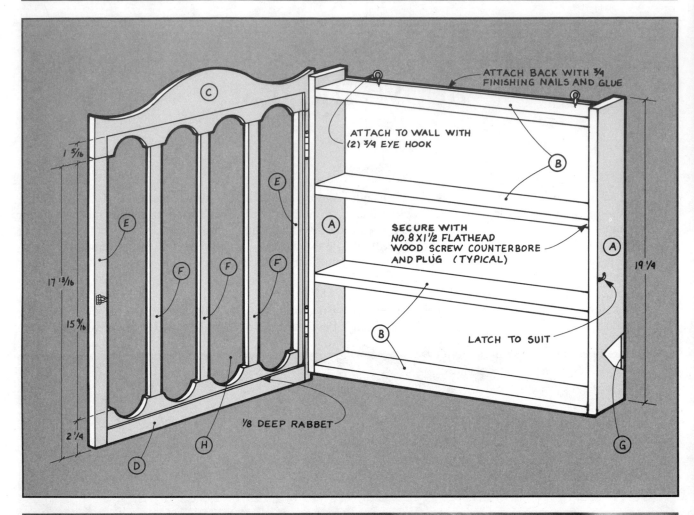

ATTACH BACK WITH ¾
FINISHING NAILS AND GLUE

C

ATTACH TO WALL WITH
(2) ¾ EYE HOOK

B

1 5/16

E

E

A

E

SECURE WITH
NO. 8 X 1½ FLATHEAD
WOOD SCREW COUNTERBORE
AND PLUG (TYPICAL)

F

F

F

A

17 13/16

19 1/4

15 9/16

B

LATCH TO SUIT

⅛ DEEP RABBET

H

D

2 1/4

G

Figure 2. *Square the rabbeted area in the top rail (C) with a wood chisel.*

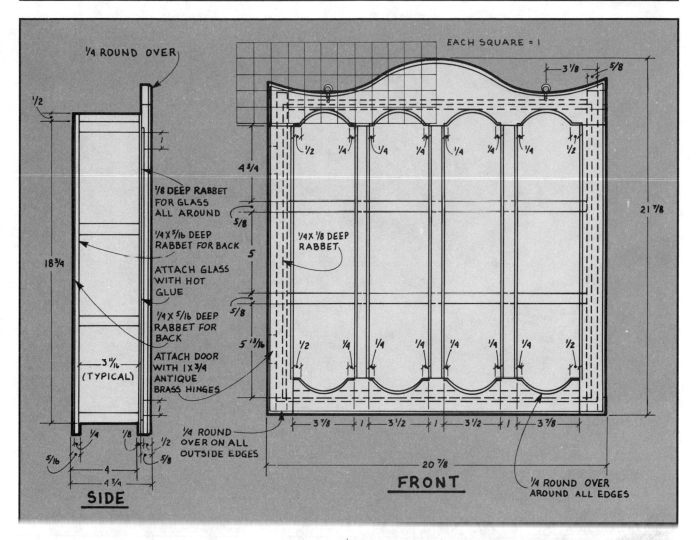

This project incorporates the use of butt joints secured with wood screws. However, if you prefer, you can use dowels instead of screws.

CONSTRUCTION

Begin by cutting out all of the project parts to their overall widths and lengths, with the exception of the middle stiles (F). Cut these three stiles to the proper thickness and width, but do not cut them to length at this time.

Rabbet the inside backs of the side workpieces (A) with a dado blade installed in your table saw. It is a good idea to finish sand the sides, the shelf/top workpieces (B) and the back (G) before assembling the project. A pad sander is ideal for the job.

Now assemble the sides to the four shelf/top workpieces with glue and No. 8 by 1½ in. flathead wood screws. Counterbore the screw holes, and fill in the recesses using wood plugs cut with a plug cutter. Install the back with glue and ¾ in. brads. The back will help to square the assembly.

Carefully lay out the contours for the top rail (C) and the bottom rail (D), but do not cut to shape at this point.

Now rabbet the top rail, bottom rail and two stiles (E) on your table saw. Notice that the rabbets in the top rail and bottom rail are much wider than those in the stiles. This is to accommodate the glass and to clear the contours that will be cut into the workpieces later.

To cut the rabbet in the top rail, attach a wood fence to your table saw's fence. Then position the saw blade to cut ⅛ in. into the material from the surface of the wood fence. Now set the saw blade to a ½ in. depth of

BILL OF MATERIALS — Covered Shadow Box

Finished Dimensions in Inches

A	Side	⅝ x 4 x 19¼ oak	2
B	Shelf/Top	⅝ x 3¹¹⁄₁₆ x 18⅝ oak	4
C	Top Rail	⅝ x 4¹⁄₁₆ x 20⅝ oak	1
D	Bottom Rail	⅝ x 2¼ x 17⅞ oak	1
E	Stile	⅝ x 1½ x 17¹³⁄₁₆ oak	2
F	Middle Stile	½ x 1 x 15⁹⁄₁₆ oak	3
G	Back	¼ x 19 x 19¼ oak plywood	1
H	Glass	⅛ x 18¹⁄₁₆ x 19 Plexiglas	1

Figure 3. *Cut out the contours in the bottom rail (D) with a band saw, as shown, or a saber saw.*

cut. Mark the top rail so that you can make stopped cuts, because the rabbet does not extend the full length of this workpiece. Make the first cut, and then continue making progressively deeper cuts until you achieve the final area to be rabbeted.

Similarly, rabbet the bottom rail. However, the bottom rail does not require any stopped rabbets. You can simply rabbet along the full length of the material. Now reset the saw blade, and rabbet the stiles (E) with your table saw.

Use a wood chisel to square the stopped rabbet in the top rail. Position the rails and stiles onto a flat surface and square the assembly. Now measure the middle stiles (F) and cut to length. Then cut the contours in the top and bottom rails with a saber saw or a band saw. Then sand the edges smooth and rout.

Lay the door workpieces on a flat surface so that the inside surfaces are facing up. This will insure that the middle stiles (F) will be flush with the outside of the door. The inside of the middle stiles should be flush with the rabbets that you cut in the stiles (E) and the rails (C, D). Apply glue to the joints, position the pieces and

Figure 4. *Sand the contours in the rails with a drum sander inserted in your drill. Make sure that you clamp the workpiece securely so that you can have both hands on the workpiece.*

clamp the assembly. It is not necessary to dowel these joints, but if you prefer, use ⅛ in. dowels. Allow the assembly to dry thoroughly overnight.

FINISHING
Finish sand the entire project and remove hardened glue with an old wood chisel or paint scraper. Any glue that is left on the project will mar the finish.

Stain the project to suit your tastes, and follow this with a coat of an appropriate sealer. After the sealer has dried, finish sand the project and then apply your final finish.

Cut Plexiglas (H) for the door. You can use regular glass, but it adds weight to the door and is not as easy to work with. Using a straightedge as a guide, make repetitive scribes with a scoring tool. Make sure that you scribe both sides of the Plexiglas, then break away the waste area. File any sharp edges on the Plexiglas before installing it. Secure it to the door with beads of hot glue.

Now hinge the door and install a latch to suit. Insert two ¾ in. eye hooks into the back of the top shelf for hanging the project. Mount the shadow box by driving two hooks in the wall to correspond with the eye hooks. If you will not be mounting the unit to wall studs, you will need a wall anchor system. Use heavy-duty wall anchors, since the shadow box is quite heavy. ❏

Knickknack Shelf

This knickknack shelf was built from oak, which offers durability and natural beauty. However, just about any wood is suitable, especially if you want to personalize the project by applying paint, antique stain, stencils or appliqués.

Give yourself a gift with this versatile knickknack shelf.

This knickknack shelf makes a great gift because it can be used for many different purposes and in many different places. The top is designed with a slotted groove for safely displaying decorative plates or family pictures. The four Shaker-style pegs can be used for hanging everything from hand-dipped candles to keys or necklaces. The dowel rod can be used to hang towels, ties or even baby blankets. Heart-shaped cutouts in the back, plus the contours in the sides, give it a country look that will warm any room. But what makes this project a real winner is that it is easy and fun to build.

TIPS

Make sure you buy the Shaker pegs (E) before you purchase the rest of the wood for the project. Otherwise, you may not be able to find Shaker pegs to match your choice of wood. A number of mail order sources offer

Shaker pegs, but they are available in limited sizes and wood types. Also, be sure to drill the holes in the back (B) to custom fit the pegs.

CONSTRUCTION

Begin by cutting all of the project parts to their overall widths and lengths. Make sure to joint all of the edges on your stationary jointer from longer material lengths.

Then rout a ⅛ in. cove all around the top (A) workpiece. Use a pilot guide with your router bit, and move the router counterclockwise around the perimeter of the top workpiece. Make sure that the workpiece is clamped securely to avoid accidents. Now use your table saw to cut a ¼ in. by ¼ in. deep by 20 in. long stopped groove into the top. This groove is used for displaying decorative plates.

Next, transfer the pattern for the back (B) and sides (C) onto the workpieces. Then cut them out with a saber

Figure 1. *Lay out the grid for the contours in the sides (C), and mark the points where the design intersects each grid line.*

Figure 2. *Connect the points with a French curve, and then cut out the shape with a band saw.*

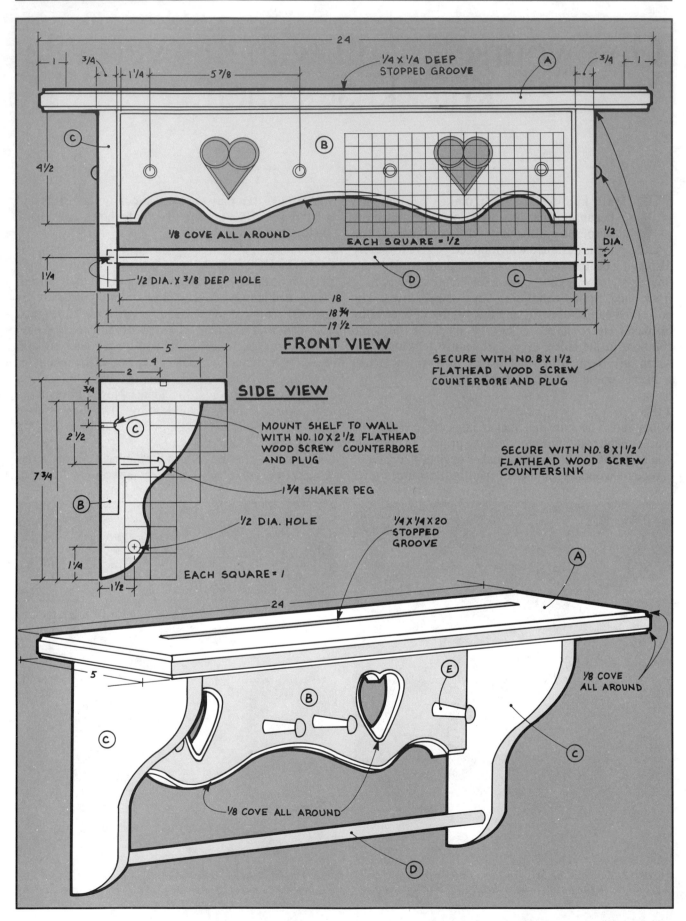

24

¼ X ¼ DEEP
STOPPED GROOVE

A

1   ¾   1¼   5⅞   ¾   1

C   4½   B   EACH SQUARE = ½   ½ DIA.

⅛ COVE ALL AROUND

½ DIA. X ⅜ DEEP HOLE   D   C

1¼

18
18¾
19½

FRONT VIEW

5   **SIDE VIEW**
4
2

¾   SECURE WITH NO. 8 X 1½
1   FLATHEAD WOOD SCREW
C   COUNTERBORE AND PLUG
2½

7¾   MOUNT SHELF TO WALL
B   WITH NO. 10 X 2½ FLATHEAD
WOOD SCREW COUNTERBORE
AND PLUG   SECURE WITH NO. 8 X 1½
FLATHEAD WOOD SCREW
COUNTERSINK

1¾ SHAKER PEG

1¼   ½ DIA. HOLE
¼ X ¼ X 20
STOPPED
GROOVE   A

1½   EACH SQUARE = 1

24

5   E   ⅛ COVE
ALL AROUND

B

C   C

⅛ COVE ALL AROUND   D

Figure 3. *Cut the stopped groove into the top workpiece (A). Install a straight bit and guide the router along the workpiece's edge with an edge guide.*

Figure 4. *Use a Forstner bit to drill 1 in. diameter holes into the heart-shaped area of the back (B). Be sure to use a backup board when drilling. Then cut out the remaining shape with a saber saw.*

saw or band saw. Drill starter holes for the heart-shaped cutouts in the back, and then cut out the section in between with your saber saw. Use a plywood cutting blade that can cut a tight radius.

Carefully sand all the contours in the back and side workpieces, using a drum sander installed in your drill press. Then with a ⅛ in. cove bit, rout a decorative cove all around the back workpiece as indicated in the illustration.

Next, locate the holes for the pegs (E) in the back workpiece and the stopped holes for the dowel (D) in the side workpieces. Drill these out with a drill press.

ASSEMBLY

Secure the back, top and sides to one another with No. 8 by 1½ in. flathead wood screws and carpenter's glue. You must predrill the holes. Note that the holes in the top should be countersunk, while those in the sides should be counterbored. As you assemble the sides to the top and the back, make sure to install the dowel (D). Apply a little dab of glue on each end of the dowel.

After securing the top, plug the hole recesses in the sides and sand flush. Complete the project by gluing and installing the Shaker pegs.

FINISHING

Give the project a fine sanding and apply a stain of your choice. Next, give the project a complete coat of polyurethane sealer, sanding when dry. Then give it a final coat of polyurethane. A satin finish polyurethane is preferred.

MOUNTING

When mounting the shelf, try to find the wall studs. The shelf should be mounted to at least one stud. Mark two mounting holes onto the back of the shelf, and drill these out to accommodate No. 10 by 2½ in. flathead wood screws. Counterbore the holes, and then use two plugs or buttons to fill the hole recesses. It is not necessary to glue these buttons in place. If the shelf is not mounted to a wall stud, substitute the screws with an appropriate fastener and wall anchor. ☐

BILL OF MATERIALS — Knickknack Shelf

Finished Dimensions in Inches

A	Top	¾ x 5 x 24 oak	1
B	Back	¾ x 4½ x 18 oak	1
C	Side	¾ x 4 x 7 oak	2
D	Dowel	½ dia. x 18¾ birch	1
E	Pegs	1¾ oak	4

Oak Drafting Table

Adjustable arms allow you to raise and lower the top, and the project can be modified to accommodate a longer or shorter straightedge.

Give yourself some workspace with this professional-style drafting table.

Most avid woodworkers do a fair amount of drafting, but rarely do they have adequate space for designing and drawing patterns. If that is your case, then this project is for you. This oak drafting table will be a functional, durable and attractive addition to any den or workshop.

The top pivots on adjustable arms to provide a large, flexible work surface. The sides are attached to the runners with knockdown fasteners, allowing the table to be dismantled easily for moving or storage. Most importantly, this drafting table will give you much-needed workspace while requiring a minimum of materials and time to build.

TIPS
We used a 48 in. parallel straightedge for this drafting table, but you may opt to modify the project to accommodate a shorter or longer parallel straightedge.

A special drafting board mat is available from drafting supply houses. This mat provides a soft, yet firm,

drawing surface. It eliminates the unevenness that can occur when drawing directly on wood.

Buy kiln-dried, knot-free lumber for the stiles (F) and side rails (G). If there is any warping in the wood, the table will not stand perfectly straight. To make the drafting table sturdier, you may want to use 1 in. wood instead of ¾ in. wood for the stiles and side rails.

CONSTRUCTION
Begin by cutting out all of the project parts, with the exception of the adjustable arms (H), to their overall lengths and widths. When cutting the oak plywood top (A), cut with the good side of the wood down, and run your circular saw along the straightedge.

Now glue the two top front/back rails (C) to the top (A) with carpenter's glue. Use bar clamps to secure the assembly, and make sure the rails are flush with the plywood top.

Joint the remaining edges of the top assembly to accommodate the two top side rails (B). Check to see if

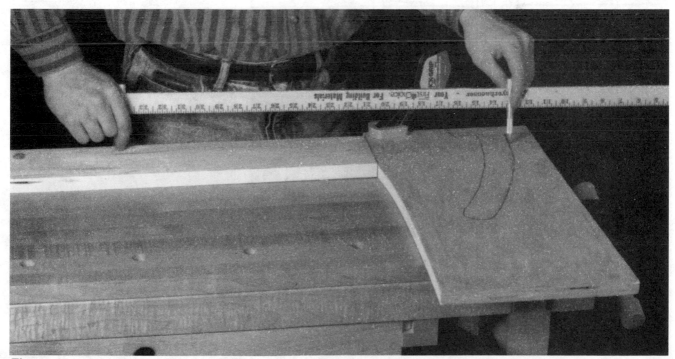

Figure 1. *Carefully lay out the adjustable arm (H) with a bar compass.*

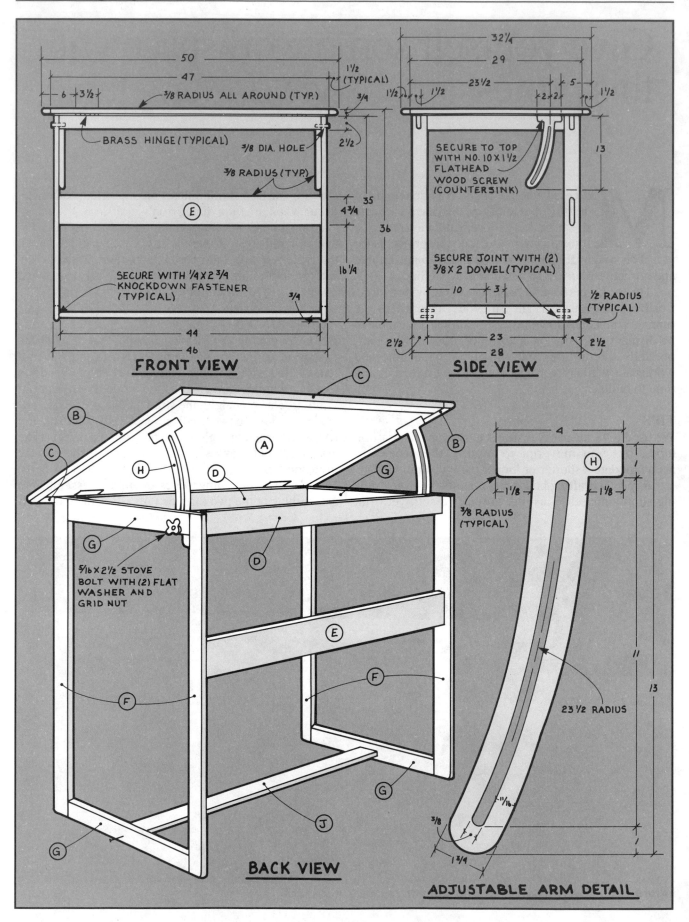

50

47

6 3½

3/8 RADIUS ALL AROUND (TYP.)

1½ (TYPICAL)

¾

BRASS HINGE (TYPICAL)

3/8 DIA. HOLE

2½

3/8 RADIUS (TYP.)

E

35

36

4¾

SECURE WITH ¼ X 2¾ KNOCKDOWN FASTENER (TYPICAL)

¾

16¼

44

46

FRONT VIEW

32¼

29

23½

5

1½

1½

2 2

1½

SECURE TO TOP WITH NO. 10 X 1½ FLATHEAD WOOD SCREW (COUNTERSINK)

13

SECURE JOINT WITH (2) 3/8 X 2 DOWEL (TYPICAL)

10

3

½ RADIUS (TYPICAL)

2½

23

2½

28

SIDE VIEW

C

B

B

A

C

G

H

D

G

5/16 X 2½ STOVE BOLT WITH (2) FLAT WASHER AND GRID NUT

G

D

E

F

F

G

J

G

BACK VIEW

4

H

1

1⅛

1⅛

3/8 RADIUS (TYPICAL)

11

13

23½ RADIUS

11/16

3/8

1¾

ADJUSTABLE ARM DETAIL

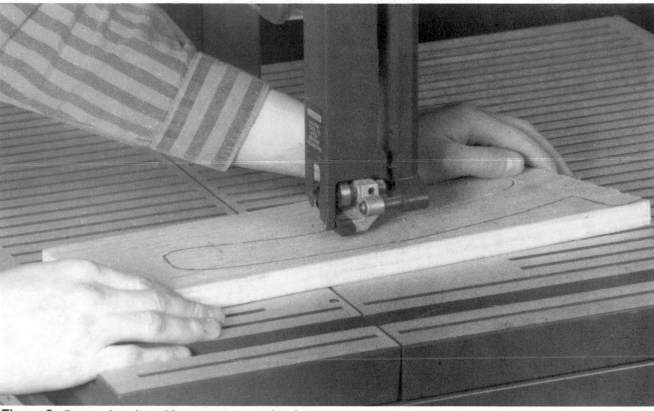

Figure 2. *Cut out the adjustable arm using your band saw.*

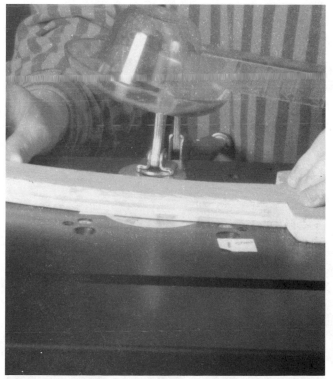

Figure 3. *Clamp a pivot guide ¹¹/16 in. from the straight bit's cutting edge. Then mark beginning and ending points for the cut on the router table. Firmly grip the workpiece as you rout. Take only a ¹/8 in. deep pass at a time. After each pass, reset the router to take an additional ¹/8 inch. Continue until you completely mill the slot.*

there are any gaps, and then drill dowel holes. A ⅜ in. diameter by 1½ in. dowel is used for each joint where the top side rails (B) adjoin the top front/back rails (C). Dry-assemble the top side rails to the top, and when everything is perfect, secure the two rails in place with glue and dowels.

Next, locate and drill dowel holes into the stiles (F) and side rails (G). Two ⅜ in. diameter by 2 in. long dowels are required for each joint. Drill the dowel holes using a doweling jig in combination with a spur bit. Remember to drill the holes about ⅛ in. deeper than the length of dowel to allow for glue expansion. Now dry-

BILL OF MATERIALS — Oak Drafting Table

Finished Dimensions in Inches

A	Top	¾ x 29 x 47 oak plywood	1
B	Top Side Rail	¾ x 1½ x 32 oak	2
C	Top Front/Back Rail	¾ x 1½ x 47 oak	2
D	Runner	¾ x 2½ x 44 oak	2
E	Runner	¾ x 4¾ x 44 oak	1
F	Stile	¾ x 2½ x 35 oak	4
G	Side Rail	¾ x 2½ x 23 oak	4
H	Adjustable Arm	¾ x 6 x 13 oak	2
I	Mat	¹/16 x 31½ x 49	1
J	Bottom Runner	¾ x 3 x 44 oak	1

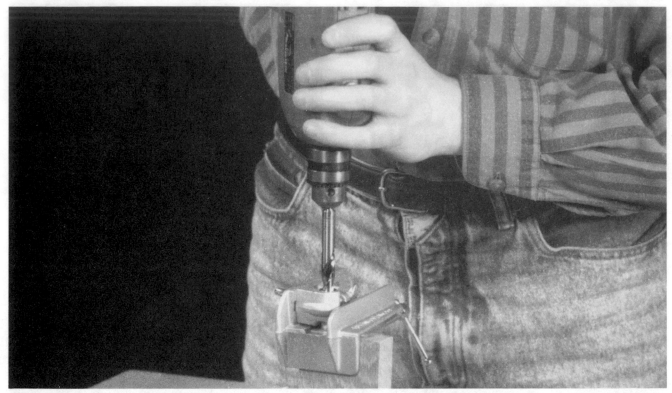

Figure 4. *Drill mating dowel holes into the side rails (G) and stiles (F). Drill the holes 1/8 in. deeper to allow for glue expansion. Here we are using a doweling jig in combination with a spur bit.*

assemble the two side assemblies, and check to make sure that the joints are tight. Then glue the assembly and secure with bar clamps.

Carefully lay out the design for the adjustable arms (H). Notice that the adjustable arms are slotted, and are located 23½ in. from the pivot points of the hinges that will be installed in the front runner (D). Use a compass to lay out the arms, then cut them out with a band saw. Before cutting the slots, equip your router table with a ⅜ in. straight bit set to cut ⅛ in. deep. Make a special guide and clamp it ¹¹/₁₆ in. from the edge of the router bit. Run the adjustable arm along the edge of the guide so that the bit will cut a slot along the length of the arm. Make a trial run first, and mark a beginning and an ending point on the router table for cutting the workpiece. Then turn on the router, and make a plunge cut to begin cutting the slot. Then slowly, keeping the workpiece firmly against the guide, work your way to the other end of the slot. Turn off the router and readjust the bit to cut ⅛ in. deeper. Again, use the starting and ending points to guide the cut. Continue in this manner until you have completely routed out the adjustable arm. Follow this same procedure for milling the remaining adjustable arm.

Joint the edges of the top assembly and the side assemblies. Then use a belt sander to round off all four corners of each assembly. Refer to the technical illustration.

Figure 5. *Secure the side to the runners (D, E) with knockdown fasteners as shown. An Allen wrench is usually needed to tighten these knockdown fasteners.*

Next, using a ⅜ in. round over bit with a pilot guide, rout all of the edges of the top and side assemblies. Similarly, rout the outside edges of the adjustable arms, but not the slots. Make sure to securely clamp one end of the workpiece while routing the other end. Under no circumstances should you try to rout the workpieces without clamping them. Now rout the showing edges of the runners (D, E) where indicated in the illustration.

ASSEMBLY

The sides are secured to the runners with knockdown fasteners. These are available through mail order catalogs or from specialty hardware stores. Knockdown fasteners provide a strong joint while allowing you to dismantle the table so it can pass easily through a doorway. Attach the sides to the runners following the manufacturer's instructions for mounting the knockdown fasteners. Make sure that the two side assemblies are resting on an absolutely flat surface when securing them to the runners.

Now locate two 3½ in. brass hinges on the front runner (D). There is no need to mortise out the area for the hinge. Secure the hinges with the screws supplied. Locate the adjustable arms 23½ in. from the pivot points of the hinges. Now secure the adjustable arm to the top (A) with two No. 10 by 1½ in. flathead wood screws. Predrill these holes and countersink the heads.

Use wedges to position the table top so it rests absolutely flat on the sides and with an even amount of space between the bottom of the table top and the top of the side rails (G). Then mark pivot holes where the slots in the adjustable arms will slide along the stove bolts. Move the table top up and down until you are satisfied that the holes to be drilled will stay in the center of the adjustable arm slots. If not, recheck to make sure that the arm's center slot is 23½ in. from the hinge's pivot point.

Once the holes to be drilled are located perfectly, drill ⅜ in. diameter holes. Use a backup board. Now secure each arm to the side rails (G) with a 5/16 in by 2½ in. stove bolt with two flat washers and a grip nut. Be sure to leave enough room between the arms and the side rails to insert a flat washer. The other flat washer is on the nut end. Grip nuts can be purchased from specialty hardware stores and come in a variety of shapes.

FINISHING

Dismantle the drafting table, and finish sand the entire project. Stain the project, and then apply several coats of a good polyurethane satin finish. Remember to sand between coats.

Reassemble the project, and cut a drafting board mat to suit the top. Use a utility knife to cut the special mat. Position the mat on top of the drafting table and make a light pencil mark along the perimeter of the mat. Remove the mat and place a strip of carpet tape along the inside of the marked perimeter. Remove the carpet tape's special backer and position the mat onto the table. The carpet tape will keep the mat flat and hold it firmly in position. When the mat eventually wears out, it can be replaced easily by lifting it up firmly and removing the old carpet tape. ❑

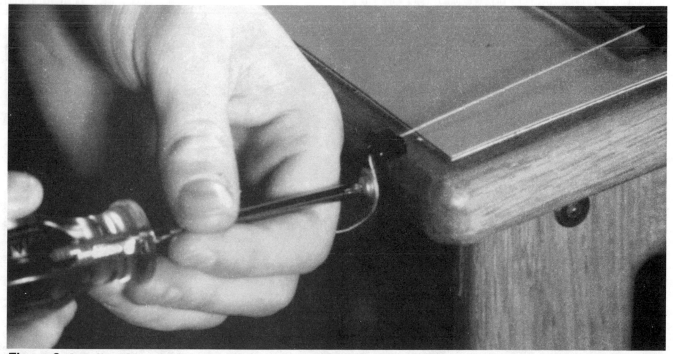

Figure 6. *Install a 48 in. parallel straightedge onto the top. These straightedges can be purchased from drafting supply houses.*

Custom-Made Waterbed

Cost-saving construction, clean lines and comfort make this project a winner.

Here's how you can throw out that old box spring and mattress, and build a better bed for less.

Once regarded as novelties, waterbeds are now commonplace. Their growth in popularity has led to better-quality mattresses that are easier and more cost-efficient to manufacture. However, waterbed frames and headboards have never been more elaborate — or expensive. This waterbed set is easy and inexpensive to make, and can be tailored to fit any mattress. Its clean lines, coupled with the comfort of a good waterbed mattress, make it the perfect replacement for that old box spring and mattress. The knockdown design allows easy disassembly, and the project can be painted to complement any decor — from master bedroom, to guest room, to children's bedrooms.

TIPS

Buy a waterbed mattress first and then build the waterbed frame and headboard to accommodate the mattress. Allow approximately ⅛ in. clearance around the perimeter of the mattress when constructing the frame.

The project is designed for easy disassembly, so it is secured entirely with wood screws. Notice that the deck supports (F) are interlocked and can be removed easily. The pedestal sides (D) and pedestal ends (E) are secured to one another with flathead wood screws. The

This story is courtesy of the American Plywood Association, P.O. Box 11700, Tacoma, WA 98411.

Figure 1. *Cut the headboard's contour with a saber saw equipped with a long cutting blade. Work slowly, and make sure the blade is perpendicular to the saw's pad.*

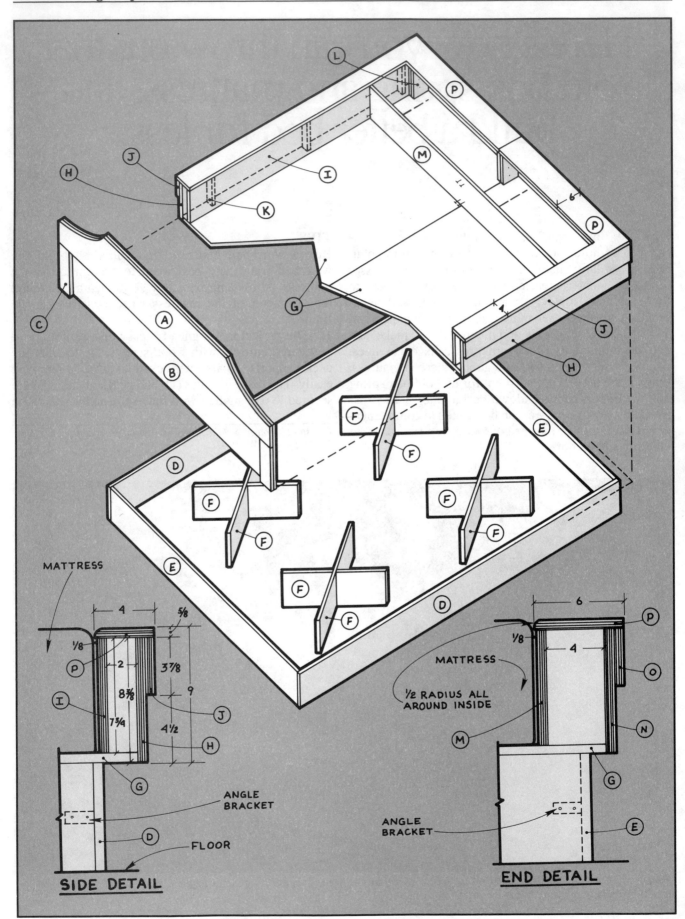

MATTRESS

4

5/8

1/8

P

2

3 7/8

I

8 3/8

9

J

7 3/4

H

4 1/2

G

ANGLE
BRACKET

D

FLOOR

SIDE DETAIL

6

P

1/8

4

O

MATTRESS

1/2 RADIUS ALL
AROUND INSIDE

M

N

G

ANGLE
BRACKET

E

END DETAIL

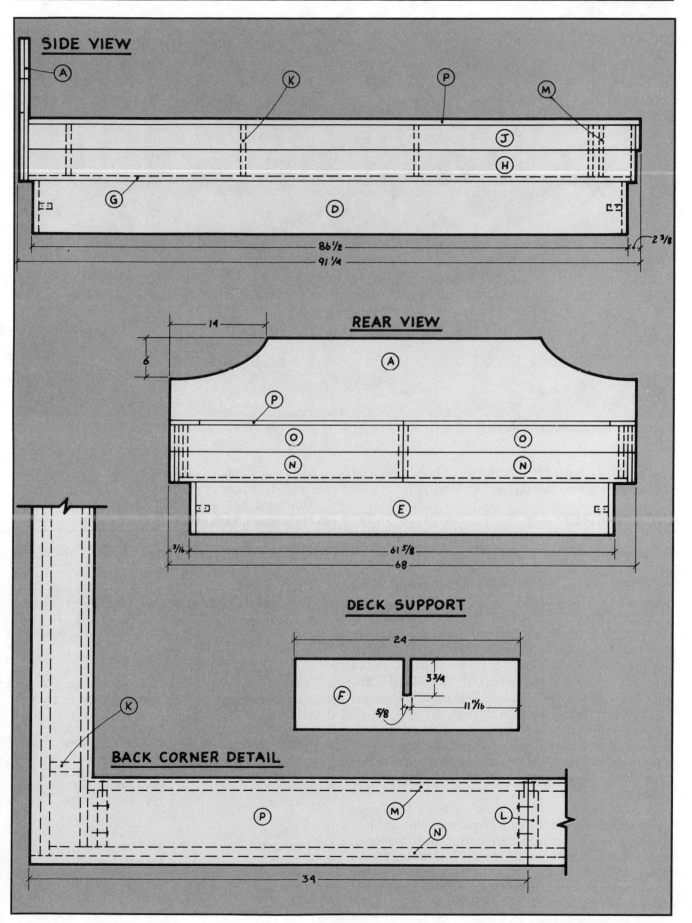

SIDE VIEW

REAR VIEW

DECK SUPPORT

BACK CORNER DETAIL

Figure 2. *Cut notches into the deck supports (F) so each pair of deck supports can be interlocked to form an X-shape.*

headboard is completely removable, as is the L-shaped frame forming the sides (H) and the deck (G).

CONSTRUCTION

Cut out all of the project parts to their appropriate widths and lengths. Note that the deck (G) is comprised of two parts, with each half secured to the sides (H).

After you have cut everything to size, joint all of the edges with a hand jointer.

Secure the pedestal sides (D) to the pedestal ends (E) with No. 8 by 1½ in. flathead wood screws, counterbored. Cover the hole recesses with wood plugs or buttons, but do not glue the plugs in place. Install L-shaped brackets to the corners of the pedestal frame with the supplied wood screws. One set of 3 in. angle brackets is sufficient for each corner.

Now measure the slots for four of the deck supports (F), and cut out the slots with a saber saw equipped with a plywood cutting blade. Insert one deck support into each slotted deck support to form four X-shaped assemblies.

Create the headboard by securing the top headboard (A) to the headboard (B) with carpenter's glue and 1 in. finishing nails driven from the top headboard. Similarly, secure the two headboard stiffeners (C) to the headboard (B).

Now lay out the contours for the top headboard and cut out with a saber saw. You must be sure that none of

the nails that you have driven into the headboard coincide with the cutout of the contour.

Now sand the contour with a drum sander installed in your portable hand drill.

The basic frame actually consists of two half sections. Each half section is comprised of an L-shaped frame secured to a plywood deck (G).

BILL OF MATERIALS — Custom-Made Waterbed

Finished Dimensions in Inches

A	Top Headboard	⅝ x 10⅞ x 68 plywood	1
B	Headboard	⅝ x 21 x 68 plywood	1
C	Headboard Stiffener	⅝ x 4 x 7¾ plywood	2
D	Pedestal Side	⅝ x 7½ x 86½ plywood	2
E	Pedestal End	⅝ x 7½ x 60⅜ plywood	2
F	Deck Support	⅝ x 7½ x 24 plywood	8
G	Deck	⅝ x 32¾ x 88⅜ plywood	2
H	Side	⅝ x 8⅜ x 89⅜ plywood	2
I	Inside	⅝ x 7¾ x 88¾ plywood	2
J	Side Rail	⅝ x 3⅞ x 89⅜ plywood	2
K	Support	⅝ x 2 x 7¾ plywood	8
L	Support	⅝ x 4 x 7¾ plywood	6
M	Inside End	⅝ x 7¾ x 60 plywood	1
N	End	⅝ x 8⅜ x 32¾ plywood	2
O	End Rail	⅝ x 3⅞ x 34 plywood	2
P	Top Rail	¾ x 34 x 90+- plywood	2

Figure 3. *Round over the inside edge of the top rail (P) with a rounding over bit equipped with a pilot guide.*

Begin constructing one of the L-shaped frames by securing a side (H) to one of the decks (G) with carpenter's glue and 1 in. finishing nails. Sink all nailheads. Now attach one of the end pieces (N) with glue and nails.

Likewise, install the vertical supports (K). Drive the nails in from the bottom of the deck, up into the supports.

Glue and nail the inside (I) in place. Once that is installed, secure the supports (L) in place.

To complete the half section, secure the side rail (J) and the end rail (O) to the frame assembly. Secure these in place with nails. Then install the top rail (P) with glue and nails.

Follow this same procedure to construct the other half section.

Place the two half sections on the bottom frame and connect them at the supports (L) with No. 8 by 1½ in. flathead wood screws. Do not glue this joint. Now attach the inside end (M) and the ends (N) with No. 8 by 1½ in. flathead wood screws, countersunk. Again, do not glue the inside end in place.

Now rout a ½ in. radius along the inside edge of the top rail (P). Attach the assembled headboard to the waterbed frame with No. 10 by 2½ in. flathead wood screws, countersunk. Do not glue this assembly, but make sure you use enough wood screws. Also, predrill all screw holes.

FINISHING

Finish sand the entire project, making sure that any areas that will come in contact with the mattress are free from any protrusions. Also, dull all sharp edges to avoid snagging bedspreads or causing injuries.

Remove all of the dust with a damp cloth, then brush on a good paint sealer. After the sealer has dried thoroughly, give the outside showing surfaces a good sanding and paint the frame and headboard to suit your room decor. You can use two or more colors to give the project more character. Be sure to apply at least two coats of paint for the best finish.

After the paint has dried, disassemble the project and reassemble in the bedroom. Carefully unfold the mattress and fill with water as specified by the manufacturer. ❐

Make Your Own Mallets

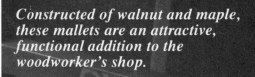

Constructed of walnut and maple, these mallets are an attractive, functional addition to the woodworker's shop.

Learn how to turn your own shop mallets — and create functional works of art.

Shop mallets are necessities for the avid woodworker. Now you can learn to make your own mallets, custom sized for almost any job and strong enough to take a pounding. By using a hardwood with an interesting grain pattern, you can turn shop mallets into works of art you'll be proud to add to your collection of tools.

TIPS

It is always a good idea to construct a mallet from one solid block of wood. However, under some circumstances you may wish to laminate lumber in order to generate an attractive and interesting-looking mallet. If you choose the latter, keep in mind that the mallet will be good for only light pounding. Heavy pounding will result in the wood splitting eventually.

Given the restrictions of a solid block of material, look for interesting grain patterns and irregularities in the wood, such as the wormholes found in the large walnut mallet that we show here.

Never finish a mallet with polyurethane. The polyurethane finish will quickly show the pounding that a mallet takes. If you want a finish, apply tung oil.

CONSTRUCTION

After you have selected the wood for your block, trim off all excess material with a band saw. If you do not have a band saw, use a bench plane to help round the material. You must round the block, or it may shake the lathe violently and fly out of the machine. The

Figure 1. *Locate the center of the turning block and draw the mallet's radius with a compass. Make sure that the block is large enough to obtain this turning radius.*

Figure 2. *Round the block on your band saw. Set the table to 45 degrees and trim 1/4 in. short of the radius you drew earlier. Afterwards, reset the table to 22 1/2 degrees and trim the remaining corners, making the block more cylindrical.*

Figure 3. *Ram the head stock center into one end of the shaped block and then mount it onto the wood lathe.*

possibility of this occurring is even greater when working with large blocks of wood. Turning square blocks of wood is also hard on wood chisels.

It is always a good idea to work from longer lengths of material when turning. Be sure to wear good eye protection and a dust mask as well.

Once you have rounded the basic turning block, mount it between the lathe centers. With the aid of your gouge, turn the basic cylinder shape, working the entire length of the material. Then turn off the machine and mark the key turning points along the cylinder. Turn the handle to the general cylinder shape.

Again mark all turning points, and use a parting tool in combination with calipers to obtain the appropriate diameter for each of the turning points.

Then gouge out the area between the turning points to approximate the basic shape of the mallet. Take great care as you refine the shape.

How you should proceed from this point is really based upon your turning experience and the tools that you have available. To further refine the shape, you can use a scraper and full-round turning chisels to smooth out the rough areas. Those with turning experience may be able to do a good job by continuing with the wood gouge.

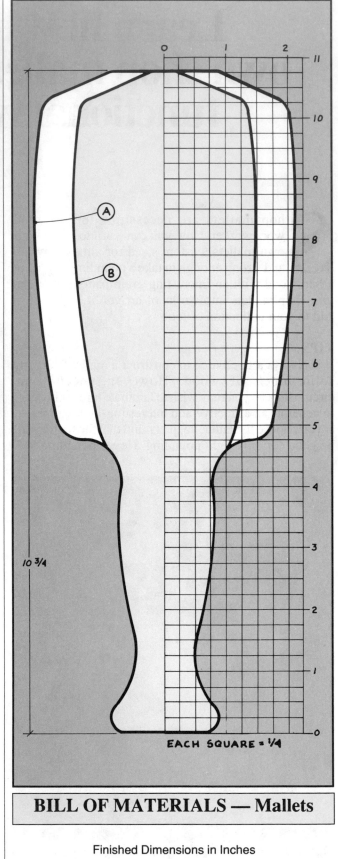

EACH SQUARE = ¼

BILL OF MATERIALS — Mallets

Finished Dimensions in Inches

A	Large Mallet	4¼ dia. x 10¾ walnut	1
B	Small Mallet	3 dia. x 10¾ maple	1

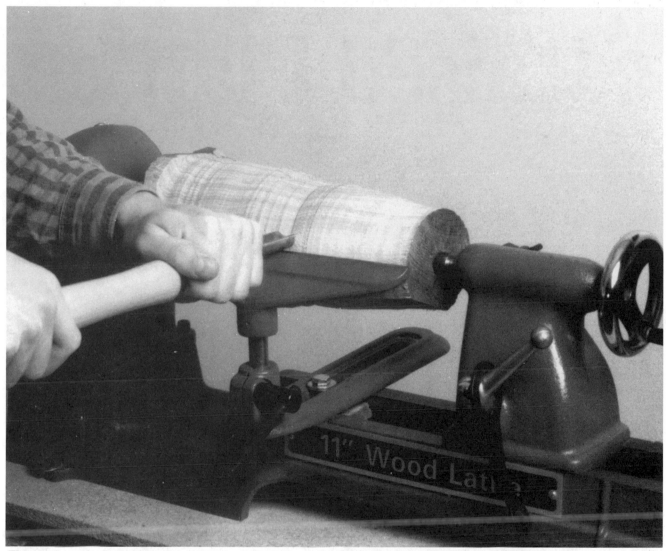

Figure 4. *Use a wood gouge to shape the mallet's basic shape. Then use a parting tool in combination with calipers to mark the turning points.*

Once the mallet has been turned to your satisfaction, sand it on your lathe. Use long strips of sandpaper, preferably those from a stationary or portable belt sander. Turn on the machine and quickly move a strip of sandpaper along the surface of the lathe. Again, you must wear good eye protection and a dust mask. Begin with coarse sandpaper and work your way to fine grit sandpaper. Periodically check your progress by turning off the machine and checking all sides of the mallet. Continue sanding until you are satisfied with the finish.

Use a hacksaw or backsaw to cut the mallet to its appropriate length. Do this on your wood lathe with the machine turned off. Then finish sand the areas that you cut off.

FINISHING
Apply a tung oil or other oil to the project, and allow it to dry before applying a second coat. Even a third coat is recommended. ☐

Raised Planter Box

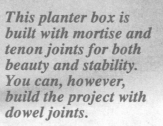

This planter box is built with mortise and tenon joints for both beauty and stability. You can, however, build the project with dowel joints.

Get your flower pots off the ground with this raised planter box.

This planter box is 27 in. high, raising flowering plants to a height where they can be more fully enjoyed. Its sturdy construction is designed to weather outdoor use, and it can be finished to match any garden furniture. Be sure to apply a good wood preservative to keep the planter box looking great for years.

TIPS
Select pine or cedar for this project, and check to make sure that the wood is absolutely straight. If you are intimidated by the mortise and tenon joints required for securing the rails to the legs, substitute with dowel joints.

CONSTRUCTION
Cut out all of the project parts to their overall widths and lengths.

Cut tenons into all four front rails (B) and side rails (C). Notice that there is a ¼ in. shoulder all around each of the ends. Form these shoulders using a mechanical miter box. Use your backsaw to cut the shoulder depth all the way around each front rail (B). Then install the workpiece in a bench vise and use a wide, sharp wood chisel to form the tenon. Follow this same technique for cutting tenons in the side rails.

Now cut mortises into all of the legs (A) to accommodate the rail tenons.

Secure the legs to all of the rails with band clamps. Now insert the side walls (I) and front/back walls (J), making sure they fit properly. Remove the walls from the assembly, then attach the wall workpieces to one another with 4d galvanized nails.

Now disassemble the legs and rails, and apply a waterproof glue to all of the mortise and tenon joints. Reassemble the rails to the legs, using two band clamps to secure all joints. Make sure the assembly is square. Allow the glue to cure for 24 hours.

After the glue has cured, remove the band clamps from the assembly and install the walls (I, J) with 3d galvanized nails driven from inside the walls.

Now attach the cleats (G, H) to the inside walls with 4d galvanized nails.

Use a spade bit to drill a series of ¾ in. diameter drainage holes into the bottom workpiece (K). Then nail the bottom workpiece to the cleats with 3d galvanized nails.

This story is courtesy of The Stanley Works, New Britain, CT 06050.

Figure 1. *Mark each of the rails (B, C) for forming the tenons. Use a mechanical miter box to cut the shoulder depths around each end.*

BILL OF MATERIALS — Raised Planter Box

Finished Dimensions in Inches

A	Leg	1½ x 2½ x 27 pine	4
B	Front Rail	1½ x 2½ x 13 pine	4
C	Side Rail	1½ x 2½ x 15 pine	4
D	Front/Back Cap	1½ x 2½ x 19 pine	2
E	Side Cap	1½ x 2½ x 14 pine	2
F	Slat	1½ x 2½ x 10	18
G	Cleat	¾ x ¾ x 14 pine	2
H	Cleat	¾ x ¾ x 12½ pine	2
I	Side Wall	½ x 15 x 15 exterior plywood	2
J	Front/Back Wall	½ x 14 x 15 exterior plywood	2
K	Bottom	½ x 14 x 14 exterior plywood	1

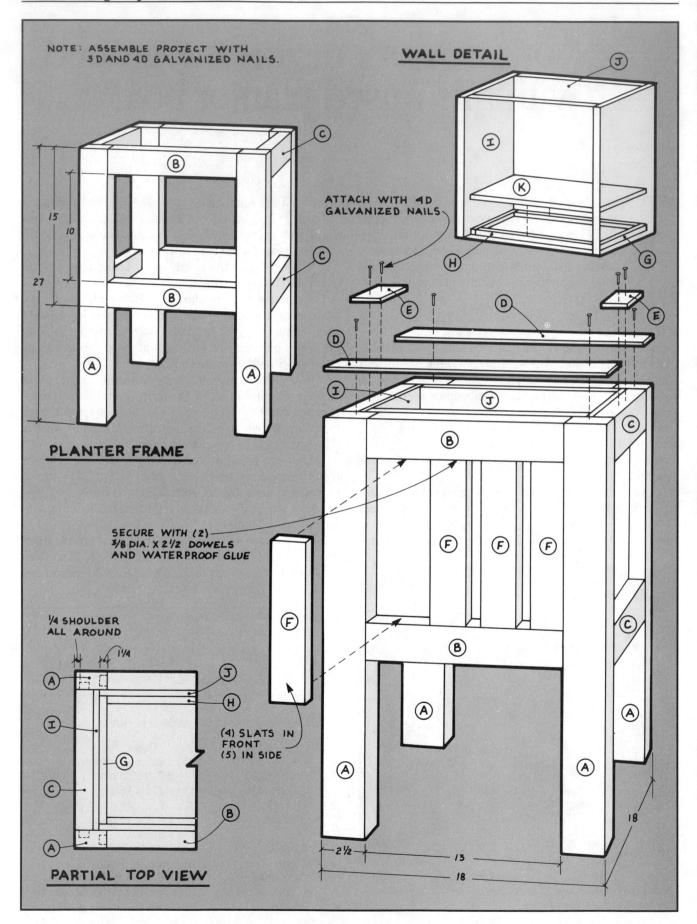

NOTE: ASSEMBLE PROJECT WITH
3 D AND 4 D GALVANIZED NAILS.

WALL DETAIL

ATTACH WITH 4D
GALVANIZED NAILS

PLANTER FRAME

SECURE WITH (2)
3/8 DIA. X 2 1/2 DOWELS
AND WATERPROOF GLUE

(4) SLATS IN
FRONT
(5) IN SIDE

1/4 SHOULDER
ALL AROUND

PARTIAL TOP VIEW

Figure 2. *Install the front rail (B) in a bench vise and remove the waste area with a wood chisel. This will form the shoulders.*

Figure 3. *Lay out the areas to be mortised for each of the legs (A). Drive the wood chisel along the area to be mortised.*

Figure 4. *Use your chisel to remove the waste area to a depth of $1^{1/4}$ inch.*

Figure 5. *Drill $3/4$ in. diameter holes into the bottom workpiece (K). About six holes are needed for good drainage.*

Attach all of the slats (F) to the walls with 3d galvanized nails. Note that the inside pieces should be positioned flush with the legs (A). Then space the remaining slats evenly.

Complete the unit by installing the front/back caps (D) and side caps (E) with 4d galvanized nails.

FINISHING

Apply two to three coats of an appropriate wood preservative. Spray on the preservative to make sure that every nook and cranny is adequately covered. ❒

SOURCES
A VHS videocassette, available from The Stanley Works, offers good tips for constructing outdoor furniture. To order a cassette, send a check or money order for $14.95 to The Stanley Works, Advertising Services, Box 1800, Outdoor Projects, Dept. OPB, New Britain, CT 06050.

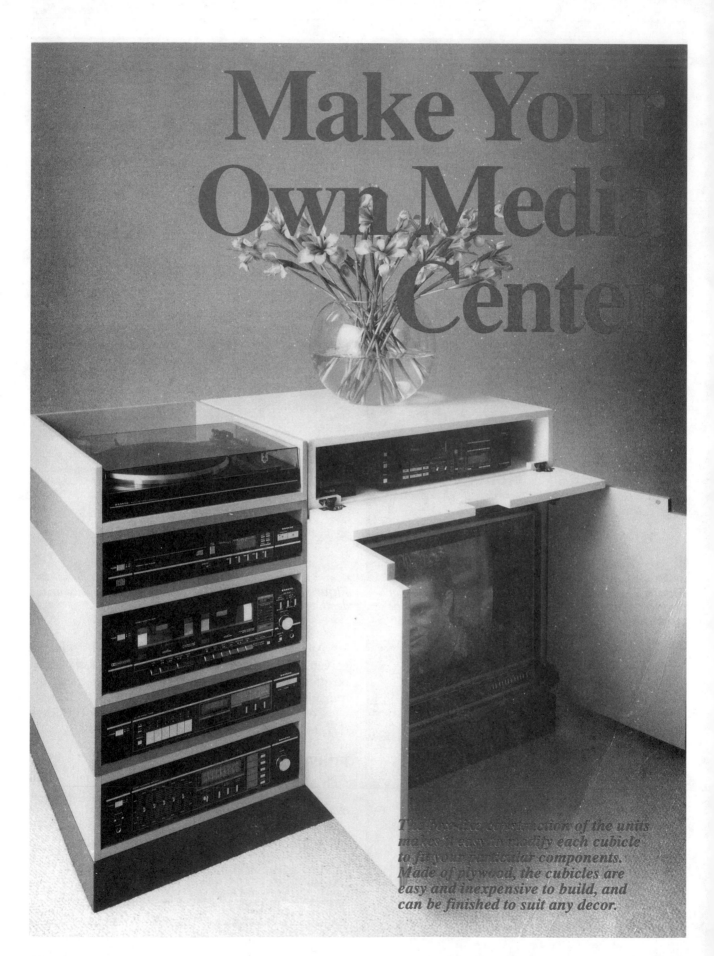

Make Your Own Media Center

The boxlike construction of the units makes it easy to modify each cubicle to fit your particular components. Made of plywood, the cubicles are easy and inexpensive to build, and can be finished to suit any decor.

Save money by making this easy-to-build media center from inexpensive plywood.

The cost of electronic equipment has come down over the years, but that is not true of the cabinets designed to hold such components as compact disc players, tuners and amplifiers. If you are having trouble finding a media center that will meet your needs at an affordable price, this project should fit the bill. Constructed of plywood cubicles, the media center is inexpensive and easy to build. It also can be modified to suit your specific components, as well as your room decor.

TIPS
Buy APA trademark A-B plywood. Inspect each sheet to insure that it is warp-free. Note that the concealed flat hinge used for the VCR door (F4) should be purchased first. This specialty hinge allows the door to be opened without interfering with the lower cabinet below it and to rest flush with the VCR bottom (F1) when closed.

This story is courtesy of the American Plywood Association, P.O. Box 11700, Tacoma, WA 98411.

BILL OF MATERIALS — Make Your Own Media Center

Finished Dimensions in Inches

A1	Turntable Bottom	1/2 x 17½ x 23⅞ plywood	1
A2	Turntable Side	1/2 x 5½ x 23⅞ plywood	2
A3	Turntable Back	1/2 x 5½ x 18½ plywood	1
B1	Disc Player Top/Bottom	1/2 x 17½ x 23⅞ plywood	2
B2	Disc Player Side	1/2 x 4⅝ x 23⅞ plywood	2
B3	Disc Player Back	1/2 x 4⅝ x 18½ plywood	1
C1	Cassette Deck Top/Bottom	1/2 x 17½ x 23⅞ plywood	2
C2	Cassette Deck Side	1/2 x 7⅝ x 23⅞ plywood	2
C3	Cassette Deck Back	1/2 x 7⅝ x 18½ plywood	1
D1	Tuner Top/Bottom	1/2 x 17½ x 23⅞ plywood	2
D2	Tuner Side	1/2 x 5⅝ x 23⅞ plywood	2
D3	Tuner Back	1/2 x 5⅝ x 18½ plywood	1
E1	Amplifier Top/Bottom	1/2 x 17½ x 23⅞ plywood	2
E2	Amplifier Side	1/2 x 6⅝ x 23⅞ plywood	2
E3	Amplifier Back	1/2 x 6⅝ x 18½ plywood	1
F1	VCR Top/Bottom	1/2 x 24⅜ x 28¼ plywood	2
F2	VCR Side	1/2 x 6 x 24⅜ plywood	2
F3	VCR Back	1/2 x 5 x 28¼ plywood	1
F4	VCR Door	1/2 x 6 x 29¼ plywood	1
G1	TV Top/Bottom	1/2 x 24⅜ x 28¼ plywood	2
G2	TV Side	1/2 x 24 x 24⅜ plywood	2
G3	TV Back	1/2 x 23 x 28¼ plywood	1
G4	TV Door	1/2 x 14⅝ x 23¾ plywood	2
H1	Base Top	1/2 x 23⅜ x 47 plywood	1
H2	Base Side	1/2 x 4 x 23⅜ plywood	2
H3	Base Front/Back	1/2 x 4 x 48 plywood	2
I	Corner Bracket	1/2 x 6 x 6 plywood	4

Figure 1. *Drill holes into the backs of all the cubicles that will hold electronic components (A3, B3, C3, D3, E3, F3, G3). Use a backup board when drilling to avoid splintering the wood.*

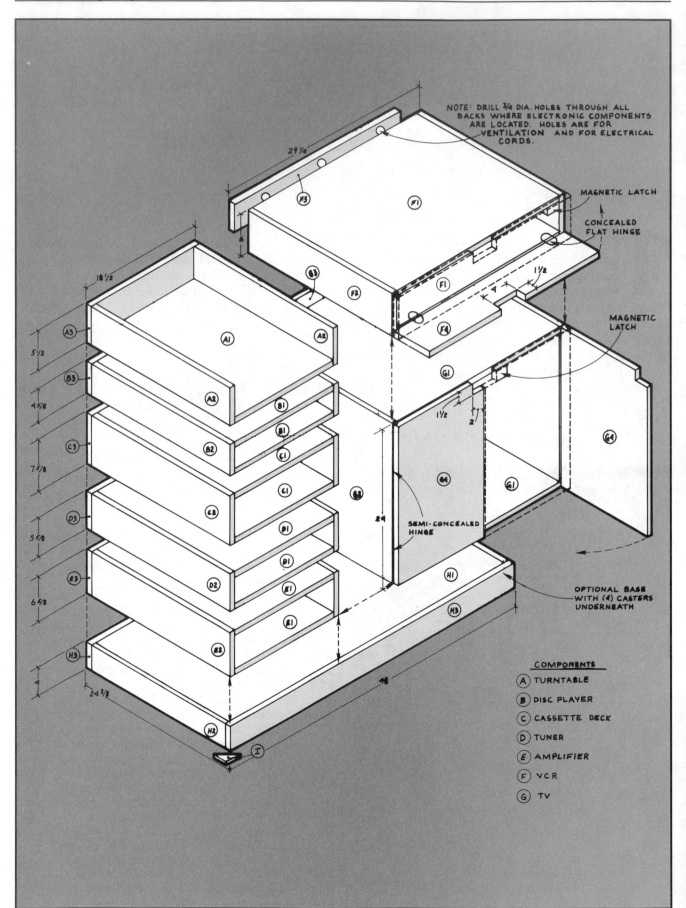

NOTE: DRILL ¾ DIA. HOLES THROUGH ALL
BACKS WHERE ELECTRONIC COMPONENTS
ARE LOCATED. HOLES ARE FOR
VENTILATION AND FOR ELECTRICAL
CORDS.

MAGNETIC LATCH

CONCEALED
FLAT HINGE

MAGNETIC
LATCH

SEMI-CONCEALED
HINGE

OPTIONAL BASE
WITH (4) CASTERS
UNDERNEATH

COMPONENTS

(A) TURNTABLE

(B) DISC PLAYER

(C) CASSETTE DECK

(D) TUNER

(E) AMPLIFIER

(F) VCR

(G) TV

Figure 2. *Carefully locate the positions for the concealed flat hinges used for the VCR door (F4). Mortise these areas out using a drill and a sharp wood chisel.*

Also, don't forget to drill ¾ in. diameter holes through the backs of the media center where the electronic components will be located. These holes are for running cords through, and also for ventilation.

CONSTRUCTION

Cut out all of the project parts, with the exception of the VCR back (F3), the TV back (G3), the VCR door (F4) and the TV doors (G4). Equip your saw with a combination blade to insure smooth cuts.

Begin constructing the media center by assembling the workpieces for the sound-system cabinet. Attach the sides (A2, B2, C2, D2, E2) to the top and bottom workpieces (A1, B1, C1, D1, E1). These workpieces make up the cubicles for the turntable, disc player, cassette deck, tuner and amplifier. Secure the workpieces with 4d finishing nails and carpenter's glue. Then attach the backs (A3, B3, C3, D3, E3), again using glue and nails.

Now assemble the cubicles for the VCR and the TV by securing the sides (F2, G2) to the top and bottom workpieces (F1, G1) with 4d finishing nails and carpenter's glue. Custom cut the VCR back (F3) and the TV back (G3) to fit your components. Once the backs are installed, cut out the VCR door (F4) and the TV doors (G4).

Form the base by securing the sides (H2) to the top (H1) with 4d finishing nails and glue. Then attach the front and back workpieces (H3), and install four corner brackets (I) to strengthen the base. Locate these corner brackets flush with the inside bottom of the base.

Mount the doors for the TV unit using semi-concealed hinges. Similarly, mount the VCR door using concealed flat hinges as indicated in the illustration.

Secure magnetic latches to all of the doors, and then check to make sure that everything fits properly.

FINISHING

Sink all nailheads and fill in the recesses with a good wood filler. Apply wood filler to any other blemishes in the wood as well. Then finish sand all of the project parts.

Carefully remove all of the dust, and apply a good coat of sealer to all of the project parts. Follow this up with a light sanding and a coat of paint in the color of your choice. When this is dry, give the project another light sanding followed by the final coat of paint. ❐

Figure 3. *Sink all nailheads and fill in with a good wood filler. Sand the project thoroughly before finishing it.*

Build a Stylish Desk Set

This handsome desk set includes a file organizer, pencil holder and paper clip tray. For the most stunning effect, use a wood with an interesting grain pattern.

You will get rave reviews with this desk set. Its classic design and natural beauty make it a gift you will want to give again and again.

This clever desk set will be appreciated by students and executives alike. In addition to being sturdy and functional, its all-wood construction gives it a look of natural beauty and permanence. You may want to build one or more of these classic desk sets. They are easy to construct and make great gifts that will never go out of style.

TIPS
It is important that you select a wood with an interesting grain pattern, such as ash, to accentuate your project. The paper clip tray (E) and the pencil holder (D) can be cut out of a solid piece of wood, or made of laminated wood. We chose the latter.

CONSTRUCTION
Begin construction by cutting out all of the project parts to their overall widths and lengths.

FILE ORGANIZER
Carefully set up your table saw or radial arm saw for dadoing the base (A) for the file organizer. Cut a test piece of material first to insure that your saw is cutting square and is not heeling. Then install a dado blade and

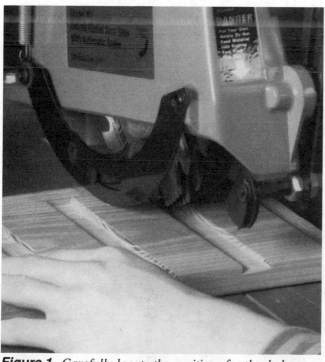

Figure 1. *Carefully locate the positions for the dadoes and rabbets in the base. Cut these out with a table saw or radial arm saw equipped with a dado blade. Work carefully and keep fingers well away from the saw blade.*

Figure 2. *Clean out the dadoed areas with a sharp wood chisel. Clamp the base workpiece to a bench to keep your fingers and hands away from harm.*

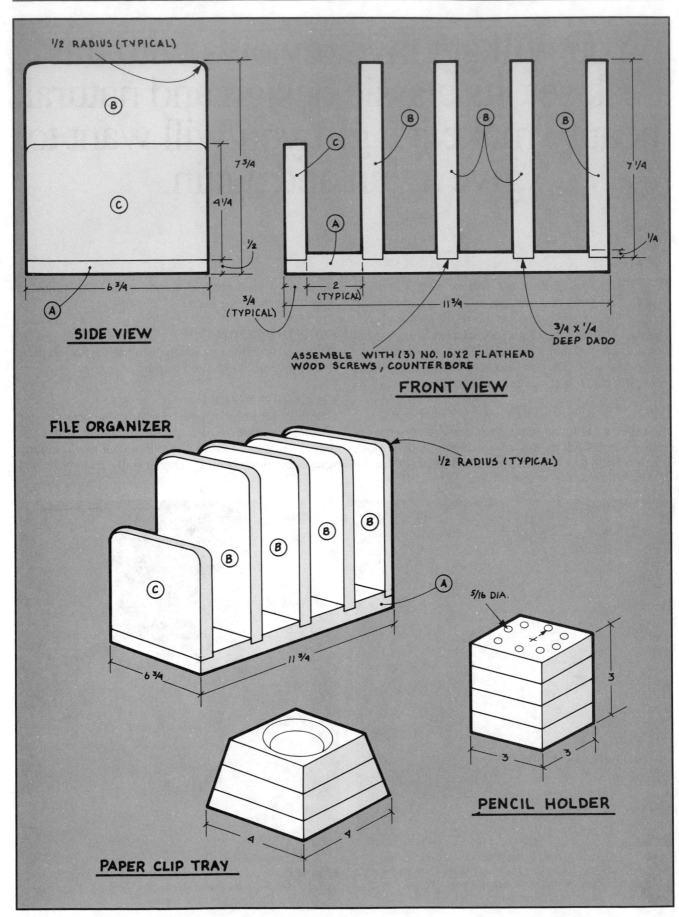

1/2 RADIUS (TYPICAL)

7 3/4

4 1/4

1/2

6 3/4

SIDE VIEW

C

A

B

B

B

B

7 1/4

1/4

2
(TYPICAL)

3/4
(TYPICAL)

11 3/4

3/4 x 1/4
DEEP DADO

ASSEMBLE WITH (3) NO. 10 X 2 FLATHEAD
WOOD SCREWS, COUNTERBORE

FRONT VIEW

FILE ORGANIZER

1/2 RADIUS (TYPICAL)

C

B

B

B

B

A

6 3/4

11 3/4

5/16 DIA.

3

3

3

PENCIL HOLDER

4

4

PAPER CLIP TRAY

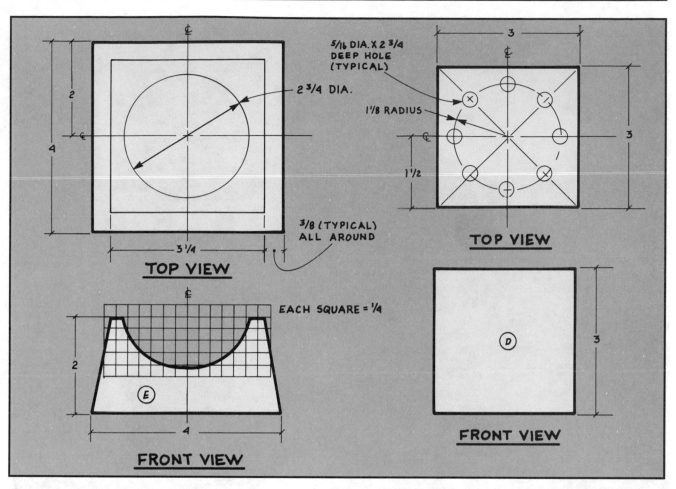

cut the dadoes in the base workpiece. With a sharp wood chisel, smooth out the bottom of the dadoes so there is no gap when the dividers (B, C) are positioned.

Now draw a ½ in. radius at the corners of each of the dividers. You can cut the radius on a band saw or a saber saw, but it is preferable to round over the radius on a stationary disk sander.

Sand the flat surfaces of the file organizer, being careful to use a pad sander to just smooth the surface. If you round over or remove too much material on the dividers, there will be gaps when the dividers are placed in the dadoed base. After sanding, install each of the dividers in its respective dado using a light dab of carpenter's glue and three No. 10 by 2 in. flathead wood screws, counterbored.

PENCIL HOLDER

Begin constructing the pencil holder (D) by cutting the basic shape on a band saw. Then sand the surface areas using a disk sander equipped with fine grit sandpaper. A stationary belt sander will work just as well.

To lay out the holes for drilling, draw diagonal lines from corner to corner. The center is where the two diagonal lines cross. Then strike a radius. Notice that the holes to be drilled coincide with the radius that you have drawn, as well as the two diagonal lines. Now use a

combination square to strike the perpendicular lines through the radius as shown in the diagram.

A drill press equipped with a spur point bit is ideal for drilling the stopped holes in the pencil holder. When drilling, clamp the workpiece in a wood clamp to give you more drilling control. If desired, slightly bevel each of the holes as you drill. Then finish sand the drilled surfaces on a disk sander or stationary sander.

PAPER CLIP TRAY

Next, round out the paper clip tray (E). Mount the block to a lathe and turn the cavity that will hold the paper clips. Use a wood gouge to create the cavity and then follow this up with a round-nose scraping tool. When finished, sand the tray area right on your lathe, beginning with a medium grit sandpaper and working

BILL OF MATERIALS — Desk Set

Finished Dimensions in Inches

A	Base	¾ x 6¾ x 11¾ ash	1
B	Divider	¾ x 6¾ x 7¼ ash	4
C	Divider	¾ x 6¾ x 4¼ ash	1
D	Pencil Holder	3 x 3 x 3 ash	1
E	Paper Clip Tray	2 x 4 x 4 ash	1

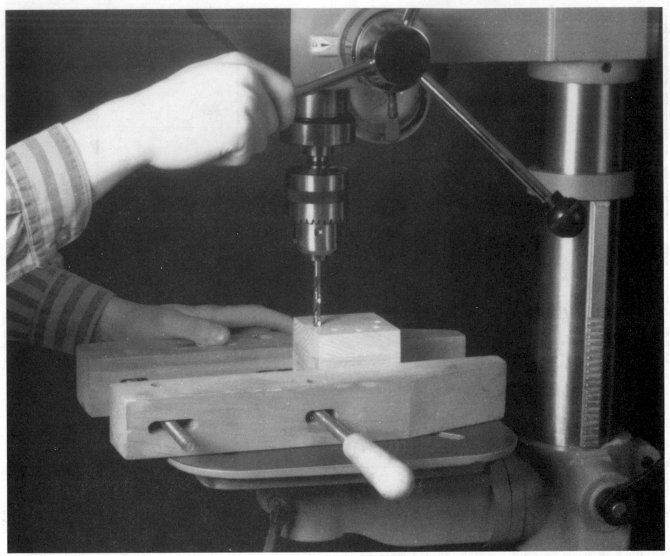

Figure 3. *Locate and drill stopped holes in the pencil holder. Set the depth of cut on your drill press, and hold the pencil holder in a wood clamp as shown.*

your way down to a fine grit. This is fine work, so use caution to avoid getting hands or forearms in harm's way. You should also wear eye protection and a dust mask during this procedure.

After sanding out the cavity, remove the paper clip tray from the lathe and cut the tapers on your band saw. As you did with the pencil holder, sand all the surfaces on a disk sander or stationary sander.

FINISHING

Finish sand the file organizer and slightly round all sharp edges on all three projects. If you opt to stain the desk set, select a light stain that will allow the beauty of the wood grain to shine through.

Apply a sealer coat and then sand lightly when dry. Follow this up with a second coat of polyurethane varnish. Satin or gloss varnish will work fine for this project. ❏

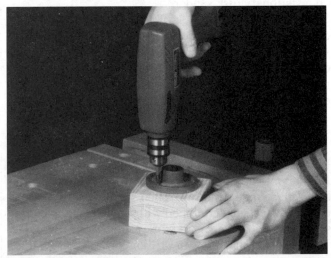

Figure 4. *Mount the paper clip tray to a lathe mount that attaches to your head stock. This blank needs to be absolutely centered on the mount. Make sure that you use short screws to avoid getting near the cavity to be formed.*

Magical Carousel

This project really lets you use your imagination and your talents. You can paint the horses, stencil them or use appliqués. Choose different color combinations for the ribbons to match the color scheme of a child's bedroom. The possibilities are nearly endless.

Bring a little magic into the life of someone special with this colorful carousel.

This whimsical carousel will never lose its magic. Four colorful horses promenade around a center dowel topped with a wooden ball. The blue streamers ending in red ribbons add to the look of youthful exuberance. Constructed of pine, the project is inexpensive and fun to make. You can follow the pattern provided for painting the horses, or create a design of your own. You may want to make several carousels to give as gifts, using different color motifs for each.

TIPS

The 1½ in. diameter wood ball (E) can be purchased at craft stores. However, you can also use a bright-colored solid rubber or plastic ball.

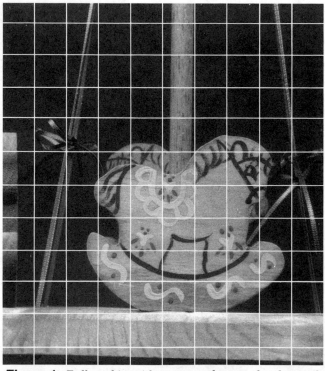

Figure 1. *Follow this grid pattern to lay out the shape of the horses (C). Each square is equal to ¹/2 inch. Also use this pattern to paint the horses.*

CONSTRUCTION

Cut out all of the project parts to their overall widths and lengths.

Now scribe the radius for the base (A) and the bottom (B) with a compass. Follow this up by cutting the radius with a band saw or saber saw. Cut next to the cutting line, but not right on it. Then edge sand the bottom and the base with a stationary disk sander, using a fine grit sandpaper.

Drill a ⅜ in. diameter hole into the bottom workpiece with a drill press. This hole must accommodate the dowel (D) yet still allow the bottom to turn freely. Now drill a ⁵⁄₁₆ in. diameter by ⅜ in. deep hole into the center of the base (A) to also accommodate the dowel.

Similarly, drill a ⁵⁄₁₆ in. diameter by ½ in. deep hole into the wood ball (E). Clamp the wood ball in a wood clamp, and mark the centerpoint for vertical drilling by making a small indent with an awl. Now drill out the hole, making sure the ball is held securely in the wood clamp.

Four ribbons will be inserted through holes drilled into the bottom workpiece (B). Locate the four ³⁄₆₄ in. holes and drill them out on your drill press. Then glue the dowel (D) to the base (A) with carpenter's glue.

Now use the grid pattern to lay out the horse shapes (C). Transfer the pattern to one of the workpieces, and cut out the shape with a scroll saw or coping saw. Use this workpiece as a pattern to cut out the remaining three workpieces.

BILL OF MATERIALS — Magical Carousel

Finished Dimensions in Inches

A	Base	¾ x 6 dia. pine	1
B	Bottom	¾ x 7¼ dia. pine	1
C	Horse	¾ x 2⅞ x 3¼ pine	4
D	Dowel	⁵⁄₁₆ x 15⅜ birch	1
E	Wood Ball	1½ dia. pine	1
F	Blue Ribbon	56 in.	1
G	Red Ribbon	5 in.	4

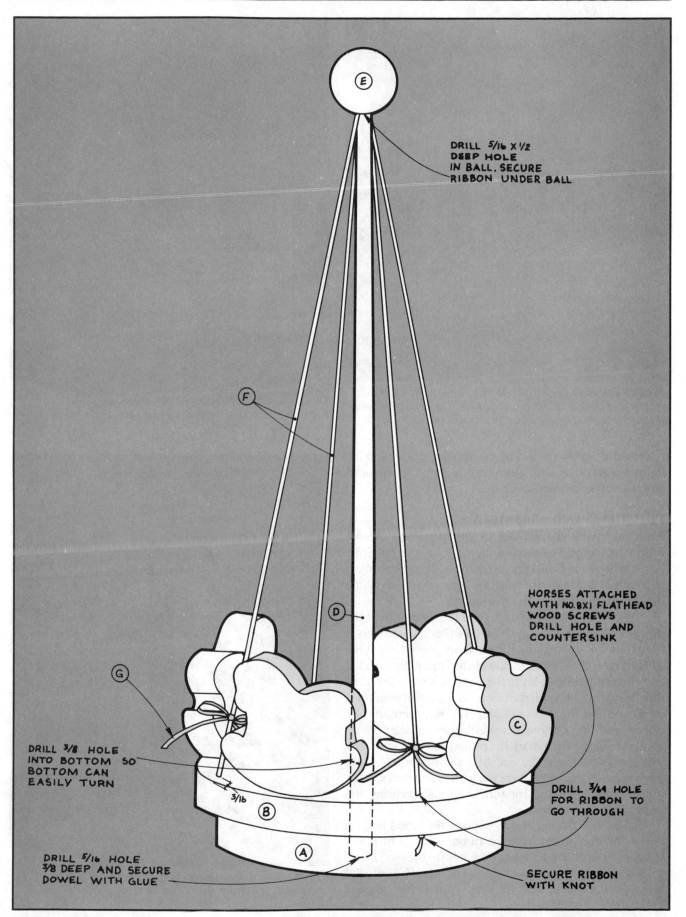

DRILL 5/16 X 1/2 DEEP HOLE IN BALL, SECURE RIBBON UNDER BALL

HORSES ATTACHED WITH NO.8X1 FLATHEAD WOOD SCREWS DRILL HOLE AND COUNTERSINK

DRILL 3/8 HOLE INTO BOTTOM SO BOTTOM CAN EASILY TURN

DRILL 3/64 HOLE FOR RIBBON TO GO THROUGH

3/16

DRILL 5/16 HOLE 3/8 DEEP AND SECURE DOWEL WITH GLUE

SECURE RIBBON WITH KNOT

Figure 2. *Insert the wood ball (E) into a wood clamp as shown and then drill the required hole. Do not try to hold the ball freehand under any circumstances.*

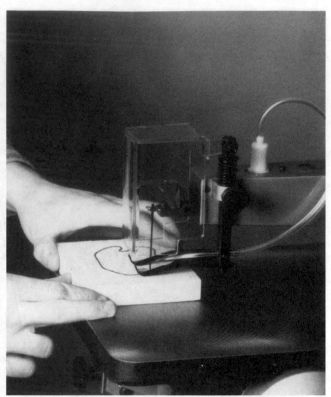

Figure 3. *Cut out the horse head with a scroll saw or coping saw.*

Sand all of the project parts. Attach the horses to the bottom workpiece with glue and No. 8 by 1 in. flathead wood screws, countersunk.

FINISHING AND ASSEMBLY

Stain and paint the project to suit. Paint the horses following the grid pattern, or create your own pattern.

Apply a satin finish polyurethane to the entire project to help seal it. Make sure you don't get any sealer inside the hole in the bottom (B) workpiece.

To assemble the carousel, feed the bottom over the dowel so that it rests on the base (A). Cut the blue ribbon into four 14 in. lengths. Then loop one of the blue ribbons over the top of the dowel and feed it through the two corresponding holes in the bottom. Knot one end of the ribbon and then pull the ribbon taut while it continues to rest on the top of the dowel (D). Keep pulling the ribbon until the bottom is raised approximately ⅛ in. above the base. Then mark the ribbon and tie a knot. For extra security, insert the end of a sharp toothpick into the bottom of the hole where the knot is and break it off. Follow this technique for threading and securing the three remaining ribbons.

Align the ribbons and then place the wood ball on top of the dowel and over the ribbons. If the fit is too snug, you may have to enlarge the hole in the wood ball.

To complete the project, tie red ribbons (G) onto the lower portion of the blue ribbons. Trim the red ribbons to the desired length. ❑

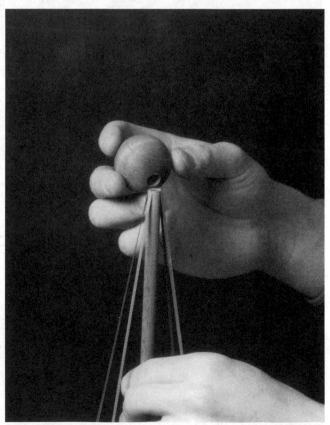

Figure 4. *Lay the ribbons across the top of the dowel (D) as shown. Attach the wood ball (E), but do not glue it in place.*

Contemporary Entertainment Center

This entertainment center was designed for today's flexible needs. The compact drop-leaf unit can be turned into a large serving counter in just seconds.

This easy-to-build, expandable bar unit provides entertainment space when you need it.

The drop-leaf design of this cabinet makes it the perfect entertainment center, whether it is used as a small bar for the family room or as a large serving counter for the "rec" room. The unit features folding leaves and leaf supports to save space and add flexibility. With the leaves folded up and the leaf supports extended, the unit becomes a full 6 ft. long. Folded down, the unit is only 40 in. long.

Both the top and the leaves are laminated to provide an easy-to-clean, durable surface. The leaf supports and the back are dressed up with prewoven cane framed by half-round moulding. Contours in the base of the unit add interest to the project and give it an elegant look. Best of all, the entertainment center is easy to build from just two sheets of plywood.

TIPS

This project is constructed from two sheets of ¾ in. A-B plywood.

We used prewoven cane to create the decorative panels on the leaf supports (K) and the back (C) of the bar. However, you can substitute with plastic laminate or by painting these areas in a contrasting color.

CONSTRUCTION

Carefully lay out all the project parts on two sheets of plywood. You should be able to also lay out the drawer front (G) and doors (F) onto the face front (A). Then use a circular saw to cut out all of the project parts to their appropriate widths and lengths. Complete the corner cuts with a saber saw. At this time, you may want to also lay out the contours in the front (A), sides (B), back (C) and leaf supports (K). Then cut out these workpieces with a saber saw. Joint the plywood edges on your stationary jointer or with a hand plane.

Notice that the leaf supports (K) are ¹⁄₁₆ in. shorter. This allows for a ¹⁄₁₆ in. clearance between the hinged supports and the leaves (E). Therefore, make light passes on your jointer until you have reached the

This story is courtesy of the American Plywood Association, P.O. Box 11700, Tacoma, WA 98411.

finished size of 35⁷⁄₁₆ inches.

Secure the sides (B) to the back (C) with 4d finishing nails and carpenter's glue. Similarly, locate and install the cabinet's bottom (Q), shelf supports (S, T) and shelf (P). Now attach the cabinet front (A) and the top (D) to the assembly with carpenter's glue and 4d finishing nails.

Apply laminate to the top workpieces (D, E). The laminate should be applied only to the tops and edges of the workpieces. There is no need to laminate the bottoms, since these will be out of sight.

Make the laminate edging by ripping a piece of laminate to width on your table saw, preferably using a carbide-tipped blade. Then apply laminate to two opposite edges of one plywood workpiece. Also apply adhesive to the laminate edging. Follow the adhesive manufacturer's instructions for set-up time. Once the adhesive is dry, carefully position the laminate edging onto the edges of the workpiece and roll the edging to insure firm contact. If you do not have an appropriate roller, then place a long length of solid wood against the laminate edging and tap with a hammer. After the edging has been applied, trim the edging to size using a router with a laminate flushing bit. Make sure you have firm

Figure 1. *Lay out the drawer front (G) and two doors (F) onto the face front (A). Then make a plunge cut with your circular saw to cut out the workpieces. Complete the corner cuts with a saber saw.*

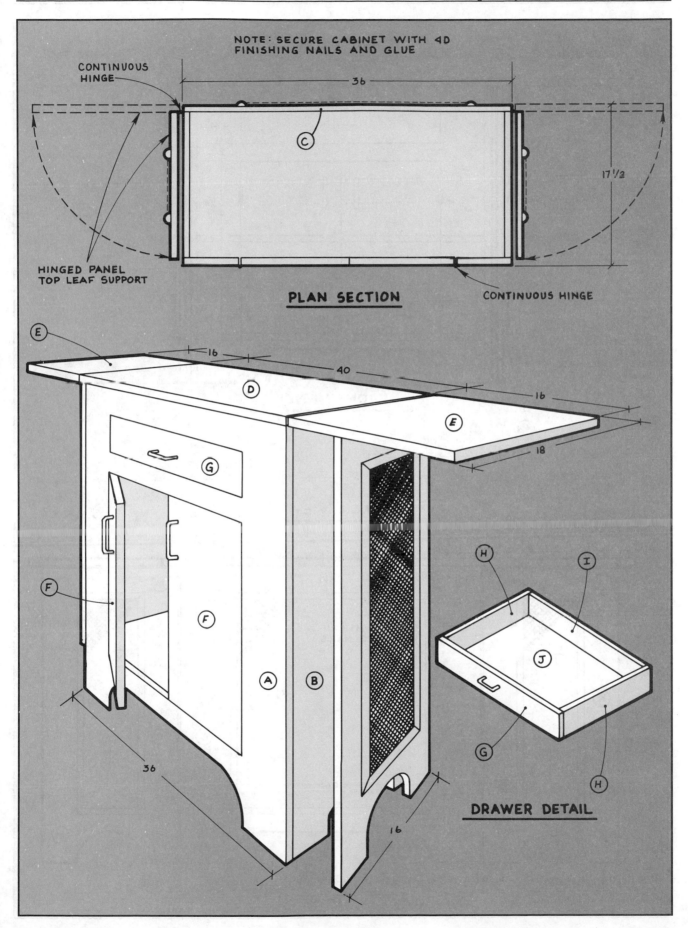

NOTE: SECURE CABINET WITH 4D
FINISHING NAILS AND GLUE

CONTINUOUS HINGE

36

17 1/2

HINGED PANEL
TOP LEAF SUPPORT

C

PLAN SECTION

CONTINUOUS HINGE

E

16

40

D

16

E

18

G

F

F

A

B

36

16

H

I

J

G

H

DRAWER DETAIL

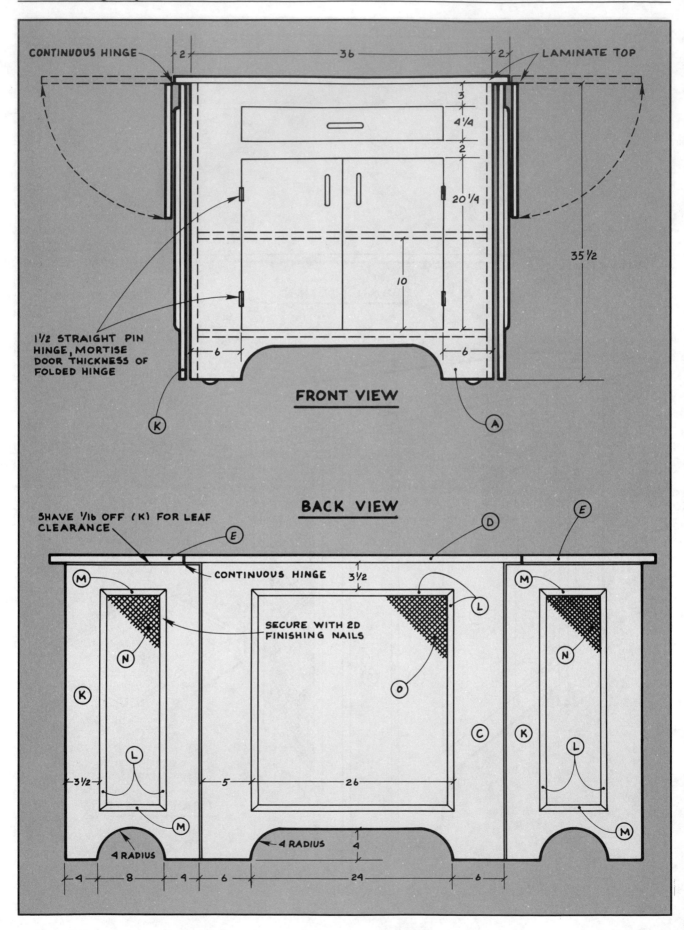

CONTINUOUS HINGE

2

36

2

LAMINATE TOP

3

4 1/4

2

20 1/4

35 1/2

10

1 1/2 STRAIGHT PIN HINGE, MORTISE DOOR THICKNESS OF FOLDED HINGE

6

6

FRONT VIEW

Ⓚ

Ⓐ

BACK VIEW

SHAVE 1/16 OFF (K) FOR LEAF CLEARANCE

Ⓔ

Ⓓ

Ⓔ

Ⓜ

Ⓜ

CONTINUOUS HINGE

3 1/2

1

Ⓛ

Ⓝ

SECURE WITH 2D FINISHING NAILS

Ⓝ

Ⓚ

Ⓞ

Ⓚ

Ⓛ

Ⓒ

Ⓛ

3 1/2

5

26

Ⓜ

4 RADIUS

4 RADIUS

4

4

8

4

6

24

6

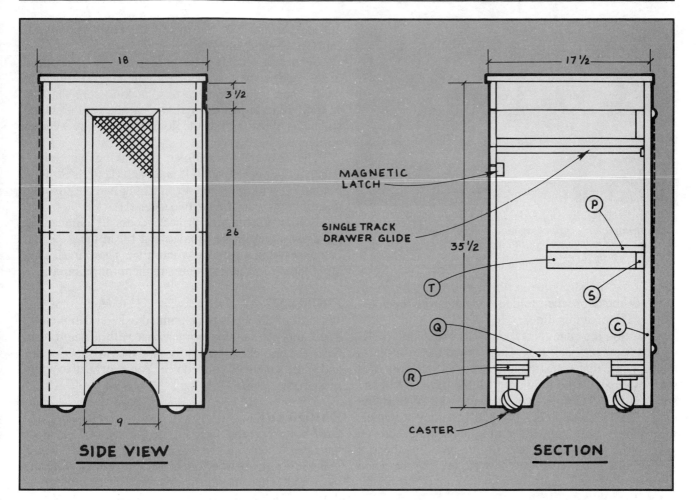

control of your router at all times. Do this for the edges of all three top workpieces. Then follow the same procedure in securing the remaining laminate edges. Once this edging has been contacted, trim these flush to the surface with your laminate trimmer. Finally, attach the laminate to the tops, being careful that they are properly aligned. It is always a good idea to cut the laminate ¼ in. oversize in width and length. This allows you some flexibility in positioning. Cut the laminate using a saber saw equipped with a plastic cutting blade. After you have rolled the surfaces of the tops, use a flushing or beveling bit to trim the laminate to its finished size.

Slightly dull all sharp edges on the project with a coarse, flat file. Work slowly and in long strokes. Do not apply too much pressure.

Then sand all of the project parts, including the edges. A pad sander is ideal for this application. Sand the contours in the front, back, sides and leaf supports using a drum sander installed in your drill.

The two doors (F) are hinged to the cabinet front (A) with 1½ in. straight pin hinges. You will need one set of hinges for each door. Mark the locations for the hinges on each door, and mortise out an area that is the thickness of a folded hinge. Instead of using a chisel to mortise out the area, use a saber saw. This simplifies the process,

BILL OF MATERIALS — Contemporary Entertainment Center

Finished Dimensions in Inches

A	Front	¾ x 35½ x 36 plywood	1
B	Side	¾ x 16 x 35½ plywood	2
C	Back	¾ x 35½ x 36 plywood	1
D	Top	¾ x 18 x 40 plywood	1
E	Leaf	¾ x 16 x 18 plywood	2
F	Door	¾ x 11¾ x 20 plywood	2
G	Drawer Front	¾ x 4¼ x 23¾ plywood	1
H	Drawer Side	¾ x 4 x 16 plywood	2
I	Drawer Back	¾ x 3¼ x 22¼ plywood	1
J	Drawer Bottom	½ x 16 x 22¼ plywood	1
K	Leaf Support	¾ x 16 x 35⁷⁄₁₆ plywood	2
L	Trim	½ x ¾ x 26 pine	8
M	Trim	½ in. half-round moulding x 9 pine	4
N	Cane	8¾ x 25¾ prewoven cane	2
O	Cane	25¾ x 25¾ prewoven cane	1
P	Shelf	¾ x 10½ x 34½ plywood	1
Q	Bottom	½ x 8 x 34½ plywood	1
R	Blocking	¾ x 4 x 4 plywood	12
S	Shelf Support	¾ x 1½ x 34½ plywood	1
T	Shelf Support	¾ x 1½ x 9¾ plywood	2

Figure 2. *Sand the rounded contours of the sides (B) using sandpaper wrapped around a large diameter dowel. Sand into the facing side of the wood to avoid splintering the showing surface.*

since a 1½ in. straight pin hinge will fit in the ¾ in. width of the door when folded. Do not attach the doors to the cabinet at this time.

Position the cane (N, O) onto the leaf supports (K) and the cabinet back (C). Then staple these in place, making sure that you stretch the cane as you work. Cut the ½ in. half-round moulding for the trim (L, M), and attach it to the perimeter of the cane with 2d finishing nails. Paint the moulding prior to installing it. Otherwise, painting the trim will be time-consuming, and you may splash paint on the cane. Before installing the trim you should also predrill the holes to prevent the wood from splitting, and carefully miter the ends of the moulding so the joints are flush.

Once the moulding has been attached, check to make sure that the cane does not extend beyond the edges of the trim. If so, trim the excess cane with a utility knife. Also check the outside perimeter of the trim for any unsightly gaps between the trim and the cabinet back and leaf supports. If there are any gaps, fill them in by applying a thin bead of latex caulk around the outside perimeter of the moulding. Then smooth the caulk bead with your finger.

Secure the blocking (R) for the casters to the bottom of the cabinet with carpenter's glue and 4d finishing nails. Then install four casters, making sure that the casters protrude just enough to clear the cabinet while still being able to roll on the floor surface — be it carpet or tile.

The drawer is assembled by making butt joints. Attach the drawer front (G) and back (I) to the drawer bottom (J) with glue and 4d finishing nails. Finish the assembly by securing the two sides (H).

Before finishing the project, recess all nailheads in the drawer and in the cabinet, and fill in the gaps and blemishes with a suitable wood filler. Then finish sand all of the project parts to prepare them for painting.

FINISHING

Wipe all of the areas to be painted using a damp cloth. Then apply a suitable primer coat with a paintbrush. Once the primer is dry, lightly sand the finish, wipe dry and apply a paint of your choice. You may need to apply two coats of paint.

HARDWARE

Drill holes for and then install the drawer and door handles. When you are drilling through the plywood, make sure you use a backup board to prevent splintering the wood. Then install the drawer with a single-track drawer glide.

Now attach the doors to the cabinet with two sets of straight pin hinges. Similarly, locate and install two magnetic latches (one for each door).

Measure lengths of continuous hinges for the each leaf and leaf support. Cut these hinges to length with a hacksaw, and then mount the hinges with the supplied screws. ❑

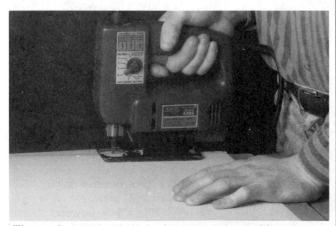

Figure 3. *Cut the laminate oversize using a saber saw equipped with a plastic cutting blade. Apply tape to the cutting area, and mark the cutting line on the tape. The tape helps minimize chipping the laminate.*

Figure 4. *Sand flat surfaces with a belt sander. Move the tool forward and backward as you work on one area at a time. Avoid staying in one place too long, or the tool will remove too much wood.*

Classic Magazine Rack

This Colonial-style
magazine rack is a classic
that will fit just about
anywhere, from the den
to the family room or
living room.

Build a magazine rack that is better than the store-bought versions.

This magazine rack has all the earmarks of classic styling. The slats are topped with a contoured rail, and the contours are echoed in the handle and the ends as well. A pantograph makes duplicating the contours fun and easy. Built of oak, the magazine rack has a look of quality that will make any woodworker proud.

TIPS

A pantograph is ideal for duplicating the contours in the ends (A), top rails (B) and handle (E) of the magazine rack. A pantograph allows you to easily enlarge or reduce designs. First you set the proportions that you want to enlarge or reduce. The pantograph's instructional manual will give you information for doing this. Tape the pattern that you want to duplicate, as well as a fresh sheet of paper, to the surface of the workbench. Then trace the project's design with a pencil to transfer the actual shape onto the paper.

Pantographs are available from a number of mail order catalogs and wood specialty shops.

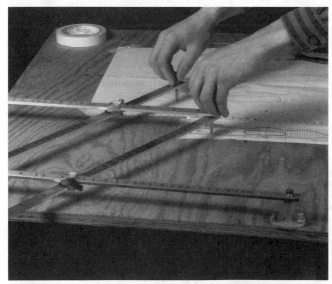

Figure 1. *Use a pantograph to duplicate the end workpieces (A). Here we taped down the design from the book and traced the end's design with the pantograph's scribe. As the pattern is traced, the pencil redraws the image to a larger proportion. Do not cut out the shape until you have cut the groove.*

CONSTRUCTION

Begin by cutting out all of the project parts to their overall widths and lengths on your table saw.

Lay out the design for the end workpieces (A), but do not cut them yet. Now form a stopped groove along the inside center of both end workpieces as shown in the illustration. This stopped groove will accommodate the divider (F).

Also cut a groove along the center of the handle workpiece (E). Next, cut a groove into the bottom rails (C) at a 17½ degree angle. Again, refer to the illustration.

Now draw the shapes for the handle (E) and two top rails (B). Then carefully cut out the shapes for the handle, top rails and ends. Use a band saw or saber saw equipped with a fine-tooth blade. Form the handle's cutout by drilling two 1 in. diameter starter holes with a Forstner bit, and then cut out the section in between with a saber saw.

Sand all of the project parts, paying particular attention to the contoured edges.

Now round over the edges of the handle, top rails and ends with a ⅜ in. round over bit. Be sure to use a pilot guide with your router. Before routing, make sure that the edges are sanded completely smooth. Otherwise, the routing will not be smooth.

Now finish sand all of the project parts. A stationary belt sander is ideal for sanding most of these small workpieces.

Next, place the side workpieces on a flat surface for assembly. Each side consists of a top rail (B), a bottom

BILL OF MATERIALS — Classic Magazine Rack

Finished Dimensions in Inches

A	End	¾ x 10¾ x 15⅞ oak	2
B	Top Rail	¾ x 2½ x 15¾ oak	2
C	Bottom Rail	¾ x 1½ x 15¾ oak	2
D	Slat	¾ x ¾ x 5⁵⁄₁₆ oak	8
E	Handle	¾ x 2½ x 15¾ oak	1
F	Divider	¼ x 11 x 16¼ oak plywood	1
G	Bottom	¼ x 4⅞ x 15¾ oak plywood	1

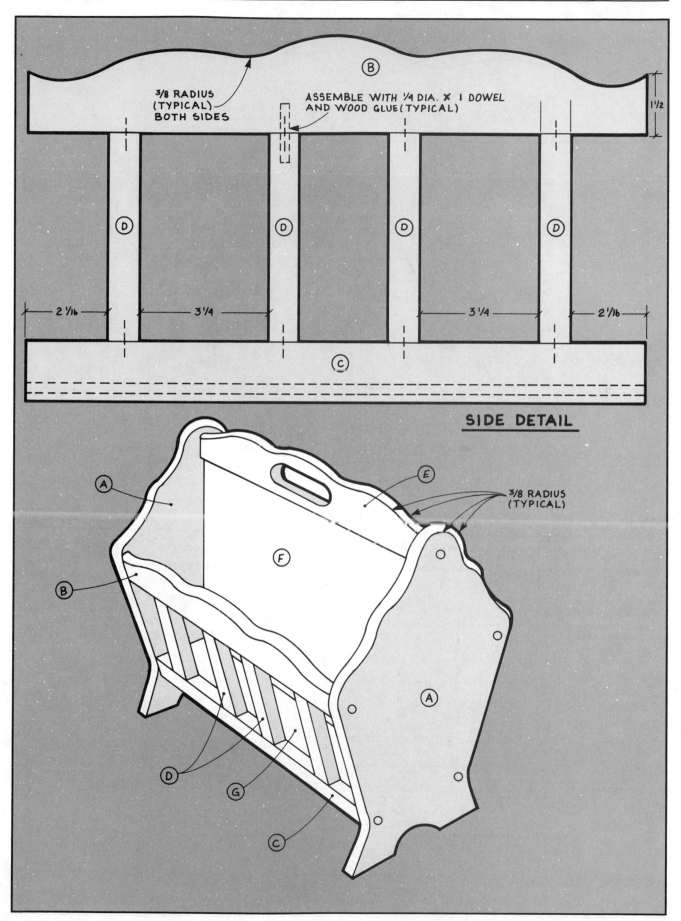

3/8 RADIUS
(TYPICAL)
BOTH SIDES

Ⓑ

ASSEMBLE WITH 1/4 DIA. × 1 DOWEL
AND WOOD GLUE (TYPICAL)

1 1/2

Ⓓ Ⓓ Ⓓ Ⓓ

2 1/16   3 1/4   3 1/4   2 1/16

Ⓒ

SIDE DETAIL

Ⓐ

Ⓔ

3/8 RADIUS
(TYPICAL)

Ⓑ

Ⓕ

Ⓐ

Ⓓ

Ⓖ

Ⓒ

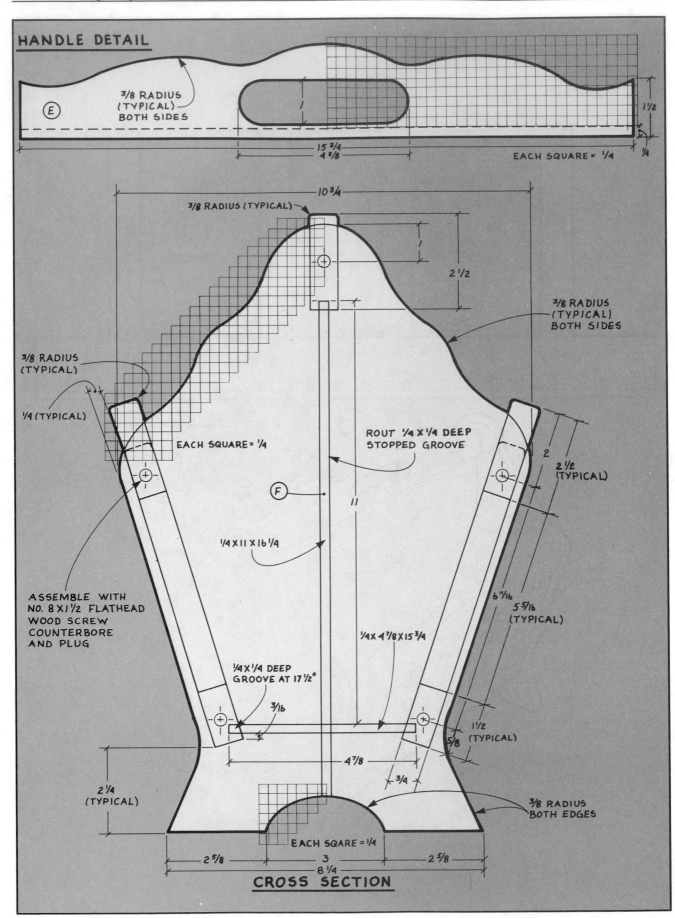

HANDLE DETAIL

E

3/8 RADIUS
(TYPICAL)
BOTH SIDES

1 1/2

EACH SQUARE = 1/4

15 3/4

4 3/8

1/4

10 3/4

3/8 RADIUS (TYPICAL)

2 1/2

3/8 RADIUS
(TYPICAL)
BOTH SIDES

3/8 RADIUS
(TYPICAL)

1/4 (TYPICAL)

EACH SQUARE = 1/4

ROUT 1/4 X 1/4 DEEP
STOPPED GROOVE

2

2 1/2
(TYPICAL)

F

11

1/4 X 11 X 16 1/4

6"/16
5 5/16
(TYPICAL)

ASSEMBLE WITH
NO. 8 X 1 1/2 FLATHEAD
WOOD SCREW
COUNTERBORE
AND PLUG

1/4 X 4 7/8 X 15 3/4

1/4 X 1/4 DEEP
GROOVE AT 17 1/2°

3/16

1 1/2
(TYPICAL)

5/8

2 1/4
(TYPICAL)

4 7/8

3/4

3/8 RADIUS
BOTH EDGES

2 5/8

3

2 5/8

EACH SQARE = 1/4

8 1/4

CROSS SECTION

Figure 2. *Groove the inside of the end workpiece (A) with your saw. Here we are using a radial arm saw set in the ripping position. Cut to the required depth and length, then stop your saw before removing the workpiece.*

Figure 3. *Drill two 1 in. diameter holes through the handhold area of the handle. Use a 1 in. Forstner bit, then cut out the waste area with a saber saw.*

Figure 4. *Cut out the shape of the ends with a saber saw equipped with a plywood cutting blade. This will minimize wood splintering.*

Figure 5. *We applied three coats of ZAR satin spray polyurethane, available in a pressurized container. This simplifies the task of finishing and provides good coverage.*

rail (C) and four slats (D). Position the workpieces and mark the joints for drilling. At each location, drill a hole to accommodate a ¼ in. diameter by 1 in. dowel. Drill about ⅛ in. deeper to allow for glue expansion.

Dry-assemble each side, using dowels to make sure that everything aligns properly. Then disassemble and apply glue to the dowels and dowel holes. Reassemble and clamp. Allow the glue to dry before proceeding.

When the glue has dried, scrape off any excess glue with an old wood chisel or a sharp paint scraper.

Locate the assembled sides to the ends (A) and mark their positions. Also insert the bottom (G). The ends are assembled to the sides with No. 8 by 1½ in. flathead wood screws. These screws are counterbored and later covered with wood plugs. Drill the holes into the ends as you drill pilot holes into the side assembly. Do this by drilling one hole into the top rail (B) and one into the bottom rail (C) of each side assembly. Drill through to

the end workpieces. If you do not drill pilot holes, there is a good chance that the hard oak will split.

Now dry-assemble the sides, bottom and center divider (F) to the two ends. Do not glue at this point. Now position the handle so that the groove in the bottom fits over the divider (F). Once the handle is positioned correctly, mark it for drilling and then drill and counterbore.

Disassemble the unit and finish sand all of the project parts. Then reassemble with carpenter's glue and wood screws.

FINISHING

Apply a stain of your choice with a clean cotton cloth. Remove any excess stain with another clean cotton cloth. Follow this up with an application of sanding sealer. When dry, lightly sand and then apply a coat of satin polyurethane. ❏

Kid's Drafting Set

This drafting set for kids has all the features of the grown-up version, including a T-square and a triangle.

This junior drafting set makes a lasting, educational gift that any kid will love.

All kids like to draw, and this junior drafting set is designed to educatc as well as entertain young minds. An authentic T-square and a triangle allow children to draw just about every geometric shape imaginable. A convenient hand-hold at the top of the drafting board provides easy portability. Constructed of lightweight yet durable birch plywood, the drafting set has a stylish "grown-up" look that kids will love.

TIPS
Buy straight, knot-free lumber and double-check your jointer and table saw to make sure that they are cutting square. If not, the drafting board will have gaps and uneven surfaces that will need to be sanded flush.

CONSTRUCTION AND ASSEMBLY
Lay out the workpieces for the triangle (G) and T-square (E, F). Rip them to the appropriate widths and lengths on your table saw. Then cut the angle of the triangle on a band saw.

Next, locate and drill the holes into the triangle as specified in the drawing. Finish sand the triangle and the T-square pieces, and then secure the T-square with

Figure 1. *The T-square and triangle are constructed from 1/2 in. thick material. If you do not have access to 1/2 in. material or a thickness planer, then resaw 3/4 in. material to a 9/16 in. thickness to allow for finishing.*

Figure 2. *Sand the resawed material on a stationary belt sander. Work from longer lengths of material and keep your fingers away from the belt.*

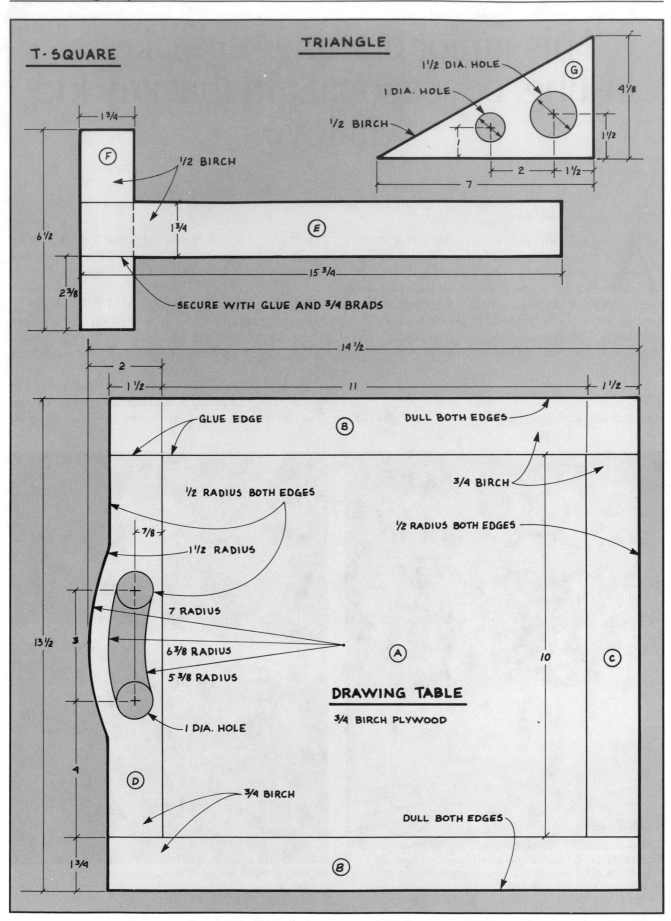

T·SQUARE

1 3/4

(F)

1/2 BIRCH

6 1/2

1 3/4

(E)

2 3/8

15 3/4

SECURE WITH GLUE AND 3/4 BRADS

TRIANGLE

1 1/2 DIA. HOLE

1 DIA. HOLE

(G)

4 1/8

1/2 BIRCH

1 1/2

2   1 1/2

7

14 1/2

2

1 1/2

11

1 1/2

GLUE EDGE

(B)

DULL BOTH EDGES

1/2 RADIUS BOTH EDGES

3/4 BIRCH

7/8

1 1/2 RADIUS

1/2 RADIUS BOTH EDGES

7 RADIUS

13 1/2

3

6 3/8 RADIUS

5 3/8 RADIUS

(A)

10

(C)

1 DIA. HOLE

DRAWING TABLE

3/4 BIRCH PLYWOOD

4

(D)

3/4 BIRCH

DULL BOTH EDGES

1 3/4

(B)

Figure 3. *Drill two 1 in. diameter holes in the area forming the handhold. Then cut out the area in between with a saber saw.*

carpenter's glue. Carefully square up the T-square and clamp into position with a C-clamp.

Next, cut the board center (A) to size. Use a plywood cutting blade in your table saw to minimize wood splintering, and cut with the good side facing up.

Cut the board top (D) and board bottom (C) to their overall widths and lengths. Do not cut the handle or the contour in the board top at this time. Now attach the top and bottom to the board center (A) with carpenter's glue. Use short bar clamps to hold the assembly in place. After the glue has hardened, joint the two edges that will be

glued to the board edges (B). Then cut the board edges and secure them to the board assembly with carpenter's glue. Again, clamp the assembly securely with bar clamps.

After the glue has completely cured, lay out the handle area and contour. Drill two 1 in. diameter holes into the handle area with a Forstner bit. Use a backup board to help eliminate wood splinters on the back side. Then cut the section between the two holes with a saber saw equipped with a plywood cutting blade. Next, cut the contour with a saber saw or band saw.

Thoroughly sand the drafting board's edges and surfaces. Be careful not to oversand the birch plywood; otherwise, you will run the risk of going through the veneer.

Rout a ½ in. radius on the bottom and top (C, D) of the drafting board. Do not rout the board edges (B). However, slightly round the board edges (B) with sandpaper. Also rout the inside of the handle on both surfaces.

FINISHING

Remove all of the dust from the drawing board, T-square and triangle and apply a wood sealer. When dry, follow this up with a coat of varnish. When that is dry, lightly sand and apply a final coat of varnish. ❏

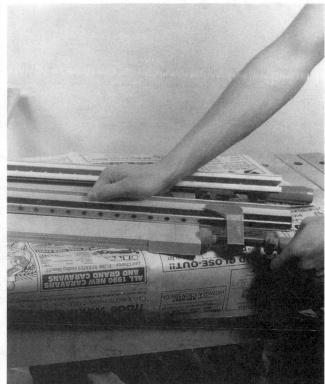

Figure 4. *Form the drafting board by edge-gluing the board center (A) to the board top (D) and board bottom (C) with carpenter's glue. Once the glue has dried, joint the two remaining edges to accommodate the board edges (B).*

BILL OF MATERIALS — Kid's Drafting Set

Finished Dimensions in Inches

A	Board Center	¾ x 10 x 11½ birch plywood	1
B	Board Edge	¾ x 1¾ x 14½ birch	2
C	Board Bottom	¾ x 1½ x 10 birch	1
D	Board Top	¾ x 2 x 10 birch	1
E	T-Square Rule	½ x 1¾ x 15¾ birch	1
F	T-Square Guide	½ x 1¾ x 6½ birch	1
G	Triangle	½ x 4⅛ x 7 birch	1

Oak Curio Cabinet

Whether hung in a hall, kitchen, bedroom or living room, this cabinet is sure to draw attention — and compliments.

Quality craftsmanship and charming looks make this cabinet a winner.

This oak curio cabinet goes just about any-where and will make a fine gift for the fussiest of folks. The decorative back features a heart cutout, a porcelain knob graces the glass door, and four open shelves provide display space for small collectibles. Constructed of oak, this cabinet boasts both beauty and durability, making it one of our all-time favorite woodworking projects.

TIPS

Instead of using glass in this project, you may wish to use Plexiglas as a substitute. It is much easier to work with and can be cut with a hand tool or with a saber saw equipped with a fine-tooth blade.

We constructed this project with oak, which is quite heavy. To mount the cabinet, we used picture wire held into the back of the project with panhead screws. It is also very important that you mount the project to at least one wall stud. If this is not possible, you will have to select and purchase a heavy-duty wall anchor system to insure that the project is properly supported.

CONSTRUCTION

Cut all of the project parts, with the exception of the rails (G), to their appropriate widths and lengths. It is important that your radial arm saw or table saw cuts square, otherwise unsightly gaps will result.

Lay out the workpieces for the rails (G) from a larger length of material. Then use your table saw to cut a ⅛ in. deep rabbet into the rails, following the details shown in the illustration. We recommend adding a wood fence to your table saw's edge guide before positioning the blade to make the ⅛ in. deep cut in the rail. That way, you will end up moving the rail with the widest portion placed against the wood fence. Do not attempt to cut the total height at one time. Instead, make repetitive passes, each time moving the saw blade ½ in. higher. After you have achieved the final height of the cut, cut the half circles with a fine-tooth blade installed in your saber saw. Then crosscut each of the rail workpieces to their appropriate lengths.

Use this technique to cut rabbets along one edge of the two stiles (F). Square the end of the rounded rabbet with a wood chisel. Then glue the door frame with carpenter's glue. You can also secure these edges by installing one dowel at each edge, but be sure to avoid the rabbeted area. Clamp this assembly on a flat surface.

Figure 1. *Form the rabbet in the rails (G) with a table saw. Work with longer material before cutting the rails to length. Install a wood fence and set the blade to cut ¹/8 in. into the wood. Make progressively deeper passes with the saw.*

	BILL OF MATERIALS — Oak Curio Cabinet		
		Finished Dimensions in Inches	
A	Top	¾ x 18 x 5 oak	1
B	Side	¾ x 4½ x 29½ oak	2
C	Bottom	¾ x 4½ x 14¼ oak	1
D	Inner Top	¾ x 4½ x 14¼ oak	1
E	Shelf	¾ x 4½ x 4½ oak	3
F	Stile	¾ x 2 x 25½ oak	2
G	Rail	¾ x 3¹⁄₁₆ x 5 oak	2
H	Glass	⅛ x 5½ x 23¾ glass	1
I	Shelf	¾ x 3¾ x 9⅛ oak	1
J	Decorative Back	¾ x 3⅛ x 18 oak	1
K	Divider	¾ x 4½ x 25¾ oak	1

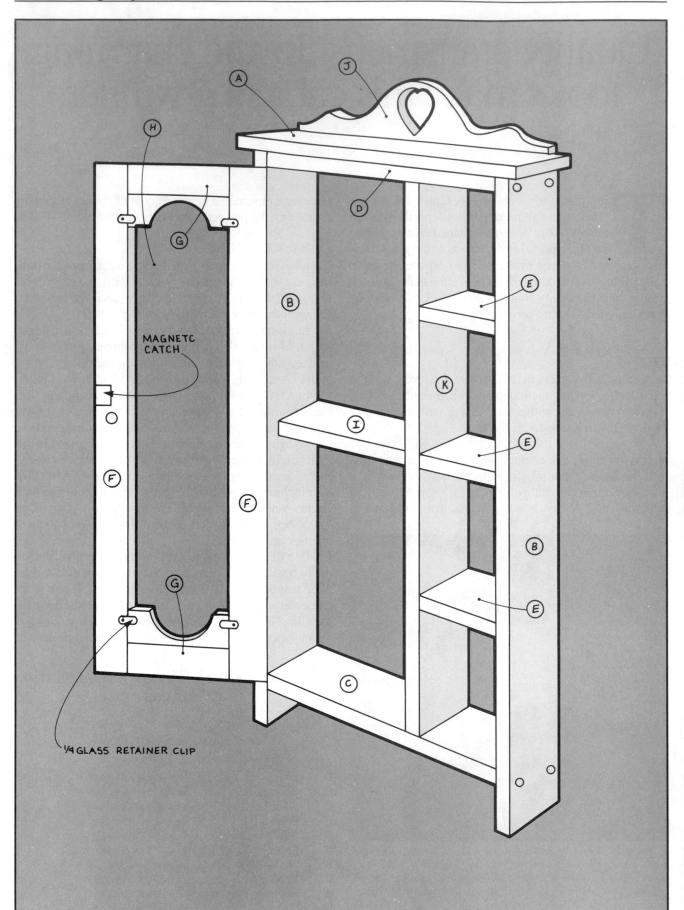

MAGNETC
CATCH

¼ GLASS RETAINER CLIP

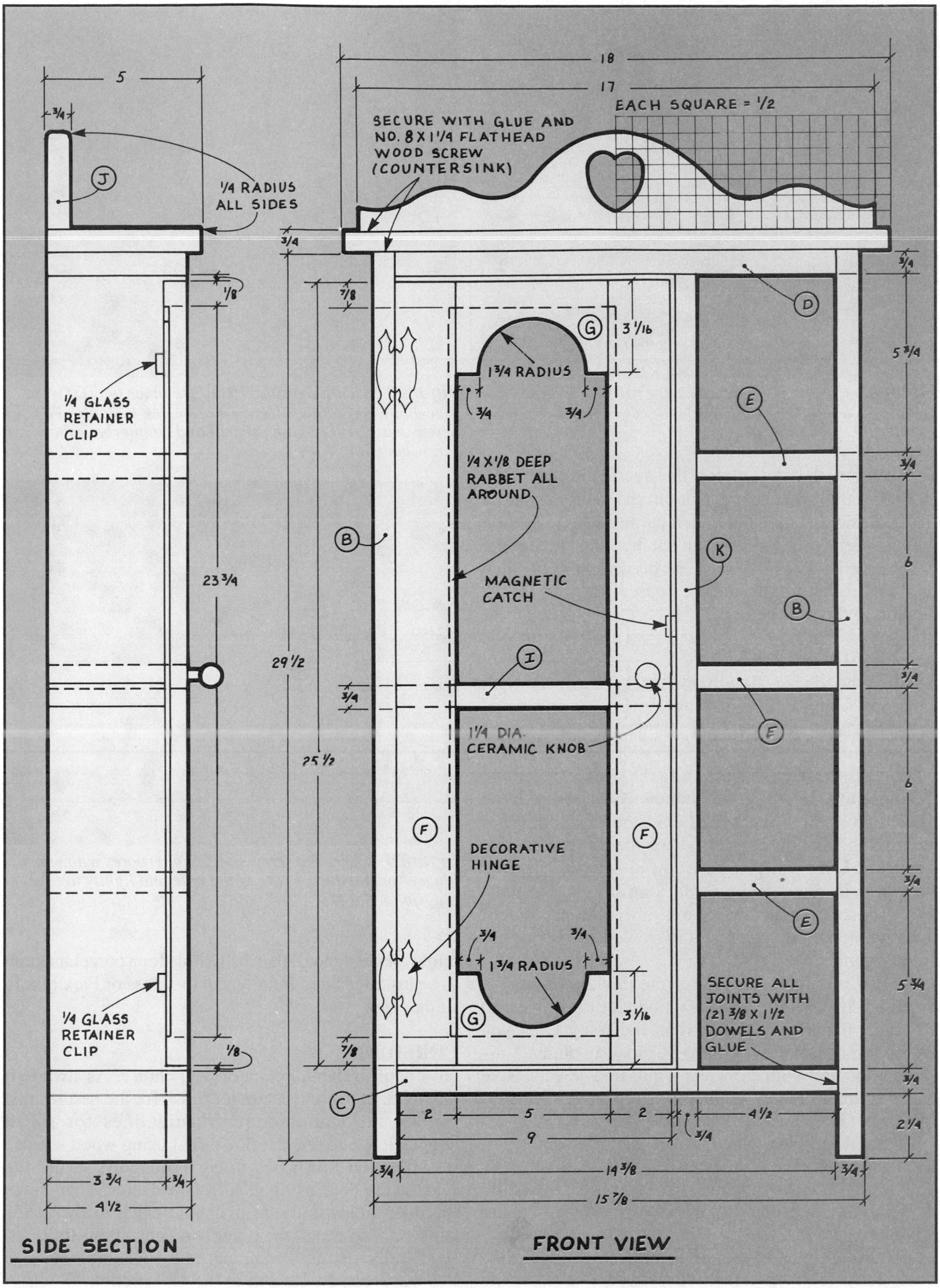
5
3/4
1/4 RADIUS
ALL SIDES
J
1/8
1/4 GLASS
RETAINER
CLIP
23 3/4
1/4 GLASS
RETAINER
CLIP
1/8
3 3/4
3/4
4 1/2
SIDE SECTION
18
17
EACH SQUARE = 1/2
SECURE WITH GLUE AND
NO. 8 X 1 1/4 FLATHEAD
WOOD SCREW
(COUNTERSINK)
3/4
7/8
G
3 1/16
1 3/4 RADIUS
3/4
3/4
D
5 3/4
E
3/4
1/4 X 1/8 DEEP
RABBET ALL
AROUND
B
K
6
MAGNETIC
CATCH
B
29 1/2
I
3/4
3/4
E
1 1/4 DIA.
CERAMIC KNOB
25 1/2
6
F
F
DECORATIVE
HINGE
3/4
E
3/4
3/4
1 3/4 RADIUS
G
3 1/16
SECURE ALL
JOINTS WITH
(2) 3/8 X 1 1/2
DOWELS AND
GLUE
5 3/4
7/8
3/4
C
2
5
2
4 1/2
2 1/4
9
3/4
3/4
14 3/8
3/4
15 7/8
FRONT VIEW

Figure 2. *Cut the half circles for the rails (G) with a saber saw. Use a fine-tooth blade to reduce wood splintering.*

Figure 3. *Secure the sides (B) to the inner top (D) with glue and wood screws. Here we are using a Stanley #8 Screw-Mate drill to both predrill and counterbore the screw holes.*

Lay out the design for the decorative back (J), including the heart shape. Cut out the heart design by first drilling a starter hole, then cutting out the section with a saber saw. Similarly, cut out the silhouette for the decorative back. Finish sand the decorative back, then rout a ¼ in. radius inside the heart shape and on the outside of the silhouette.

ASSEMBLY

Secure the decorative back to the top (A) with carpenter's glue and No. 8 by 1¼ in. flathead wood screws. Make sure that you countersink these wood screws.

Dry-assemble the cabinet on a flat surface by joining the inner top (D), sides (B), bottom (C) along with the divider (K) and shelves (E, I). Square this unit. After everything is square, mark all of the workpieces for doweling. Use a drill press or a doweling jig to drill holes for two ⅜ in. diameter by 1½ in. long dowels. You must work carefully, otherwise there may be slight misalignments that can result in slanted shelves or unsightly gaps.

After you have drilled for the dowel holes, dry-assemble if possible. You may find that the dowels fit so snugly that they cannot be removed easily. Once you are convinced that everything is properly aligned, assemble the unit with carpenter's glue and dowels. Note that it is not necessary to dowel the top (A) and decorative back (J) in place.

After the glue has dried, secure the top assembly (A, J) to the cabinet with carpenter's glue and No. 8 by 1¼ in. flathead wood screws. Drill for the screws underneath the inner top (D), making sure that you countersink for the screws.

Thoroughly sand the entire project, including the door. Then joint the door's edges where necessary to

Figure 4. *Cover the screw hole counterbores with wood plugs. Apply a dab of glue to the hole and lightly tap the plugs into place.*

allow for clearance. Also drill a hole for a porcelain knob to be installed later. Finally, cut the glass or Plexiglas to fit the door.

FINISHING

Now apply a stain or paint of your choice. As always, it is important to apply a quality finish for the best results. Follow the manufacturer's guidelines for finish application, and test the finish first using wood scraps.

After the finish has dried thoroughly, secure the glass to the door using glass retainer clips. Then hinge the door and install one magnetic catch to the inside cabinet. Also install the porcelain knob at this time.

Finally, mount the cabinet to the wall according to the instructions discussed in the Tips section. ❏

Elegant Welch Buffet

Built from plywood and requiring only basic tools and woodworking techniques, this buffet makes a great family project that can be completed in a weekend.

Build this easy-to-make, attractive buffet in just one weekend!

Simplicity and elegance are the keynotes of this design. Whether you are a novice woodworker or a seasoned pro, you'll appreciate this project's straightforward construction and use of inexpensive materials. Built from plywood, the buffet has simple butt joints for easy assembly, and the pre-manufactured legs make construction a snap.

Decorative moulding covers much of the showing edges, giving the project its refined look. The moulding is particularly striking when painted in a contrasting color. Two shelves and a pair of drawers make the unit as functional as it is attractive, whether it is used as a china display cabinet or as a writing desk.

TIPS
This easy-to-make project features butt joints, with moulding decorating the edges that would ordinarily be exposed. You can use just about any type of moulding you like. However, remember that the moulding should be wide enough to cover the plywood's ¾ in. thickness.

CONSTRUCTION
Cut all of the project parts slightly oversize. However, do not cut the moulding at this time. Then joint all of the edges until you achieve the appropriate width and length for each workpiece.

Figure 1. *Lay out the design for the front apron (G), and cut it out with a saber saw equipped with a fine-tooth plywood cutting blade.*

BILL OF MATERIALS — Elegant Welch Buffet

Finished Dimensions in Inches

A	Top/Bottom	¾ x 11⁷⁄₈ x 31½ plywood	2
B	Side	¾ x 11⁷⁄₈ x 30 plywood	2
C	Front	¾ x 5⁷⁄₈ x 30 plywood	1
D	Back	¾ x 30 x 30 plywood	1
E	Shelf	¾ x 10 x 30 plywood	2
F	Desk Top	¾ x 24 x 36 plywood	1
G	Front Apron	¾ x 8⁷⁄₈ x 36 plywood	1
H	Side Apron	¾ x 8⁷⁄₈ x 22½ plywood	2
I	Leg	3 x 3 x 33¼ turned leg	4
J	Back Apron	¾ x 8⁷⁄₈ x 36 plywood	1
K	Desk Bottom	¾ x 22½ x 34½ plywood	1
L	Drawer Front	¾ x 2¾ x 11¾ plywood	2
M	Drawer Back	¾ x 2 x 10¼ plywood	2
N	Drawer Side	¾ x 2¾ x 16³⁄₈ plywood	4
O	Drawer Bottom	¾ x 10¼ x 16³⁄₈ plywood	2
P	Drawer Guide	¾ x 1½ x 22½ pine	4
Q	Drawer Moulding	³⁄₈ x 1 x 2¾ pine moulding	4
R	Drawer Moulding	³⁄₈ x 1 x 11¾ pine moulding	4
S	Top Moulding	¾ x ¾ x 33 pine moulding	1
T	Top Moulding	¾ x ¾ x 12⁵⁄₈ pine moulding	2
U	Side Moulding	½ x ¾ x 30 pine moulding	2
V	Shelf Moulding	½ x ¾ x 30 pine moulding	2
W	Bottom Moulding	¾ x ¾ x 33 pine moulding	1
X	Bottom Moulding	¾ x ¾ x 12⁵⁄₈ pine moulding	2
Y	Table Moulding	¾ x ¾ x 37½ pine moulding	1
Z	Table Moulding	¾ x ¾ x 24¾ pine moulding	2

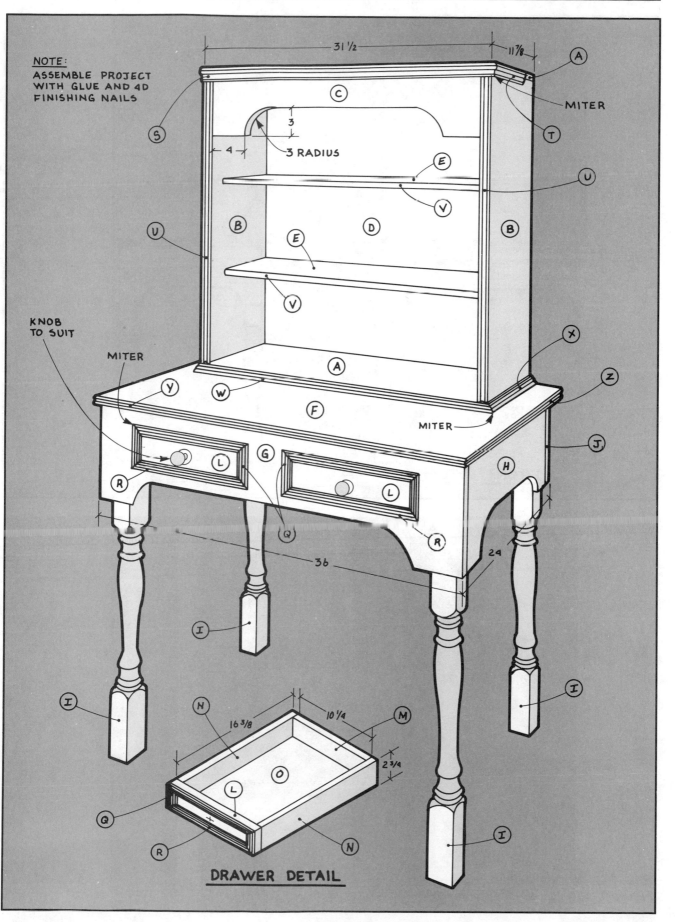

NOTE:
ASSEMBLE PROJECT
WITH GLUE AND 4D
FINISHING NAILS

31 1/2

11 7/8

Ⓐ

MITER

Ⓢ

Ⓒ

3

3 RADIUS

4

Ⓣ

Ⓔ

Ⓤ

Ⓥ

Ⓤ

Ⓑ

Ⓔ

Ⓓ

Ⓑ

Ⓥ

KNOB
TO SUIT

MITER

Ⓧ

Ⓐ

Ⓩ

Ⓨ

Ⓦ

Ⓕ

MITER

Ⓙ

Ⓛ

Ⓖ

Ⓗ

Ⓡ

Ⓛ

Ⓠ

Ⓡ

36

24

Ⓘ

Ⓘ

Ⓘ

Ⓝ

16 3/8

10 1/4

Ⓜ

2 3/4

Ⓛ

Ⓞ

Ⓠ

Ⓡ

Ⓝ

Ⓘ

DRAWER DETAIL

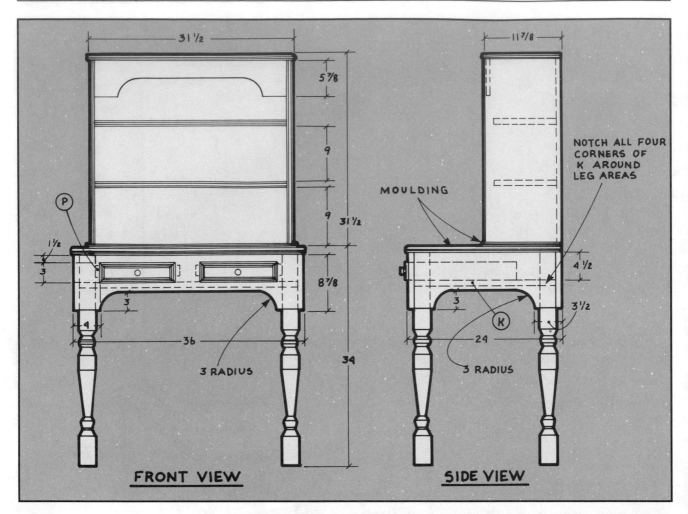

FRONT VIEW

31 1/2

5 7/8

9

9

31 1/2

1 1/2

3

8 7/8

3

4

36

3 RADIUS

34

P

MOULDING

11 7/8

NOTCH ALL FOUR
CORNERS OF
K AROUND
LEG AREAS

4 1/2

3

3 1/2

24

K

3 RADIUS

SIDE VIEW

Figure 2. *Miter the moulding for the drawer faces (Q, R) with your power saw.*

Figure 3. *Cut out the drawer openings by making a plunge cut with your saber saw as shown.*

Now lay out the designs for the front (C), front apron (G), side aprons (H) and back apron (J). Cut out the designs using a saber saw equipped with a plywood cutting blade. Finish sand the contours with a drum sander installed in your drill press.

Carefully lay out the drawer openings onto the front apron. The waste will become the drawer fronts (L). Make a plunge cut with your saber saw to avoid blemishing the wood for the drawer fronts.

Secure the front, back and side aprons to one another with carpenter's glue and 4d finishing nails. Then install the desk top (F).

Next, secure the four premanufactured legs (I) in place. They should be flush with the bottom of the desk top. Now install four drawer guides (P). Center the four guides. They should be flush with the left and right side of each drawer opening so that the drawers will be guided properly. Secure these drawer guides by driving nails into the front and back aprons. The guides also need to be glued.

Notch the desk bottom (K) so the desk bottom will pass over the legs. Position the desk bottom so it is flush with the lower opening of the drawer cutouts. In other words, the drawer bottoms will ride against the desk bottom. Make sure that the desk bottom is square.

Assemble the upper unit by securing the two shelves (E) and the top/bottom workpieces (A) to the two sides (B). Square the unit by inserting the back (D) in place. Now attach the upper unit to the desk top with glue and nails.

Assemble the drawers by securing each drawer front (L) and drawer back (M) to the two drawer sides (N). Then install the drawer bottom (O).

Custom cut all of the moulding for the drawers, the upper unit and the desk top. You will need a miter box to form the miters for most of these joints. Pay particular attention to the side moulding (U). This moulding must be a little shorter in height so it will fit under the adjacent top moulding (S, T) and the bottom moulding (W, X). Install the moulding with glue and 1 in. brads. Make sure you predrill these holes to avoid splitting the fragile moulding.

FINISHING

Sink all nailheads, and fill in the recesses and any blemishes with a wood filler. Now finish sand the entire project and remove the dust.

Paint the project in one or two colors. Before painting, apply a coat of paint sealer followed by a light sanding. Then brush or spray on two coats of paint, sanding between coats. ❏

This project is courtesy of the American Plywood Association, P.O. Box 11700, Tacoma, WA 98411.

Techniques

Clamping Know-How

When clamping wide boards it is always a good idea to alternate the position of the bar clamps. Thus, the bar of one clamp fits under the workpiece, the next fits over, the next bar under, etc.

Whether long, short, big or small, here's how to get the most from your clamps.

We never seem to have enough clamps around the workshop. We need long ones for gluing projects like table tops, and short ones for smaller items. However, what is more important than buying a lot of clamps is buying the right clamps to suit your purposes. For most of the projects in this book, you will need two basic clamps: One is a long bar clamp for gluing up table tops, and the other is a C-clamp for surface-gluing and holding down projects after assembly.

This primer on clamping will show you the basic techniques for edge-gluing and surface-gluing pieces of wood. And, most importantly, it will show you some clever tools that allow you to really clamp down on your work.

INSPECT THE JOINTS

When edge-gluing, make sure that the edges are perfectly square and not rounded over. Whether you use a stationary jointer or a hand plane, the better the jointed

Figure 1. *Lay out the bar clamps for clamping groups of boards, and position spacer boards so the workpieces will rest on the spacers. The spacers should be the same height. Bar clamps come in various shapes and sizes.*

Figure 2. *Now place the boards to be clamped on the spacers as shown. Check the gaps between the boards to make sure you will have a tight fit. If not, joint the boards.*

Figure 3. *Adjust the bar clamps to prepare them for clamping the actual workpieces. This process will insure the bar clamps are long enough and are ready to tighten the workpieces. Most bar clamps have preformed slots for adjusting.*

edge, the easier it is to glue and the better it will appear. If there are any gaps in the joints, the project will be less than perfect.

Some novice woodworkers often try to fix gaps by drawing the edges together with clamps, using excessive force. However, over time the tension on the wood may cause it to separate, leaving unsightly blemishes in the project.

HOW TO POSITION THE CUPS

When edge-gluing, there is an ongoing controversy about whether the cups of each workpiece should be facing in the same direction or alternately placed. In other words, should the cups all face down (or up), or should they be alternated so that one is up and the next one is down? There are good reasons for using both methods, and the controversy has not been resolved. Your own experience with surfacing will tell the tale. However, your judgment should be based on the interesting grain patterns that you can achieve by organizing the wood. Each piece of wood to be glued is an important part of the project's overall look.

Figure 4. *Remove the workpieces and lay down one layer of newspaper or wax paper. Wax paper keeps the glue from sticking to the clamps.*

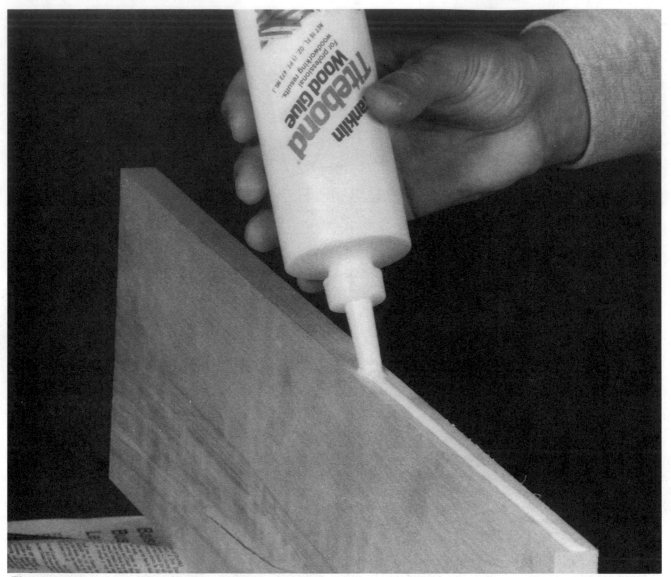

Figure 5. *Position the first board as shown and run a bead of carpenter's glue.*

WHAT CLAMPS AND HOW MANY?

The types of clamps that you need are based on the kind of work that you do. It is always a good idea to have at least four bar clamps that extend beyond the largest lengths that you will be clamping together. For gluing large surfaces, we recommend that you have at least four 48 in. bar clamps.

Like everything else in your workshop, the type of bar clamp that you buy is really based on how much you can afford. The big, heavy-duty ones cost significantly more than light-duty ones. However, keep in mind that a heavy-duty clamp will last you a lifetime.

Similarly, C-clamps come in a variety of shapes and sizes, but we suggest having a minimum of two 6 in. C-clamps.

A vast variety of clamps are available, like band clamps and wood clamps, but we have confined our discussion to those that are used primarily for edge-gluing, surface-gluing and holding down workpieces for processing.

WHAT TYPE OF GLUE?

There is a multitude of glues available, all of which are quite suitable for edge-gluing and surface-gluing workpieces. However, the most appropriate is carpenter's glue. It is made specifically for this purpose and is strong and nontoxic. It can be used safely by children as well, and for that reason it is found everywhere from drug stores to lumberyards.

Elmer's and Titebond are two of the most common brands of carpenter's glue.

The amount that you apply should be based on this fundamental rule: *only apply as much glue as it takes to get the job done*. In other words, a light gluing application will not result in a strong joint. However, overgluing will result in a strong joint — and an oozing mess of

Figure 6. *Spread the glue over the surface of the edge with a brush or a strip of wood. Then lay down the board in position.*

Figure 7. *Do not place glue onto the edge of the adjoining workpiece. Apply glue to the other edge of the next workpiece.*

Figure 8. *Apply light pressure to the clamps as you move from one board to the other. Adjust the boards so they are flush on the good side.*

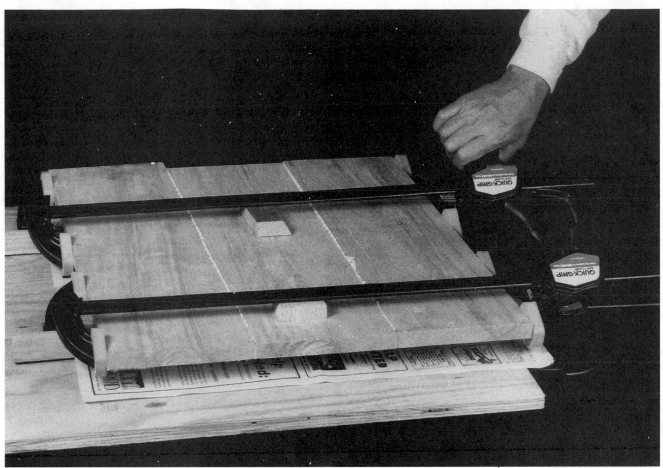

Figure 9. *Once the workpieces are perfectly aligned, tighten each bar clamp until glue oozes out. Do not overtighten to the point where the boards begin to bend, or where you are exerting excessive force.*

Figure 10. *Apply glue to one of the workpieces that is to be surface-glued. Then smooth the glue with a brush or a scrap piece of wood.*

excess glue. For example, removing excess glue from workpieces forming a butcher block top is terribly messy. If you allow the glue to dry without cleaning it up beforehand, the glue will form a formidable glaze that clogs sanding belts and wreaks havoc upon your power tools.

REMOVING GLUE

There is continued controversy about when and how to remove glue from wood. Some suggest wiping the glue that has oozed out from the joint with a damp, clean cloth while the glue is still wet. Others contend that you should allow the glue to harden, and then remove the residue with an old wood chisel or paint scraper. Again, which method you use is really a matter of choice. However, both sides will agree that it is not a good idea to remove excess glue with a sanding belt, because the glue tends to clog the pores of the belt. ❏

SOURCES
Vise-Grip and Quick-Grip clamps: American Tool Companies, Inc., P.O. Box 337, DeWitt, NE 68341.

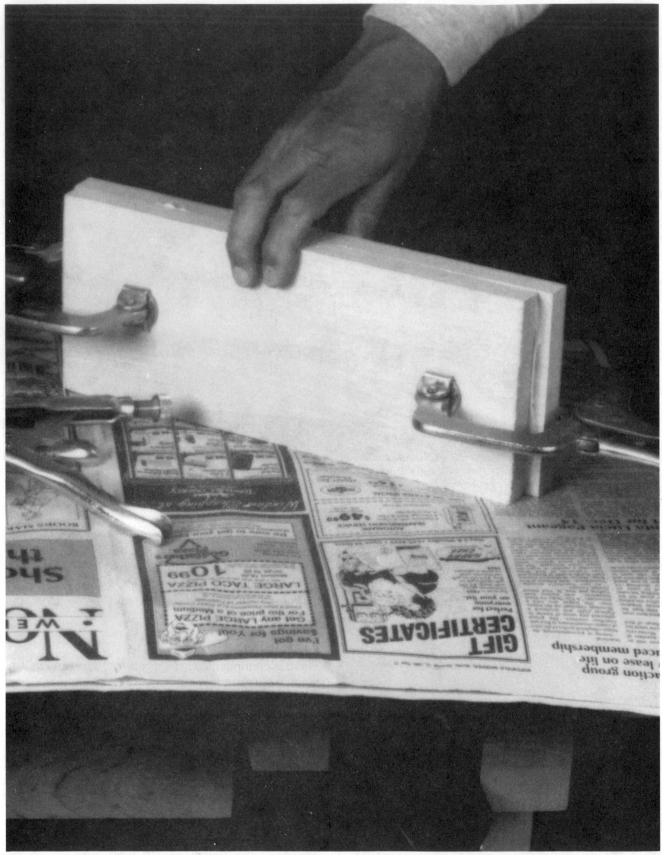

Figure 11. *Apply clamps to the center of the workpieces being surface-glued. Wood often has a slight cup. Thus, when you place the cup down, applying pressure will also draw down the edges. The result is a better glued seam. However, don't forget to clamp the edges as well.*

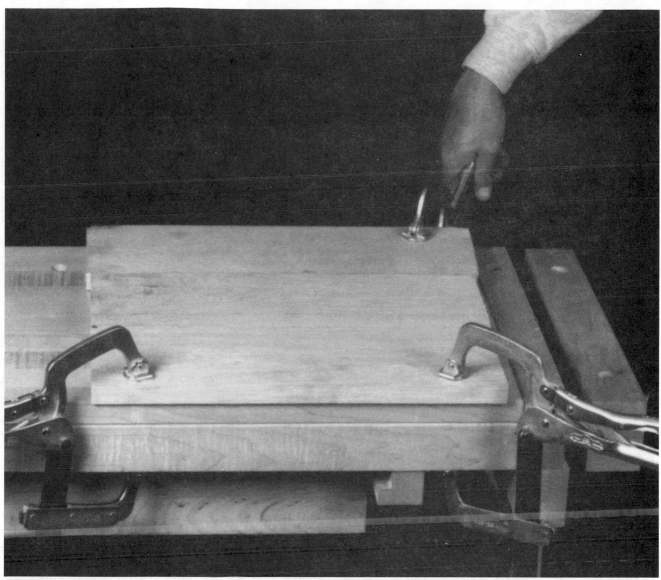

Figure 12. *Always clamp workpieces that are being processed with power and hand tools. This Vise-Grip C-clamp features swivel pads and quick adjustment.*

Figure 13. *Small clamps are just as important as big clamps, but are for smaller tasks.*

Figure 14. *This bar clamp is quite unique in that the jaw quickly adjusts to fit the material being clamped.*

Figure 15. *If your clamp does not have a soft pad to prevent it from denting your wood, install a smooth wood pad as shown.*

Figure 16. *Remove the glued workpiece, and scrape away the dried glue with a paint scraper or old wood chisel.*

Drill Press Basics

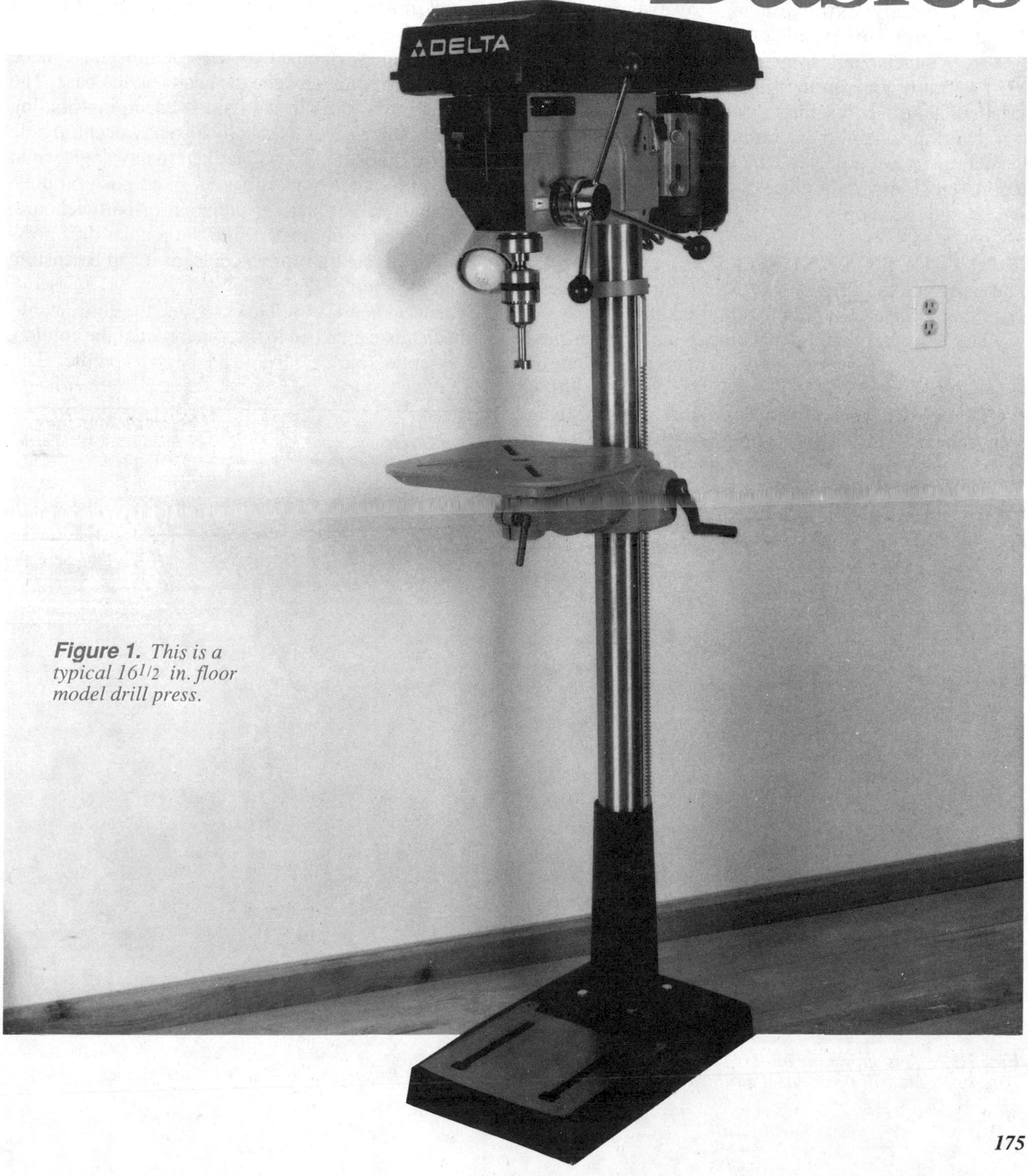

Figure 1. *This is a typical 16¹/2 in. floor model drill press.*

Learn how to buy and set up a drill press.

The drill press was designed originally for the metalworking trades. However, with the availability of cutting tools, jigs and attachments, the drill press is now one of the most versatile tools in the shop. It not only drills into metal, but also bores into wood and performs other woodworking operations such as mortising and sanding. In fact, after the table saw, the drill press is easily the second most important piece of equipment in the average home workshop.

CONSTRUCTION AND SIZES

The conventional drill press (Fig. 1) consists of these main parts: the base, column, table and head.

The base supports the machine. Usually, it has pre-drilled holes for fastening the drill press to the floor or to a stand or bench.

The column, generally made of steel, holds the table and head and is fastened to the base. Actually, the length of this hollow column determines whether the drill press is a bench model or a floor model. Floor models range in height from 66 to 75 in.; bench models range from 23 to 48 inches.

The table is clamped to the column and can be moved to any point between the head and the base. The table may have slots in it to aid in clamping holding fixtures or workpieces. It usually also has a central hole through it. Some tables can be tilted to any angle, right or left, while other models have a fixed position only. An auxiliary table made of plywood or particleboard, which can be readily fastened to the regular drill press table, is available on some models, or it can be custom made in the shop.

The term *head* is used to designate the entire working mechanism attached to the upper part of the column. The essential part of the head is the spindle. This

*This story is courtesy of Delta's book titled **Getting the Most Out of Your Drill Press**, and is published by Delta International Machinery Corp., 246 Alpha Dr., Dept. PS92, Pittsburgh, PA 15238.*

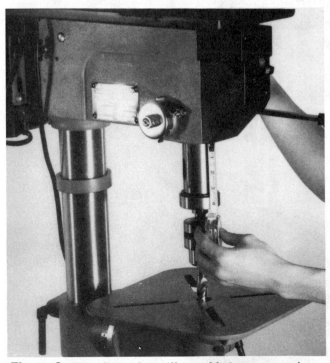

Figure 2. *This shows the quill travel being measured. This 16$\frac{1}{2}$ in. drill press has a quill travel of 3$\frac{3}{8}$ inches.*

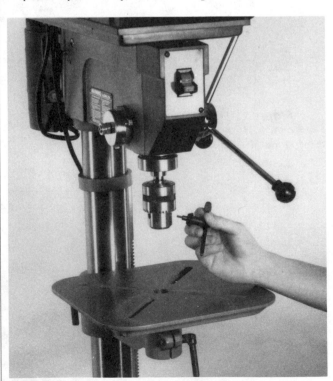

Figure 3. *This shows a standard geared chuck and key.*

Figure 4. *A 16¹/2 in. drill press can drill 8¹/4 in. to the inside of any material.*

revolves in a vertical position and is housed in bearings at either end of a movable sleeve, called the quill. The quill, and hence the spindle which it carries, is moved downward by means of a simple rack-and-pinion gearing, worked by the feed lever. When the feed handle is released, the quill is returned to its normal "up" position by means of a spring. Adjustments are provided for locking the quill and presetting the depth to which the quill can travel. Incidentally, the quill usually has a stroke or travel of from 2 to 3¼ in. in most home workshop models (Fig. 2).

The typical drill press has a ½ in. capacity geared chuck with a key. This chuck (Fig. 3) offers the best grip for most work. Most drill press accessories fit directly into the geared chuck.

The spindle usually is driven by a stepped-cone pulley or pulleys connected by a V-belt to a similar pulley on the motor. The motor usually is bolted to a plate on the head casting in the rear of the column. The average range of speeds is from 250 to about 3,000 revolutions per minute (rpm). Because the motor shaft stands vertically, a sealed ball-bearing motor should be used as a power unit. For average work, a ¼ or ¾ horsepower motor meets most needs.

The capacity or size of the drill press is determined by the distance from the center of the chuck to the front of the column. This distance is expressed as a diameter. For example, a 16½ in. drill press (Fig. 4) will drill a hole through the center of a round piece of stock that is 16½ in. in diameter. The actual distance from the center

Figure 5. *A cast-iron base and table gives the necessary support and stability for heavy drilling applications.*

of the chuck to the front of the column is 8¼ inches. Conventional drill press sizes for home workshops generally range from 8 to 17 inches.

WHAT TO LOOK FOR IN A DRILL PRESS

Because the drill press is one of the most versatile of power tools, it is essential that it should have the qualities and operating features that permit it to be utilized fully. Listed are a number of features to look for when buying a drill press for the home workshop:

- ⇨ The entire drill press should be solidly constructed to allow for long life and prolonged precision work.

- ⇨ The table and base (Fig. 5) should be ribbed for strength and rigidity. They also should be slotted. The table should have slats or ledges on the sides for clamping the work. (This offers convenience and safety to the user.) The table should be ground flat for accurate work, and the base should also have a flat surface for holding large workpieces. The table should be easily adjusted up or down, left or right, for adapting to different drilling situations.

- ⇨ The head should be cast iron, which offers excellent support and protection for the most im-

portant parts of the drill press — the motor, quill and pinion shaft.

- ⇨ The drill press should be equipped with a chuck that is tightened by a wrench or key rather than by hand. The chuck should have a ½ in. capacity so it will accommodate bits of various sizes and accessories. Many drills feature a taper-mounted chuck. By having a taper-mounted chuck, the runout is practically eliminated and the user is assured of accurate drilling. Some chucks feature a self-ejecting key, which insures that the key is not left in the chuck accidentally.

- ⇨ The depth-adjustment gauge allows the user to drill many holes at the same depth as the original hole. It eliminates any guesswork and allows precise, accurate drilling.

- ⇨ The drill press should have an adjustable motor bracket support that is sturdily constructed to support the motor, yet is easily movable to assure proper belt tension.

- ⇨ The drill press should have a selection of speeds for drilling wood, metal, plastic, glass and ceramics. Some drills feature a triple pulley arrangement (Fig. 6) for easy selection of 12 different speeds, ranging from a low of 250 rpm to a high of 3,000 rpm.

- ⇨ Be certain you can get proper replacement parts and service if needed.

- ⇨ A complete line of accessories will help you get the most from your machine. Accessories available from the manufacturer of the tool that you buy are designed for your particular tool. This eliminates having to use makeshift arrangements in order to use your tool to its best advantage.

- ⇨ It pays to equip your workshop with the best in power tools. Choose a drill press produced by a manufacturer who has established a record of quality and reliability.

BITS AND DRILLS

To be technically correct, you *bore* a hole in wood (even though twist bits are used) and *drill* a hole in metal. Today, however, this terminology is not followed rigidly, and usually the two terms—bore and drill—are used interchangeably in discussion of power drills. However, the bits used to cut into wood and those used to cut into metals are usually different from each other.

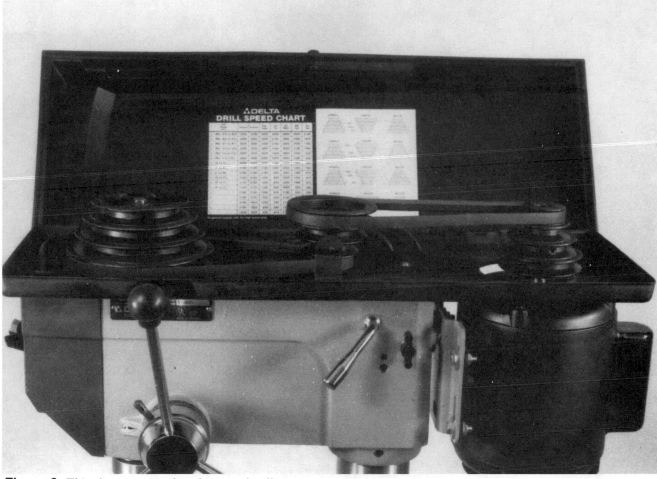

Figure 6. *This shows a typical twelve-speed pulley arrangement.*

Wood Bits. Several types of wood bits are used for boring wood with a drill press. Figure 7 shows the two common styles of wood bits: the one on the right is a machine spur bit; the one on the left is a spade bit.

A *machine spur bit* has a brad and lip point and is one of the cleanest, fastest-cutting bits for dowel holes. The opening in the spiral of a machine spur bit is called the *throat*. In some styles of machine spur bit the throat is designated by the term *flute*. Both terms mean the same thing. These bits come in standard sizes from ¼ to 1 in. and are generally available in thirty-seconds of an inch.

To drill larger holes in wood a *spade* or *speed-type bit* is generally recommended. A spade bit is flat and has a brad point. Bits of this style range from about ⅜ in. to as large as 1½ inches. They relieve the chips easily, and binding is not much of a problem.

Spade or speed bits have a tendency to split not only the front surface of the wood, but the back surface as well. The front surface can be drilled without splintering by starting the hole slowly. (That is, do not press too hard. Also, be sure the bit goes in square to the wood.) The back surface can be drilled clean without splintering

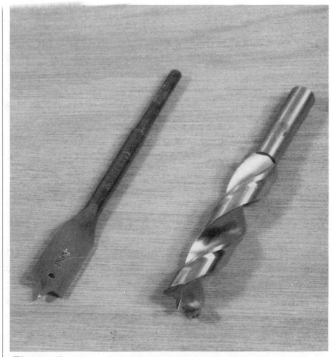

Figure 7. *Here are typical wood boring bits: the spade bit is on the left and the machine spur bit is on the right.*

Figure 8. *A fly-cutter tool adjusts to cut large-diameter holes into wood.*

by using either of two methods: First, as soon as the pilot (the center of the bit) comes through the back, stop drilling. Complete the hole by drilling from the back. Second, place a piece of scrap behind or under the workpiece. Drill through the workpiece and into the scrap piece.

Holes larger than 1½ in. can be cut with a *rotary hole saw*. This is literally a saw bent into a circle. It will make a clean, round hole in anything a hacksaw will cut, including metal, plastic and composition board. The pilot bit of the hole saw's mandrel, or shaft, can be centered on a punch mark to locate a large hole with great accuracy. The most popular sizes of hole saws range from ¾ to 2½ in. in diameter. Some come with fine-tooth blades that cut slowly but smoothly, while others come with several teeth for quick but rough cutting. The task of the rotary hole saw is to remove a diameter of wood. Therefore, the tool must cut completely through the wood's thickness. To accomplish this, manufacturers make these saws for various cutting depths. Thus you can buy a tool to cut ¾ in. plastic or another to cut through a 1½ in. thick floor joist.

One-size rotary hole saws are more expensive. More economical is the type with a shaft, or mandrel, on which saws of various sizes can be mounted. The cup-like saw shells range from approximately ⅝ to 2½ in. in diameter and are deep enough to cut through ¾ in. thick material. (A few are designed to cut up to 2 inches.) Be sure to tighten the chuck for maximum grip when using a hole saw, since its large diameter puts great stress on the spindle. At any angle other than 90 degrees, the hole saw will start cutting on one edge instead of all around. So take pains to start the pilot drill straight. In thick or hard wood, withdraw the saw occasionally to clear the chips and help cool the hole saw.

Fly-cutter-type circle makers (Fig. 8) are available for cutting holes from ½ to 8 in. in diameter. Actually, the size of the hole is controlled by loosening a set-screw and then sliding the cutter blade in or out. For best results when cutting circles in wood, cut halfway through each side of the wood, or back up the wood so the cutting blade does not tear and splinter the wood as it comes through. The cutter blade should be set back behind the center drill bit approximately ½ in. (where the flutes end

Figure 9. *Sanding drums are ideal for smoothing contoured workpieces.*

on the drill bit), so the blade will be held firmly in place when it begins to bite into the wood. Since the circle cutter has an off-center load, it works more smoothly and with less vibration at slower speeds. When using a fly-cutter, be sure that the workpiece is securely clamped to a solid surface.

With either the rotary hole saw or fly-cutter, splintering of the far side of the work will be prevented if you bore the hole about halfway through and then finish cutting it from the other side of the work. The pilot hole, having passed through the work, centers the tool for its second cut.

What we have covered is only a sample of the many bits available to you. Most can be used on a drill press, with one exception: *Never use a self-feed bit on your drill press.* A self-feed bit has a screw at the end. This bit will quickly dig into the material, attempting to swing the workpiece itself. Or if the workpiece is tightly clamped, the motor will stop. This operation is dangerous to both you and your machine.

Twist Drills. While twist drills are designed for drilling metal, they can be used to make holes in most materials — wood, plastic, ceramic or other materials. They often are rated as the most efficient of all cutting tools, based on the length of the cutting edge in proportion to the amount of metal that supports it. This is a tool that will stand a tremendous amount of abuse and still keep cutting. Nevertheless, any drill will work better and last longer if properly ground.

The lip or cutting edge of a drill is that part of the point that actually cuts away the metal when a hole is drilled. Ordinarily, it is as sharp as the edge of a knife. A point angle of 118 degrees should be maintained for general work. However, for extensive drilling in wood, a much sharper angle should be used.

The standard 118 degree angle drill is easily checked with a drill-point gauge. Gauges in a variety of styles can be purchased at a nominal cost, or can be made from sheet metal. The markings on the edge need not be exact, since they are used only to check the length of one lip against the other. In use, the drill body is held against the edge of the gauge, and in such a position that the angular edge is over the cutting lip of the drill. The gauge will then show whether one edge of the point is at the correct angle. Besides being ground to the correct angle, both lips must be exactly the same length. If not, the resulting hole will be out of round and larger than the drill.

The shank is the part of the drill that fits into the spindle or chuck of the drill press. Drills used on the drill press commonly have straight shanks to fit the adjustable chuck on the machine. It is also possible to mount taper-shank drills by using a taper-shank spindle.

Twist drills are made of either carbon-steel or high-speed steel. High-speed steel drills, made of an alloy that usually contains tungsten, chromium and vanadium, are designed expressly for work on metal and can take considerable heat without weakening or becoming dull. Usually, high-speed drills can do their work without the use of a coolant. The carbon-steel drills are softer, and are used solely on wood and soft metals or plastics. They cost much less than the harder high-speed steel drills but will wear quickly and become distorted if overworked. When drilling soft metals, they require a flow of cooling liquid on the tip to prevent burning. Carbide-tipped drills are also available. These are primarily used for drilling masonry, ceramics and extra-hard materials.

DRILL PRESS ACCESSORIES

Proper accessories enable you to do more jobs, and to do them easier and faster. Here are some of the more common accessories available for most drill presses.

Sanding Drums and Abrasive Sleeves. Sanding on curved surfaces can be accomplished on the drill press with the use of a sanding drum (Fig. 9). Various sizes of sanding drums are available. Aluminum oxide-coated sleeves for metal, and garnet-coated sanding sleeves for wood, are made up in different grits and sizes to fit the various drums.

Disk sanding also can be done on the drill press. Although designed primarily for portable drill work, the typical 1/4 in. shank-arbor adapter will fit a standard drill press geared chuck, and the 5 in. rubber backing pad can be attached to the adapter by a screw and washer.

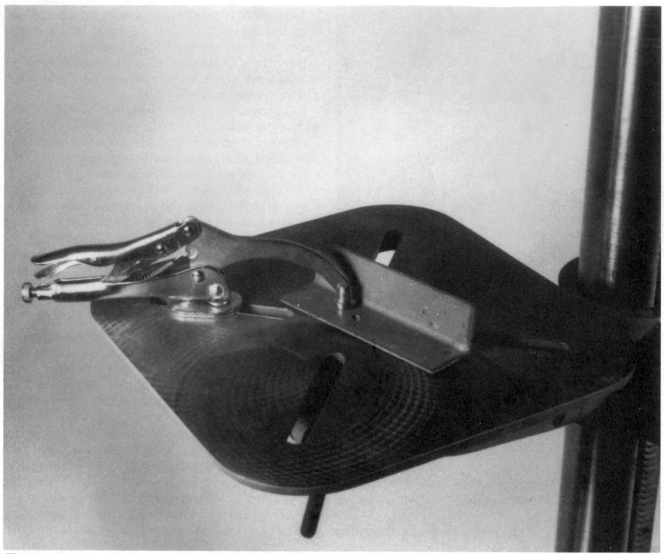

Figure 10. *All workpieces should be firmly held in place. The Delta clamp is ideal because it slides within the slots cut into most drill press tables.*

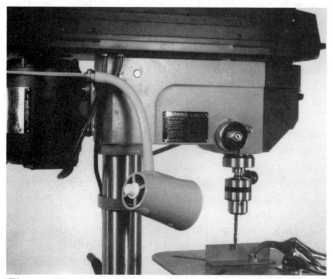

Figure 11. *It is a good idea to purchase a work lamp. This one attaches to the drill press.*

Various grades of sanding paper can be installed on the pad. *Note:* Do not use a backing pad that is larger than 5 in. on a standard drill press.

Buffing wheels and *polishing bonnets*, 5 in. and less, also can be used on the drill press. Other valuable portable drill accessories include *rotary rasps, rotary files* and a *flexible shaft with a chuck.* The rotary rasps are handy for fast wood removal, slotting and shaping. Rotary files can be used for filing metals, elongating holes and slots, removing burrs and scale, light milling and other similar metal finishing operations. The flexible shaft permits you to employ the drill press as a power source to drill, sand or shape anywhere within the reach of the shaft. Most flexible shafts are about 40 in. long.

Vises and Hold Downs. To drill a small workpiece with a drill press, either hold the workpiece in a drill press vise of some type or clamp the work securely to the table. C-clamps are excellent for holding small, flat

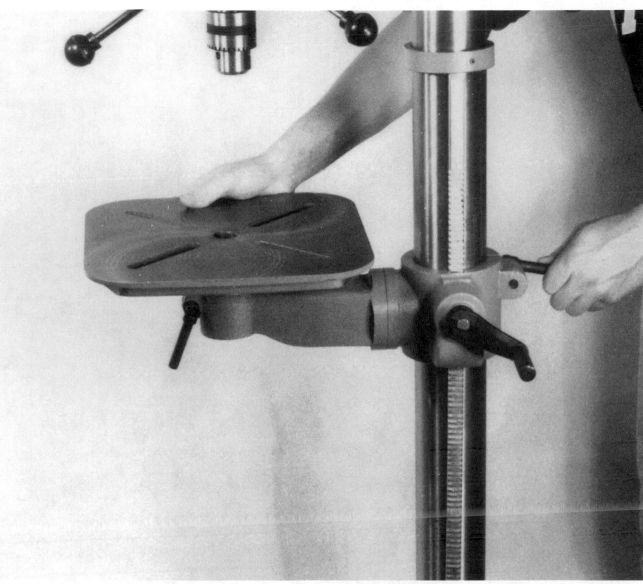

Figure 12. *Periodically you need to drill holes at angles other than 90 degrees. This is why an adjustable table is ideal. This table moves up and down, swings left and right, and tilts.*

workpieces and, in many cases, for securing a long, unwieldy piece to the table to assist you in holding it. For another useful clamp, see Fig. 10.

Lamp Attachment. Many workers want a lamp that is conveniently attached to the machine, since it is important to keep sufficient light on the work at all times. The lamp attachment shown in Fig. 11 is available complete with shade, socket and cord, and mounting bolts.

Numerous other drill press accessories available are listed in Delta's *Getting the Most Out of Your Drill Press* book.

DRILL PRESS TABLE
Most home shop drill presses manufactured today feature a tilting work table (Figs. 12 and 13). Usually, such tables can be tilted by loosening a nut under the

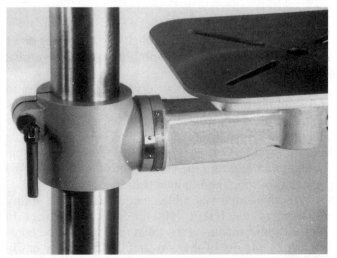

Figure 13. *This tilting table has built-in angle graduations for precision work.*

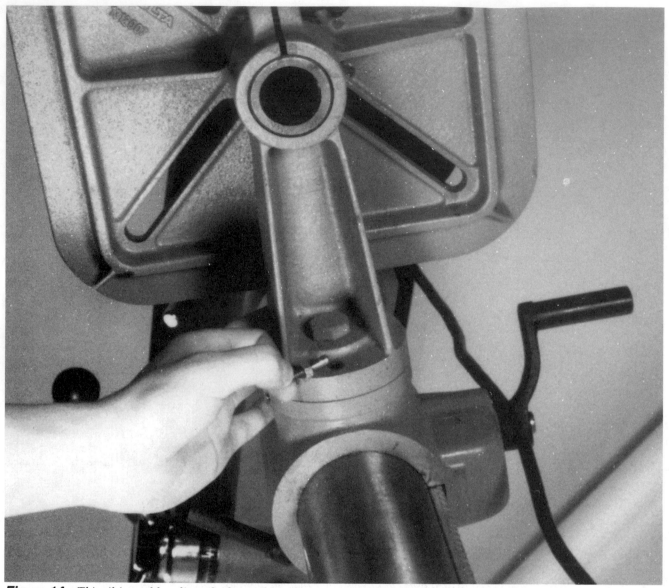

Figure 14. *This tilting table adjusts by loosening a nut, removing a locking pin and tilting the table to the desired angle.*

table (Fig. 14). A pin fitting through corresponding holes provides a positive stop at both horizontal and vertical positions.

The advantage of a floor drill press is its ability to adjust to the height of the work. Therefore, it is important that the table can be quickly set up for a drilling operation. To speed table set-up, a rack and pinion table assembly (Fig. 15) is invaluable. Unlock the table bracket lock and turn the handle until the table is at the proper position. Then tighten the table bracket lock.

Another important table characteristic is its ability to swing around, left or right, for drilling alignment. In fact, in some situations the table may have to be completely swung out of the way and this should be easily accomplished by loosening the table bracket lock and rotating the table left or right.

Safety Goggles. Safety goggles or a safety face shield should be worn when operating any power tool, including the drill press.

BEFORE OPERATING THE DRILL PRESS
It is important to know your drill press before operating it. The information provided here is of a general nature but appropriate for most drill presses. For specific data on your drill press, carefully check the owner's manual that came with it. By using the owner's manual, along with the information provided here, you will be able to get the most out of your drill press.

INSTALLATION
When setting up the drill press in your shop, make sure to locate it where you can easily handle any workpiece.

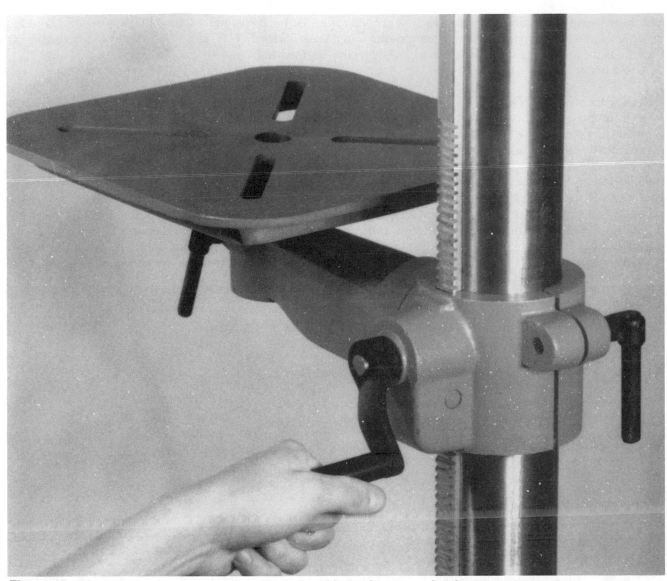

Figure 15. *The rack and pinion mechanism allows the table to adjust to any height.*

Good overhead light is of utmost importance, even if the tool is equipped with a lamp attachment. A nearby storage area to keep your bits and other accessories handy is a good step-saver to consider as well.

While the bench-type drill press can be mounted on the workbench, its operation will prove more satisfactory when mounted on a wood or steel stand of its own. (A steel stand usually can be purchased with the drill press.) When mounting the drill press to the bench, use bolts and nuts to fasten the base of the machine to the bench top. If there is any tendency for the drill press to tip over, slide or "walk" on the supporting surface during operation, the stand (floor model) or bench must be secured to the floor.

On a wooden floor, the bench and stand models can be secured with lag bolts. On concrete, use masonry bolts and anchors.

Connecting the Drill Press to Power. A separate electrical circuit should be used for your power tools. This circuit should not be less than 12 gauge wire and should be protected with a 20-amp time-lag fuse. If an extension cord is used, use only a three-prong extension cord in a grounded three-pole receptacle. The wire rating of the extension cord should be matched with the motor amperage of the tool and length of cord. Replace or repair damaged or worn cords immediately. Before connecting the motor to the power source, make sure the switch is in the "OFF" position and that the electric current is of the same voltage as that stamped on the motor nameplate. All line connections should make good contact. Running on low voltage will damage the motor.

The drill press must be grounded to protect the operator from electric shock. The motors for small drill presses are usually wired for 120 volts, single-phase, and are equipped with an approved three-conductor cord and three-prong grounding type plug to fit a properly grounded three-slot receptacle. The green conductor in the cord is the grounding wire. Never connect the green wire to a live terminal.

DRILL PRESS ADJUSTMENTS

Most drill presses are thoroughly tested, inspected and accurately aligned before leaving the factory. However, moving parts will wear, and the abrasive action of dust and dirt adds to this wear. Rough handling during transportation also can throw the machine out of alignment. Eventually, adjustment and realignment are necessary in any machine to maintain accuracy — regardless of the care with which the tool is manufactured.

Quill Adjustments. The quill travels in a bored hole in the head casting. These parts will remain accurate indefinitely if kept clean and lubricated according to instructions.

The spindle is raised or lowered by the hand lever. The quill can be locked at any desired point in its travel by tightening the quill locking screw. This is an especially desirable feature for operations such as sanding. Any play that might develop between the head and quill after considerable use can be taken up by partially tightening the quill locking screw.

For operations such as sanding, where the quill is clamped in place, always keep the quill as high as the work will permit so that any side thrust will be transmitted directly to the head casting.

Belt Tension. The belt should be just tight enough to prevent slipping. Excessive tension will reduce the

Figure 16. *The belt is tensioned by moving the motor bracket to the required position.*

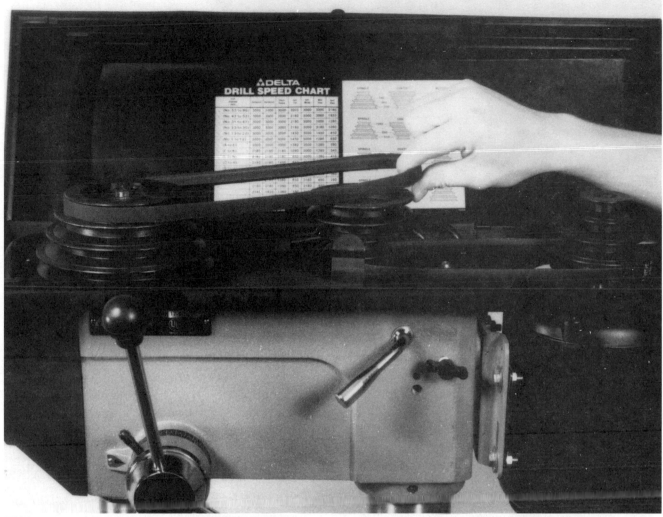

Figure 17. *This is how the belts are placed to obtain a 3,000 rpm spindle speed.*

life of the belt, pulleys and bearings. Correct tension is obtained when the belt can be flexed about 1 in. out of line midway between the pulleys, using finger pressure. To adjust belt tension, follow the manufacturer's instructions found in the owner's manual. Generally, this is accomplished by moving the motor bracket to the required position (Fig. 16).

If the drill press is equipped with a 1,725 rpm motor, the typical spindle speeds are approximately 250 to 3,000 rpm. The highest speed of 3,000 rpm is obtained when one belt is positioned on the smallest pulley of the spindle and the largest pulley of the center pulley, while the other belt is placed on the smallest pulley of the center and the largest motor pulley (Fig. 17).

Similarly, to obtain the slowest speed of 250 rpm, place the first belt over the largest spindle pulley and connect it to the smallest center pulley; run the second belt over the largest center pulley and the smallest motor pulley (Fig. 18). When you change the belt position to change speed, *always disconnect the machine from its power source.*

Figure 18. *Now the spindle speed is set to its slowest speed of 250 rpm.*

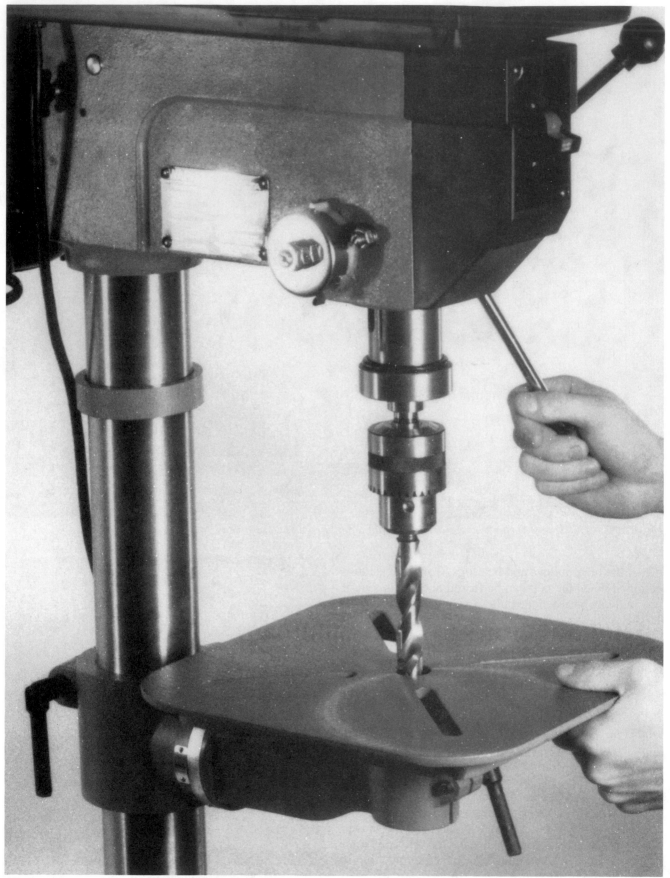

Figure 19. *Center the work table under the drill.*

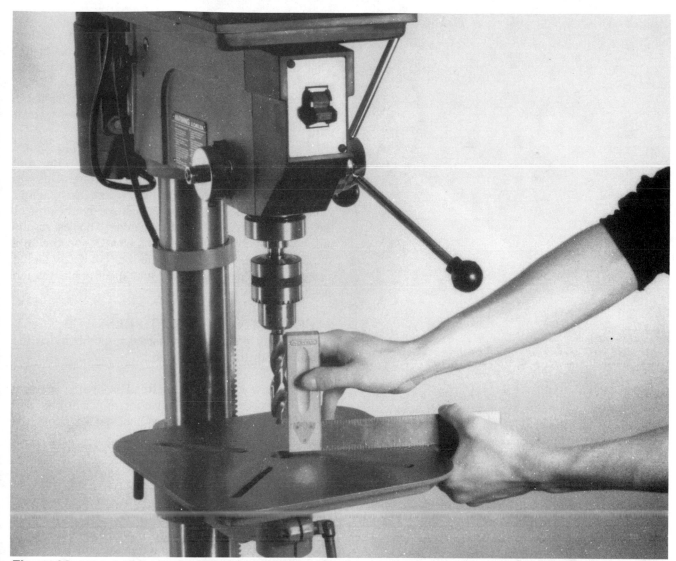

Figure 20. *To insure that the adjustable table is set 90 degrees to the drill, check with a square as shown.*

Inserting Drills. The standard geared or keyed chuck is opened and closed with the chuck key provided. It also can be worked by hand, although the final grip tension must be applied with a wrench. Be sure the drill's shank is centered between the chuck's jaws and is properly secured in the chuck before the power is turned on. Do not apply further pressure with pliers or wrenches after you have hand-tightened the chuck with the chuck key.

Always remove the key immediately after you use it. Otherwise, the key will fly loose when the drill motor is started and may cause serious injury. Self-ejecting chuck keys are available.

Centering the Table. In average drilling operations, the hole in the center of the table should be directly under the drill so that the drill, after going through the work, will enter the hole in the table. When through drilling is being done, the quill always should be brought down first without the work in place to make sure that the drill enters the table opening (Fig. 19).

Check to see if the head is set perpendicular to the table by placing a drill bit in the chuck. Then place a combination square on the table, as shown in Fig. 20. If not square, readjust the table until the drill bit is perpendicular to the table.

Adjusting the Spindle Return Spring. For the purpose of automatically returning the spindle upward after a hole has been drilled, a coil spring enclosed in a metal case is fitted to the side of most drill presses. (Check your owner's manual for the exact details.) Generally, this spring is adjusted at the factory and usually requires no further adjustment. If, however, the spindle fails to return to a normal position, or if the return is too rapid, the tension should be adjusted. This is done by loosening the locknuts that hold the case in place. They should not be completely removed, but simply backed off about ¼ in., enough so that the case can be pulled out to clear the bosses on the head. As the case is pulled out, it must be held tightly to prevent the

Figure 21. *Here the spindle return spring is being adjusted.*

spring from unwinding (Fig. 21). The case is turned clockwise to loosen the spring; counterclockwise to tighten it. When the quill is up, two full turns from a non-tension position should give the proper tension. Before tensioning the spring, it is well to slack it off entirely. It should be noted that the exact method of adjusting the spindle return spring varies with different models and makes of drill presses. Consult the owner's manual supplied with your machine for specific details.

LUBRICATION

On all drill presses, a coat of paste wax or a rub-down with a piece of wax paper will protect the surface of the table. Wiping with a slightly oiled cloth will discourage rusting of the column and quill. Also lubricate the spline and quill with a light machine oil. Make sure to read your tool's instructional manual for additional lubrication points.

SPEED AND FEED

Factors that determine the best speed to use in any drill press operation include: the kind of material being worked, size of hole, type of drill bit or other cutter, and the quality of the cut desired. The smaller the drill, the greater the required rpm. The speed should be higher for soft materials than for hard ones.

On most drill presses it is impossible to get the *exact* recommended speed, but you can come close by adjusting the drive belt on the step-cone pulleys. You will find a chart giving the various speed ratios available with your particular drill press somewhere in the owner's

manual or on the tool itself. Regardless of the speed selected, remember that the tool should cut steadily, smoothly and without excessive vibration, no matter what the material. Decreasing or increasing rpms is sometimes necessary because of differences in boards, even boards of the same type of wood. After some experience with your machine, you will know which pulley step is best in each case.

Feed is the amount of pressure you apply to control penetration. Too much pressure will force the tool beyond its cutting capacity and result in rough cuts and jammed or broken tools. Too light a feed, particularly with metal or other hard material, causes overheating of the tool and burning of the cutting edge. The best results will be obtained by matching the correct speed with a steady feed pressure that lets the tool cut easily and at an even rate. The proper feed and speed make the job easier.

SAFETY WITH THE DRILL PRESS

A few safety precautions must be remembered while operating a drill press. They are:

⇨ Know your drill press. Read the owner's manual very carefully. Learn its applications and limitations, as well as the specific potential hazards peculiar to it.

⇨ Always wear safety goggles or a face shield.

⇨ Be sure that the chuck key is removed from the chuck before turning on the power. Using a self-ejecting chuck key is a good way of insuring that the key is not left in the chuck accidentally. Also to avoid accidental starting, make sure the switch is in the "OFF" position before plugging in the cord. *Always disconnect the drill from the power source when making repairs.*

⇨ Never attempt to use a hand auger bit in a drill press. Use only drills and bits designed for machine use. Consult the owner's manual for recommended accessories. The use of improper accessories may present hazards.

⇨ Hold the workpiece firmly so that it will not fly or spin off the table. It is generally best to fasten the workpiece securely with clamps or hold it in a vise. This is especially true when drilling or boring small workpieces.

⇨ Keep the guard on the spindle pulley to prevent your hair and clothing from getting caught. In fact, no loose clothing, gloves or jewelry should

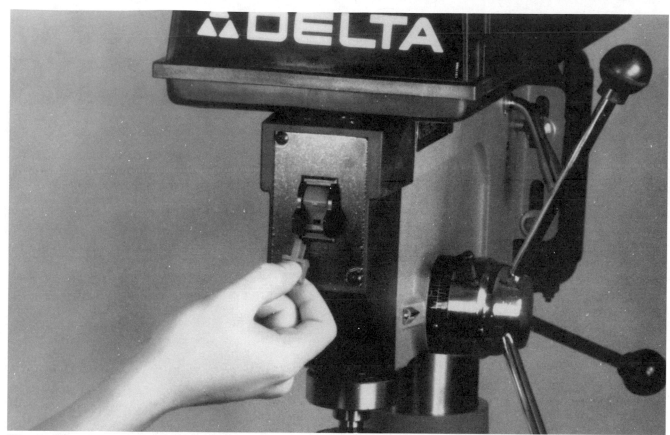

Figure 22. *The chuck key should be removed from the drill press at the end of each operation to prevent unauthorized tool use. Self-ejecting chuck keys also are available.*

be worn when working on the drill press. A hair net is recommended for long hair.

⇨ Use the recommended spindle or chuck. Most operations can be done successfully with the 0 to ½ in. capacity geared drill chuck.

⇨ Be sure the drill bit or cutting tool is locked securely in the chuck. Remember that all adjustments should be made with the power off.

⇨ Adjust the table so that the hole in the table center is beneath the drill, or set the depth stop to avoid drilling into the table. It is a good idea to place a piece of wood beneath the workpiece to prevent this.

⇨ Do not use too high a spindle speed. Stay as close to the recommended speeds as possible. If there is any doubt, use the lower speed. The wrong application of high speed can burn up the cutting tool and/or workpieces, and can hurl the work off the table with considerable force. Too slow a speed with a heavy feed can cause the tool to dig into the workpiece, which can stall the motor or break the cutting edges. *Always*

disconnect the machine from the power source when changing speeds or making adjustments.

⇨ On deep cuts, raise the bit frequently to clean the chips out of the hole. If the drill becomes stuck in the hole, turn off the machine before attempting to raise the bit.

⇨ Use a brush to keep the table and workpiece free of sawdust or chips. Always disconnect the machine from the power source before cleaning.

⇨ When using sanding drums and other abrasive accessories, make sure the work area is well ventilated.

⇨ Never try to stop the machine by grabbing the chuck after the power is turned off. Do not run the tool unattended. Turn off the power, and do not leave the drill press until the chuck comes to a complete stop.

⇨ To make your drill press kid-proof, it is a good idea to position the key to the "OFF" position and remove the switch toggle (Fig. 22). ❐

Credits

Story contributors:

American Plywood Association
P.O. Box 11700
Tacoma, WA 98411

Delta International Machinery Corp.
246 Alpha Drive
Pittsburgh, PA 15238

The Stanley Works
New Britain, CT 06050

Product contributors:

American Tool Companies, Inc.
P.O. Box 337
DeWitt, NE 68341

Minwax Company, Inc.
15 Mercedes Drive
Montvale, NJ 07645

Skil Corporation
4300 West Peterson Ave.
Chicago, IL 60646

United Gilsonite Laboratories
Box 70
Scranton, PA 18501